Apt Imaginings

Thinking Art

Series Editors

Noël Carroll and Jesse Prinz, CUNY Graduate Center

*

Thinking Art fills an important gap in contemporary philosophy of art, focusing on cutting edge ideas and approaches to the subject.

Published in the Series:

ATTENTIONAL ENGINES:
A PERCEPTUAL THEORY OF THE ARTS
William P. Seeley

APT IMAGININGS:
FEELINGS FOR FICTIONS AND OTHER CREATURES OF THE MIND
Jonathan Gilmore

GAMES: AGENCY AS ART
C. Thi Nguyen

Apt Imaginings

*Feelings for Fictions
and Other Creatures of the Mind*

JONATHAN GILMORE

OXFORD
UNIVERSITY PRESS

OXFORD
UNIVERSITY PRESS

Oxford University Press is a department of the University of Oxford. It furthers
the University's objective of excellence in research, scholarship, and education
by publishing worldwide. Oxford is a registered trade mark of Oxford University
Press in the UK and certain other countries.

Published in the United States of America by Oxford University Press
198 Madison Avenue, New York, NY 10016, United States of America.

Library of Congress Control Number: 2019954851
ISBN 978-0-19-009634-2

1 3 5 7 9 8 6 4 2

Printed by Integrated Books International, United States of America

For Ginevra

All effects of art are merely effects of nature for the person who has not attained a perception of art that is free, that is, one that is both passive and active, both swept away and reflective. Such a person behaves merely as a creature of nature and has never really experienced and appreciated art as art.

Schelling, Philosophy of Art

Contents

Acknowledgments   ix

1. Introduction   1
2. Cognitive Imagining and Literary Fictions   17
3. Evaluative Emotions   44
4. Apt Emotions and Normative Continuity   85
5. Defending Discontinuity   102
6. Epistemology of Fiction and Rational Imagining   134
7. Tragedy and Desire   155
8. Discrepant Affects   176
9. Artistic Functions   201

Bibliography   227
Index   255

Acknowledgments

Although often identified with solitary reflection—a home for the intellectual recluse—philosophy really is a collaborative enterprise. This book would have been much worse, and might not have been at all, were it not for the generous responses I've received to its arguments over the years of its gestation. For particularly helpful exchanges, I am grateful to Bianca Finzi-Contini Calabresi, David Carrier, Noël Carroll, Gregory Currie, Arthur Danto, Susan Feagin, Stacie Friend, Berys Gaut, Tamar Gendler, Lydia Goehr, Gregg Horowitz, Shelly Kagan, Jerrold Levinson, Aaron Meskin, Eric Mandlebaum, Alexander Nehamas, Jérôme Pelletier, Jenefer Robinson, Barbara Sattler, Matthew Noah Smith, Brian Soucek, and Catherine Wilson. Immature versions of its contents were presented at, inter alia, the American Society of Aesthetics and British Society of Aesthetics conferences, workshops on fiction at the Institut Jean Nicod, École Normale Supérieure, the Yale Department of Philosophy faculty lunches, and talks at New York University, Princeton, Uppsala, Temple, and the Graduate Center, CUNY. I thank the participants in those forums for criticism and encouragement. I also wish to acknowledge the generous support of the National Endowment for the Humanities for a 2013–2014 Fellowship that allowed me to develop the core arguments of this volume; Columbia University, where, as a Visiting Scholar in 2015, I was almost able to complete it; and the essential Upper West Side café, Tarallucci e Vino, where over many long afternoons the book was finished.

Chapters 4 and 5 are a substantial expansion of my "Aptness of Emotions for Fictions and Imaginings," published in *Pacific Philosophical Quarterly*; Chapter 6 revises my "The Epistemology of Fiction and the Question of Invariant Norms," *Philosophy*; Chapter 7 draws substantially on "That Obscure Object of Desire: Pleasure in Painful Art," in Levinson, ed., *Suffering Art Gladly*; Chapter 9 appropriates the substance of "A Functional View of Artistic Evaluation," *Philosophical Studies*; and some short passages and examples have been lifted from

"Grief and Belief," *British Journal of Aesthetics*, "Ethics, Aesthetics, and Artistic Evaluation," *Journal of Value Inquiry*, and "Imagination," *Routledge Companion to the Philosophy of Literature*. I thank the editors and publishers of those venues for their permission to incorporate that material in this book.

Apt Imaginings

1

Introduction

In this introduction, I identify a very general dilemma that plays a pronounced role in descriptive and explanatory claims about the arts. On the one side is the pull of *continuity*, in which our engagements with the contents of fictions and other imagined creations are said to be modeled on our engagements with ordinary real-world states of affairs. On the other is the pull of *discontinuity*, in which such representations are posed as offering potentially sui generis sorts of experiences that resist assimilation or reduction to those we encounter in the everyday.

1.1. Continuity and Autonomy

Late in Henry Fielding's picaresque novel *Tom Jones*, the surgeon-barber Partridge accompanies Jones to the playhouse to see a production of *Hamlet* starring David Garrick. The narrator tells us that after first denying Jones's identification of one of the actors with the Ghost—"No, no, sir; ghosts don't appear in such dresses as that," and then accepting it, Partridge

> fell into so violent a trembling that his knees knocked against each other. Jones asked him what was the matter, and whether he was afraid of the warrior upon the stage? "Oh, la! sir," said he, "I perceive now it is what you told me. I am not afraid of anything, for I know it is but a play . . . yet . . . if that little man there upon the stage is not frightened, I never saw any man frightened in my life." . . . And during the whole speech of the Ghost he sat with his eyes fixed partly on the Ghost and partly on Hamlet, and with his mouth open; the same passions which succeeded each other in Hamlet succeeding likewise in him.

Partridge's confused tangle with what is life and what is art continues after the curtain falls: objecting to the audience's praise for Garrick's performance, he insists the actor's achievement is only what one would expect: "why, I could

Apt Imaginings. Jonathan Gilmore, Oxford University Press (2020). © Oxford University Press.
DOI: 10.1093/oso/9780190096342.001.0001

act as well as he myself. I am sure if I had seen a ghost, I should have looked in the very same manner, and done just as he did. And . . . any man . . . that had had such a mother, would have done exactly the same."[1]

We are told that Partridge expresses "the simple dictates of nature, unimproved indeed, but likewise unadulterated by art." Yet his responding as if the characters of the play, not just their performers, inhabit his own world, is not so easily explained away by naiveté. For the tendency to evaluate, empathize with, and emotionally respond to beings one knows don't exist is shared by even those who fully appreciate what is real and what is only a creature of the mind.

One can feel sadness over a fictional character's death, cringing embarrassment for hapless people in a sitcom, resentment in imagining being slighted by a rival, jealousy from visualizing one's wholly faithful lover in the arms of another, desire that the unalterable past be different, arousal over images of simulated sex, shame or glee over some action that one only fantasizes about performing. These circumstances are of course very different, and sometimes it is difficult to determine whether someone's affective responses are activated only by her imagining some state of affairs, or imply the presence of a relevant belief. Most sports fans who subject the opposing team's players to lacerating verbal abuse (along with imprecations about their mothers) don't really believe that they're mortal enemies, yet there are some fans for whom such enmity may be real. And, while both believers and atheists visiting Amiens Cathedral can feel the awe and disassociation from one's mundane self that the edifice's soaring vaults and brilliant light are designed to evoke, for one group this is an experience of faith, and for the other something akin to imagining or simulating what it would be like to enter a space suffused with the divine.[2]

In any case, despite their ubiquity, it may seem odd that we have these emotional responses to what we take to be made up or imagined; odd because, at first glance, emotions seem inexplicable if felt for what one believes not to exist. Why feel fear of something that is no danger; pity for someone who can't suffer? Hamlet thus objects to the player who tears up while performing the role of Aeneas recounting his travails (and Priam's slaughter) to Dido:

---

[1] Fielding (1750/1999, 611–613).
[2] For the problem of how to characterize the experience by non-believers of religious works of music, see Neill and Ridley (2010).

And all for nothing!
For Hecuba.
What's Hecuba to him, or he to Hecuba,
That he should weep for her?[3]

That question—why do we have feelings for what we know doesn't exist—is a long-standing one.[4] Yet, however we resolve our puzzlement over the phenomenon Hamlet condemns, it is remarkable how much of our lives is given over to experiences that in one way or another draw on contents of the imagination. These include not only being transported by fictions into an alternative world, such as the court of Elsinore or the city of Troy, but also finding one's way through everyday negotiations with the actual one. Hypothetical and counterfactual thinking, fantasizing, pretending, visualizing, dreaming, entertaining ideas, employing metaphorical descriptions, mentally retracing one's steps to discover where one left one's keys, and so on, employ what appears to be the same capacity to represent some states of affairs without one's representation being wholly constrained by one's current sensory experiences and beliefs. There are of course important differences among these and other forms of imagining, and some philosophers argue that there is no single concept of the imagination that can serve in all the multifarious explanatory contexts in which the notion is employed.[5] For the moment, I will speak of imagining, simpliciter, and only later, where relevant, distinguish the particular forms relevant to the explanatory context of our engagements with fictions.

In the history of philosophy there has been substantial ambivalence over the capacity of the mind to summon forth ideas that may bear little representational correspondence and alethic commitment to the actual world. On one side is the recognition of imagination's power. Descartes notes in *The Passions of the Soul* our ability "to imagine something non-existent—in thinking about an enchanted palace or a chimera," and Hume in the *Enquiry* remarks that "[t]o form monsters, and join incongruous shapes and appearances, costs the

---

[3] *Hamlet* 2.2.536–37.
[4] Radford (1975), who brought to prominence in Anglo-American aesthetics the puzzle of how to characterize such emotions, suggests that there is something potentially incoherent in emotional responses to what we don't believe exists.
[5] Some philosophers treat imagining, conceiving, and supposing as occupying distinctive functional roles. Chalmers (2002), for example, identifies the relevant general attitude to be conceiving and treats imagining as one of its subclasses, distinguished by being imagistic. Peacocke (1985), by contrast, treats imagining and conceiving as distinct. See Kind (2013) for the general argument against a univocal explanatory concept.

imagination no more trouble than to conceive the most natural and familiar objects."[6] On the other side, there is the worry about its putative freedom from rational constraints. Locke, for example, uses the terms "wanton," "extravagant," and "chimerical" in describing the imagination. Hume refers to "loose and indolent reveries of a castle builder," and Samuel Johnson calls it "a licentious and vagrant faculty, unsusceptible of limitations and impatient of restraint."[7] The touchstone for many critics of the imagination in its relation to the arts is, of course, Plato, whose own imagined fictional character Socrates, with varying degrees of correspondence to the real one, proposes in the *Republic* that dramatic poetry, absent a last-minute reprieve, must be exiled from the ideal state. The charge leveled there is that the pretenses of poetry evoke emotions for states of affairs and characters that don't, in Plato's severe estimation, merit the evaluations that those emotions seem to entail. An actor performing the role of Achilles gives himself over to extravagant expressions of grief over the death of Patroclus, and the part of us (the enraptured audience) that "hungers for the satisfaction of weeping and wailing" responds accordingly, however unmerited such putatively irrational feelings of loss might be. Thus, Plato does not object to the fact that we feel emotions for what is merely fictional—what Hamlet decries—but to a corruption in our identification of the proper evaluative grounds of those feelings, whether engendered by events in real life or dramas on the stage.[8]

When the contents of the imagination were seen as pertaining solely to a shadowy realm of appearances segregated from reality, the mental attitude had only a limited purchase on philosophical theorizing, whose primary domain is the nature of this world, not the indefinite contents of what can be conjured up in thought. However, the situation has radically changed in the past few decades due to a key insight shared by many theorists: that the imagination is not a peripheral or dispensable dimension of our mental lives but, rather, pervades ordinary experience and cognition. Indeed, the concept of the imagination now enters into a diverse array of explanatory contexts, including our knowledge of metaphysical possibility (or non-epistemic modality in general), empathy, prediction of behavior, the nature of delusion

---

[6] Descartes (1649/1988, 226); Hume (1777/1975, Sec. II, para. 13).

[7] Johnson (1751).

[8] Anticipating the pleasure in the experience of such inappropriate lamentation, the rational part of the soul "relaxes its guard," giving full rein to that response to what is seen on stage when it might restrain it in virtue of being inappropriate or unmerited in relation to relevantly similar states of affairs in real life. See Halliwell (2002, 78–79).

and mental illness, memory, dreaming, the use of scientific models, and, of course, the experience of art.[9]

One way to address the imagination is to analyze its contents: what events, objects, or states of affairs it represents. But another way, which is employed in this book, is to address its grounds or justifications—why it has those contents and why certain emotional, desire-like, and cognitive responses to those contents follow. The deep question that I want to explore is to what extent we can model our engagements with such counterfactual phenomena on analogous forms of experience in the real world. What is the relationship, to put it roughly and too grandly, between art and life? I refer to this as the *continuity* question. It can be posed in two senses: descriptive and normative.

Descriptively, the question is whether our evaluations, emotions, desires, and cognitive representations can be explained in a way that is largely indifferent to their genesis in, alternatively, imagination and belief. Normatively, the question is whether the kinds of reasons that can serve in the justification or criticism of such responses are invariant across imagined and real-world contexts.

Although in the first few chapters of this volume I address evidence bearing on the descriptive/explanatory question, the normative question, especially in relation to fiction, is my study's central concern. Are the normative criteria governing the aptness, fit, or rationality of our emotional, cognitive, and conative engagements with the actual world continuous with the norms governing those attitudinal engagements with fictional works of art and objects of the imagination? Commitments to, or against, the invariance of such norms have been implicit, albeit not always recognized, in reflection on the psychology of fiction from ancient philosophy's attempts to reckon with the nature of artistic expression to contemporary accounts of artistic autonomy, art and ethical criticism, and the cognitive utility of thought experiments.

Some writers posit that the same norms govern our responses to states of affairs represented in fictional works of art and analogous real states of affairs. Others see it as part of a proper engagement with fictions that certain ordinary norms governing real-world responses are suspended; norms indexed to fictional contexts operate in their place. In the latter perspective,

---

[9] For the role of imagining in children's play and development, see Leslie (1987); Harris et al. (1993); in social cognition and the prediction of behavior, see Currie and Ravenscroft (2002); Nichols and Stich (2003); Goldman (2006b); in creativity, see Gaut and Livingston (2003); Boden (2004); Carruthers (2007); in memory and planning, see Schacter et al. (2012); Harris et al. (1993); Goldman (1992); in modal reasoning, see Lewis (1986); Rosen (1990); in metaphysical theorizing, see Gendler and Hawthorne (2002); in dreaming, see McGinn (2004); in scientific models, see Toon (2012).

for example, it may be appropriate to feel admiration for the clever and attractive criminal in a film without that entailing that any such attitude would or should be felt toward a person who is similar in relevant respects in real life.

The dilemma is that, on the one hand, it seems that when we respond to the contents of representations that are make-believe or fictional, we employ the same representational, affective, behavioral, and evaluative capacities that serve us in engaging with the real world. My feelings, for example, for a character in a fiction seem to be generated by the same mechanisms—of, e.g., empathy—and subject to the same norms—of, e.g., proportionality and evaluative correctness—as my emotions directed toward real people. Likewise, the faculties that I use to discover what is true in the real world—perception, inference, testimony, and so on—seem to be analogous to those I use to discover what is the case—what is represented as true—in a fictional world. Finally, it seems that if I desire something to occur in a fiction, this is because I would tend to desire an analogous thing in a comparable scenario in real life.

Ancient philosophical conceptions of the imagination, insofar as they overlap with ours, seem to adopt that continuity view. Plato's criticism of Homer's epics and the great tragedies for leading audiences to identify with poor exemplars of virtue wouldn't make sense if he didn't think that the feelings people had for such representations were subject to the same norms as when elicited by actual states of affairs. Aristotle might appear to adopt a contrary view in his observation in the *Poetics* that "we enjoy looking at the most exact portrayals of things whose actual sight is painful to us" (he refers to pictures of corpses as an example).[10] However, that he sees such pleasure as peculiar, and requiring an explanation, implies a background assumption that, all things being equal, our responses to what is represented in works of art normatively and descriptively track our responses to analogous things that we take to be real.

By contrast, Romantic and modernist thought typically take it to be a distinctive feature of our engagement with art that the normal rules or principles for our traffic with the real world can be suspended. We can feel sympathy for fictional characters whose real-life counterparts we would only despise; we can imagine some scenario to hold in a fiction without any reason to believe

---

[10] *Poetics* IV. In *De Anima*, Aristotle (2016) contrasts thinking about some distressing state of affairs with visually imagining it, and seems to imply that the latter experience is less affecting because when visually imagining such things we "are just as if we had seen the terrible or audacious things in a picture" (3.3.427b21–4).

such a state of affairs could come to be in real life. We feel pleasure in and desire to see certain kinds of fictional representations of violence and suffering, when we would not feel such pleasure or have such desires before such things outside of art. In this perspective, how we respond to events represented in a work of art, and in our fantasies and other imaginings, does not, prima facie, tell us how we would or should respond if they really occurred.[11]

In this book, I address the debate between *continuity* (i.e., a commitment to invariance) and *discontinuity* (i.e., a commitment to invariance's denial) in four interrelated ways. I ask:

Do the criteria for the aptness of our emotional responses to what we take to be real apply invariantly to those emotions we have toward what we take to be only imagined or fictional? Or might a feeling for some state of affairs in a fiction be apt despite being inapt or unfitting in response to a like scenario in real life?

Must our desires for some state of affairs within a fictional work of art cohere with our desires for comparable states of affairs outside the story? For example, if we desire that a character in a tragedy, such as Cordelia in *King Lear,* somehow survive her narratively mandated fate, does this entail that we desire the play to be performed in an idiosyncratic fashion—with a happy ending? Also, can it be appropriate for us to desire something to occur within a narrative even if it would be irrational, unethical, or otherwise wrong for us to desire an analogous thing to occur in the real world?

Do the criteria that tell us whether we are epistemically rational in what we take to be true apply invariantly to our imagining of what is true in (what are the contents of) a fiction? In short, is make-believing rational in the same sense as believing?

And are the evaluative norms that govern our sympathies, alignments, or identifications with fictional characters, and the moral norms that govern our approval or condemnation of fictional states of affairs, consistent with those that govern our evaluations in real life?

Although there may be no univocal answer to these questions taken together, I see each as probing and potentially giving determinate characterization to the grounds and limits of the autonomy that is often claimed for products of the imagination. That is, the debate over continuity should be

---

[11] Characterizing the point, Susan Feagin (1984) writes, "the freedom of imagining is freedom *without* responsibility. . . . Pleasure in what one imagines can be as fickle or as base as one likes, without consequence" (50).

seen against a background of a larger, much less tractable, clash between two perspectives on art:

The first treats the experience of art as an extension in relevant dimensions of what is available to us outside of artistic contexts. This view realizes itself in forms of theoretical reduction (e.g., of art to ordinary artifacts); an assimilation of paradoxical artistic phenomena to everyday states of affairs; and an aspiration to reach greater explanatory power and theoretical simplicity with tools developed in the empirical sciences to study domain-general affective, cognitive, and behavioral processes.

The second perspective, by contrast, is expressed in the identification of potentially sui generis experiences of art, such as a kind of emotion or insight that aesthetic objects alone can furnish. There great stress is laid on the essential embeddedness of certain kinds of expression in their respective artistic media, as in the putative heresy of translation vis-à-vis poetry, or in Tolstoy's famous claim that, if asked to say what *Anna Karenina* expresses, he could answer only by writing the same novel from the beginning.[12] We also see this anti-reductionist approach in theories that speak to putatively "ineffable" features of an engagement with art, seeing it not as an extension of ordinary experience but as one that is different (morally, cognitively, and so on) in kind. Thus, in his lectures on literature, Nabokov cautions us to address each work of art as the "creation of a new world," and to approach it as "something brand new, having no obvious connections with the world we already know."

Let me now identify where the view I defend stands in relation to its opponents.

1.2. Related Theories

I argue for normative discontinuity: make-believing is not epistemically rational in the same sense as believing, and the norms governing our desires, emotions, and moral evaluations vis-à-vis what is internal to a fiction can be inconsistent with those governing our responses to relevantly similar things in the real world.

The case for discontinuity faces two kinds of opponents. One kind affirms a thesis of discontinuity but only through denying that certain fiction-directed

---

[12] "If I were to try to say in words everything that I intended to express in my novel, I would have to write the same novel from the beginning," in a letter to Nikolai Strakhov (April 26, 1876/1978).

responses are of the same relevant kinds as their real-world counterparts. Thus, Kendall Walton assigns the emotions elicited by what we know to be make-believe to a class of "quasi-emotions": states generated within a pretense that exhibit the phenomenological dimensions of, but do not play the same explanatory role as, ordinary emotions.[13]

Whether such quasi-emotions fail to qualify as "real" emotions may be only a verbal dispute, but many readers of Walton take him to be asserting a metaphysical thesis, that such emotions are only pretend. Gregory Currie and Alvin Goldman likewise construe desires for fictional states of affairs as "i-desires" or desires held "off-line," i.e., as imaginative counterparts of real desires.[14] These and like-minded philosophers thus may appear to settle certain questions about continuity at one stroke through denying that affective states belong to the same relevant kind across the real/fictional divide. For if fiction-directed emotions and desires are not real, it would seem to be otiose whether the norms governing our emotions and desires are invariant across real-world and fictional states of affairs. I argue, by contrast, for a less sweeping discontinuity thesis, one that preserves realism about those fiction-directed affective states but shows that, nonetheless, their fit with their objects is governed by a different set of norms.[15]

The second kind of opponent, more broadly represented among Anglo-American philosophers of art, assumes or defends the correctness of continuity or invariance: the criteria governing the correctness, fittingness, or aptness of emotions, desires, evaluations, and representations of states of affairs are the same whether those token mental states are elicited within the context of imagined experiences or genuine engagements with the actual world.[16] When we seek to discover what is (fictionally) true in a story, and when we respond emotionally, or with desires or moral evaluations to what we only imagine to be true, we are subject to the same relevant norms as

---

[13] In an alternative explanation of the view expressed in his (1990), Walton (1997/2015) remarks that fiction-directed emotions are, indeed, real emotions. However, his construal assigns them an explanatory role distinct from that of reality-directed or belief-based emotions in virtue of his denial that the fiction-prompted emotions are felt about fictional entities.

[14] Currie and Ravenscroft (2002).

[15] Note that proponents of the idea that art furnishes sui generis kinds of experiences, i.e., those with no relevant analogues in ordinary life, present a comparable discontinuity claim through asserting a disjunction between those contexts—art and life—in light of which no question of continuity can arise. Schopenhauer's claim that music represents joy in general, not that everyday emotion provoked by a particular state of affairs, suggests that at least for some such responses, we cannot compare like with like across real experience and that occasioned by art.

[16] See, e.g., de Sousa (1987); Feagin (1996); Wilson (1986); Goldie (2000); Robinson (2005); Matravers (2014); Livingston and Mele (1997); and Meskin and Weinberg (2003).

those governing the fit of our beliefs, emotions, desires, and evaluations concerning the real world.

These thinkers and I both appeal to the substantial recent empirical literature in the psychology of the emotions and the counterfactual imagination.[17] However, I argue that such research supports claims of only *descriptive* continuity between the processing of our responses to fictions or imaginings and our responses to our actual environment. Such continuity fails to hold, I show, in the *normative* dimensions of our responses. Indeed, responses that would be irrational or inapt when directed at some state of affairs in real life may be rational or apt when formed in response to an analogous state of affairs that is imagined or represented by a fiction. Here, contra a dominant strain in studies of affect and automatic processes, I illustrate a way in which assessing the rationality of a mental disposition or tendency requires consideration of the particular, context-specific functions for which it is activated.[18]

More specifically, I argue that the functions of our engagements with fictions and other objects of the imagination license a departure in those engagements from real-world affective norms. That is, the kinds of reasons that we countenance in genuine justifications or criticisms of our responses to works of the imagination depend on the purposes of our engagement with those works. In this respect, my account draws on considerations of practical reason, whereby the norms governing our engagements with (1) works of fiction, (2) objects and events in real life, and (3) other states of affairs represented via the imagination are derived from the distinct and not always mutually consistent aims or functions by which those engagements are constituted.

I should note that in what follows I refer to *the* purpose (aim, function, point) of our engagement with a work of art, but this is artificial and only for simplicity of exposition. For in encounters with even a minimally complex fictional work, let alone those of significant artistic substance, there are typically multiple ends at play, and realizing one may not be compatible with realizing another. Furthermore, although I argue that the norms governing our responses in certain practices of fictional engagement are derived from the context-specific functions those kinds of responses serve, this does not mean that such functions are always or regularly consulted to determine such norms. Rather, the functions, aims, purposes, and so on may be

---

[17] For example, work by Damasio (1994); Gordon (1990); Byrne (2007); Johnson-Laird (1983); Harris (2000); Nichols and Stich (2000).

[18] See, for example, the approaches of Kahneman and Tversky (2000); Blackburn (1998).

embedded in the practices themselves, and brought to awareness only under some conditions, such as when the contours of the practices are challenged.

If my argument for discontinuity is sound, it has certain implications for those debates over autonomy I have canvased. As we will see in Chapter 5, discontinuity threatens such things as the idea that a person's emotional response to fiction is an unmediated reflection of his or her character and genuine desires; the thought that stories evoke a reader's responses by giving her reasons for them that would apply in the real world; the claim that we can learn from a fiction when it provides a simulation of states of affairs that we might encounter in actual experience; and the methodological assumption employed in a wide range of psychological research that scientists can study the nature of emotions by exposing test subjects to acknowledged fictional representations (e.g., short films) in which those emotions are elicited.

My methodology in this book is to address the nature of the emotions and other affective states *across* real and imagined contexts: in this respect, I depart somewhat from the standard approaches to the emotions that take as their primary explananda our affective responses to the real world and, only by extension, show how those theories also apply to our emotional responses to what we imagine. That approach tends to be motivated by the assumption that our affective responses to imaginings reflect secondary, indirect, exploitations of capacities that, in evolutionary and developmental processes, were acquired for dealing with actual situations. If the imagination allows us to feel emotions for what we know is not real, this may only reflect the value, for example, of being able to anticipate the consequences of certain behaviors by merely mentally representing ourselves as carrying them out. Kim Sterelny calls such imaginings that are not necessarily motivational "decoupled representations," and emphasizes their role in supporting adaptive behaviors that spring from "coupled" or truth-apt representations.[19]

The reasons for that approach become clear when we see how it helps explain the development of the capacity for counterfactual thought in the face of suspicions that, given the threats to survival and reproduction faced by early hominoids, the cost of thinking in ways that are non-veridical would be too high for the imagination to have bestowed adaptive benefits. Perhaps cavemen couldn't afford to daydream.

However, that emphasis on the truth-apt foundations of our imaginative activity can seem exaggerated in light of how much of our time is

---

[19] Sterelny (2003).

spent in, and how much of our well-being is dependent on, the many varieties of counterfactual thinking that don't seem aimed at representing the world as it is.[20] Our capacity to experience powerful affective responses to fictions may instead be explicable from the standpoint of evolution as a *spandrel*, in the sense used by Stephen Jay Gould and Richard Lewontin to describe biological features that, although only an indirect result of the evolution of other features, acquire functional characteristics.[21] In response to worries that withholding a direct adaptive role from imaginative experiences somehow diminishes them, we should point out that compelling questions can be raised about the experiences afforded by the role of actual spandrels in cathedrals' decorative and representational programs, independent of questions about their origins.

In any case, the contrasts I draw in this volume between fiction-directed and real-world-directed responses should not be taken to imply that fictions are to be identified by their falsity. For it is very difficult to find any satisfactory way of distinguishing fictions from nonfictions on the basis of correspondence to the facts. Fictions contain many straightforwardly true propositions, and they elicit us to make many straightforwardly true inferences from their contents; conversely, nonfictions contain statements that are literally false (as in the use of metaphors), and exhibit narrative-like structures (e.g., claims about beginnings, climaxes, and endings) that are imputed to the real world but belong only to the form of representation itself.[22] Then there are fanciful cases in which we can imagine an author writing what she takes to be solely fictional, and which we would count as a fiction, but which happens to correspond to what is genuinely true.[23] Beyond those considerations, even when the statements of a fictional work of art are false, the insights the work is designed to lead us to—such as some moral discovery based on a parable— may be true, just as, inversely, a documentary may be literally true in all it says but cause us to form beliefs that are false (via, e.g., a manipulation of saliencies and constraints on the information that's provided). Finally, some genres and traditions don't fit easily into categories of fiction and nonfiction.

---

[20] Bloom (2010).
[21] Gould and Lewontin (1979). Their comparison of such features was to the triangular form created from the intersection of two adjacent arches in a Gothic cathedral. Although such areas were incorporated into the visual program of the cathedral, their presence can be explained not through an attempt to realize that function but through the creation of other functional elements, from which they result.
[22] Gilmore (2000).
[23] Davies (2007) and Currie (1990) offer theories of fiction that specifically accommodate this possibility.

Awkward questions emerge when undergraduates, taught that Thucydides is one of the first historians, notice his reassurance to readers of *Peloponnesian War* that when generals didn't say what they ought to have in an important speech, he substitutes the oratory that would have been appropriate to the occasion.

Hence, in what follows, I take fictionality to be a function, not of the falsity of a representation, but (minimally) of its place within a practice involving prescriptions to engage in pretense or make-believe. In this practice, authors or works prescribe audiences to imagine certain things, and audiences engage in that imagining because of their awareness of such prescriptions. The extension of this concept of fiction is that broad class of representations designed to prompt complex imaginings, a proper engagement with which does not require an evaluation of their truth.[24] A fiction asks us to imagine certain things to be true, e.g., that Dr. Watson served in the Second Anglo-Afghan War. Some of that which it asks us to imagine to be true is true, e.g., that there was a Second Anglo-Afghan War. Here the opposition between nonfiction and fiction is orthogonal to that between truth and falsity.[25]

Relatedly, although I contrast our attitudes toward the contents of imaginings with those toward the "real world," I acknowledge that the contents of fictions and imaginings are in some sense parts of the real world. Our world contains fictional and imagined representations according to which certain facts hold, such as that Sherlock Holmes's nemesis is Moriarty, Mimi dies of consumption, Godot never arrives, one has an alternative career, lover, or kitchen cabinets, the little monster who resembles one's own child in pajamas is very scary, and so on. Philosophers have developed highly sophisticated theories of how to account for the metaphysical status of such fictional characters and the constituents of fictional states of affairs—some treating them as actually existing abstract artifacts, others explaining away our reference to them so as not to impute any genuine existence.[26] My point is only that these contents of fictional and imagined representations do not

---

[24] On prescriptions to imagine, see Currie (1990); Walton (1990); Lamarque and Olsen (1996); Davies (2007); Stock (2017). On why such prescriptions can count as only a necessary, not sufficient, condition of fictionality, see Friend (2008).

[25] Empirical research showing significant differences between readers' experiences of narratives identified as false (fabricated but purporting to be true) and those identified as fictional suggests that the theorized independence between the true/false distinction and the nonfiction/fiction distinction is reflected in reading practice. See, e.g., Appel and Malečkar (2012).

[26] For a survey, see Friend (2007).

belong to a different world, but, minimally, to various, often not entirely true, representations of our world.[27]

Thus, in what follows I distinguish between our responses to what we identify as facts about the world and what we identify as the contents of fictions and imaginings. This is a distinction in our responses made with reference to our mental attitudes, not the actual metaphysical status of the responses' objects. Also, psychology doesn't always respect ontology; my interest is in the explanatory and normative relevance of the distinctions people make between what they take to be imagined and real, whatever the best metaphysical and semantic theory of fictional or imaginary objects might be.

Finally, a point that is more general than the others. The relationship between literature, the imagination, and affective experience is of fundamental importance. But I do not think that understanding here is helpfully advanced through panegyrics to the ineffability of art or by the (more excusable) rhetorical defenses of the values of the arts marshalled against threats by censorship, pedagogical marginalization, and distractions of more easily digestible media. Instead, I call on certain lines of thought in philosophy and the empirical sciences that may appear to be too dry, too rationalizing, or too abstract to expose what is so important to us about aesthetic forms. Handled carefully, however, these modes of inquiry offer ways of grounding what might have seemed only a debate over intuitions. Indeed, in what follows I hope to show that certain prima facie highly plausible views of our affective engagements with fictions do not survive scrutiny. However, I acknowledge that the style of such analysis sometimes seems to do violence to its object. What Wordsworth said of deciphering nature may hold as well for art: "We murder to dissect."

1.3. Chapter Plan

Here is a brief plan of what follows. In Chapter 2, I offer a summary of the general framework within which this work proceeds: a broad family of explanations of mental representation identified as the cognitive theory of the imagination. I then show how that general theory must be modified and supplemented when employed in the characterization and explanation of the

---

[27] Currie (2014).

particular kind of imagining constitutive of our engagements with works of fiction.

In Chapter 3, I sketch a general theory of the emotions that aspires to accommodate both traditional philosophical conceptions of the emotions as cognitively inflected evaluative appraisals and more recent empirical approaches that highlight the automatic and subdoxastic dimensions they often exhibit. Adopting an approach parallel to that taken in Chapter 2, I then show how that general theory of the emotions must be modified and supplemented to account for the particular kinds of emotions elicited in the imaginative experiences afforded by works of art.

In Chapter 4, I begin to delineate the debate between normative continuity and discontinuity by establishing what they have in common: a commitment to apt, fitting, or rational emotions. This chapter offers a characterization of that concept of aptness and then turns to the argument in favor of continuity: the claim that the criteria of aptness governing our responses to the contents of artistic representations conform to those governing our responses to analogous states of affairs in real life.

In Chapter 5, I look at what turns on the debate between continuity and discontinuity. In other words, I show why, beyond our interest in characterizing the grounds of fiction-directed emotions, we should care about which account is correct. Then, after diagnosing what I take to be two prima facie plausible but ultimately inadequate defenses of the discontinuity thesis, I turn to what I think is its best defense.

In Chapter 6, I ask if the same case that was made for discontinuity of norms governing our emotions can be developed for only the cognitive part of those emotions, that is, the respect in which they represent some fact about their objects. In other words, I ask whether invariance holds between the grounds of our affectively neutral and real-world-directed representations and those directed at the contents of fictions. Is "make-belief" rational in the same sense as belief?

In Chapter 7, I address the question of invariance vis-à-vis our desires for fictions, particularly those such as tragic dramas that elicit mutually inconsistent desires. Both emotions and mere representational states such as belief and imagining have a mind to world (or "world" of fiction) direction of fit, and their aptness can be assessed with reference to that relation. Desires, however, require a different kind of treatment because they have a different direction of fit; they aim for the world to be changed to fit their contents rather than for their contents to fit the world. An important question I ask here is whether desires *as such* are subject to any standards of aptness over which the existence of discontinuity or continuity across fictions and real life could be identified.

In Chapter 8, I turn to a puzzling feature of our engagement with certain kinds of fictions, albeit one whose possibility is provided for by the discontinuity thesis. This is the problem of *discrepant affects*: why we sometimes find ourselves taking pleasure in fictional events that we would deplore in real life; align ourselves with or even admire fictional characters whom we would find despicable if they were encountered in the actual world; and form desires for events to occur in fictions that, in our actual experience, we want to prevent. I argue that such responses reflect an appropriate fiction-motivated breakdown in the quarantine separating how we really value things and from how we only imagine doing so.

Finally, in Chapter 9, I seek to defend a claim that I regularly advert to in the preceding chapters: from a very broad perspective, the norms governing our affective, desire-like, and evaluative engagements with works of art reflect the functions the works are designed to serve. Here I argue for that claim against both those who assert that works of art have no function (a notion of the artistic autonomy gestured to earlier in this chapter) and those who would identify a set of particular functions all works of art have qua art. Although throughout this volume I focus on the representational aptness of our responses to art, to the exclusion of moral forms of aptness, I conclude this chapter by showing how the functional view has the resources to explain how and when moral considerations enter into our evaluation of fictions in artistic terms.

2

Cognitive Imagining and Literary Fictions

> "Painters and Poets," someone objects, "have always had an equal
> right to do whatever they wanted." We know it and we both seek this
> indulgence and grant it in turn. But not to the degree that the savage
> mate with the gentle, nor that snakes be paired with birds, nor lambs
> with tigers.
>
> —Horace, *Ars Poetica*, 1–13

This study proceeds within two interrelated explanatory frameworks. One is
a cognitive theory of the imagination, the other is an evaluative theory of the
emotions. In §2.1, I identify some of the major commitments of the imagination framework and, in §2.2, I show how it is to be applied, with adjustments,
to the imaginative representations elicited by literary fictions.

2.1. The Cognitive Theory of the Imagination

I will begin here by sketching some of the main tenets of a prominent
framework in philosophy of mind that I'll refer to as the *cognitive theory of
the imagination*. I will then suggest where that theory needs to be amended
to capture peculiarities of our imaginative engagements with works of art.[1]

There is a broad consensus among theorists of the imagination that imaginings can be type-identified, like other mental states, in virtue of their functional role.[2] That is, beliefs, desires, and imaginings (as well as other states)
are each to be individuated from one another not by their contents but by
the typical patterns of interactions they (the types of which they are tokens)

---

[1] For major cognitive theories, see Walton (1990); Leslie (1987); Gordon (1986); Goldman (1992);
Harris (2000); Currie and Ravenscroft (2002); Nichols and Stich (2000).
[2] Nichols (2006a, 8).

Apt Imaginings. Jonathan Gilmore, Oxford University Press (2020). © Oxford University Press.
DOI: 10.1093/oso/9780190096342.001.0001

respectively share with other elements of the mind and behavior.[3] The idea here is that we can characterize the essence of some kind of mental state by collecting ordinary folk-psychological observations—largely platitudes—about how that mental state is typically causally connected to various causes (such as beliefs, desires, and perceptions) and effects (such as beliefs, desires, behavior, and emotions).[4] For example, if I believe a proposition p, I will tend to assert that p under appropriate conditions; behave in ways appropriate to it being true that p; deny what saliently contradicts it; rely on it in inferences; and so on. Thus, an instance of imagining that p is distinguished from believing or desiring that p (and other token attitudes we might adopt with the content p) not by some special tagging or proprietary kind of content, but by the typical roles imagining plays in the causal networks connecting sensory inputs, our other kinds of mental representations, and our behavior.[5] Generalizations about such roles are then perhaps subsequently revised for the sake of greater explanatory power within a given psychological theory. The result, ideally, is the discovery of a distinctive causal profile, perhaps one that specifies counterfactual dependencies, for each kind of mental state by which their token instances can be identified.[6]

As noted in §1.1, appeals to the imagination, historical and contemporary, enter into such a wide variety of explanatory contexts that it is an open question among philosophers of mind whether across these uses the capacity that is referred to is the same. In other words, it is unclear whether we can identify a canonical set of causal generalizations about imagining that would serve in all contexts to individuate a person's token imaginings from her other mental states. However, some standard distinctions, each of which holds ceteris paribus, are as follows:

---

[3] See Block (1996). Because imaginings play many inferential roles analogous to those of beliefs, the former are often identified in theories with reference to the latter, as *simulated beliefs, bracketed beliefs, decoupled representations,* or *offline beliefs.*

[4] Some terminological distinctions: I use the following conventional terminology to describe our mental states: an *attitude,* or *propositional attitude,* is a content-bearing state that is defined by its distinctive functional role, that is, a tendency to interact in particular ways with other elements of the mind and behavior. A token of any such attitude contains a *content,* such as a representation of some proposition or fact. A *mental state* is an attitude plus its content, e.g., a belief that p is a mental state with the content p that is functionally distinct from other mental states such as an imagining or desire with the content p.

[5] Appealing to causal-functional roles in distinguishing mental attitudes such as beliefs, desires, and imaginings does not exclude the possibility that, in the particular case or in general, different attitudes may also be distinguishable, not essentially but diagnostically, by their particular phenomenologies. Some writers argue that intentional states or propositional attitudes can have a robust phenomenological character. See Strawson (2009); Horgan and Tienson (2002); Pitt (2004).

[6] Lewis (1972); Shoemaker (1984).

Our imaginings are often, although not exclusively, caused and constrained by our will, unlike our occurrent beliefs, which depend much more on our other occurrent beliefs and perceptions. That is, a person's mental state does not typically count as a belief if it is not grounded in relevant ways in his or her other beliefs and experiences. A will to believe does not belong among those grounds. I can arrange conditions by which I intend to make it likely that I will come to form a certain belief, but my intention itself cannot cause me to form the belief. Likewise, my perception of a real object (in any sense modality) is counterfactually dependent on the object and tends to change involuntarily along with changes in the object or my physical relation to it. By contrast, my sensory imagining of an object exhibits a much greater freedom, where its appearance can be a consequence of how I choose to represent it to myself. Of course, such freedom does not entail omnipotence: I may fail in carrying out the intention to imagine some content because, e.g., I merely lack the imaginative capacities or the relevant experiences that are required to do so. In his *Sixth Mediation*, Descartes notes that whereas one can conceive of the idea of a chiliagon, one cannot visually imagine it, a point confirmed when one tries to visualize the 1,000-sided figure as looking different from a figure with 10,000 sides.[7]

Furthermore, beliefs, perceptions, and some other mental states such as remembering are subject, arguably, to a constitutive norm of aiming at what is true. Imaginings, by contrast, are not always comparably constrained. If my beliefs happen to be false or my perceptions delusionary, they fail to be satisfied qua beliefs or perceptions. This is not the case with generic imagining, which, as such, bears no such essential normative connection to what is the case—although, as we'll see, particular imaginings can be subject to contextually imposed norms of correctness.

Finally, imaginings, unlike beliefs, tend to be context-dependent. What I imagine depends on the particular circumstances that motivate the imagining. Watching a film provokes one set of imaginings, reading a novel, planning a trip, and daydreaming provoke different imaginings. Beliefs, however, tend to be context-independent: once formed, if suitably connected to my other beliefs, they remain stable elements in what I believe, if not always consciously so. Also, whereas what I now believe affects the acceptance,

---

[7] "It is true that since I am in the habit of imagining something whenever I think of a corporeal thing, I may construct in my mind a confused representation of some figure; but it is clear that this is not a chiliagon. For it differs in no way from the representation I should form if I were thinking of a myriagon, or any figure with very many sides" (1988, 111).

rejection, and revision of other potential beliefs I may form, imaginings don't get added to a single general stock that is brought to bear on an assessment of any other imagining that might arise. This distinction makes it possible to imaginatively represent, successively, many conflicting states of affairs— say, the New York City of Spider-Man, Henry James, and post-apocalyptic fantasies—without any impetus to reconcile their mutual inconsistencies.

Of course, not every reference to the imagination bears a commitment to some mental attitude that is essentially distinguished from the others. Consider how sometimes what we call an instance of imagining is readily susceptible to redescription in ways that eliminate any explanatory role for an appeal to the concept, or its behavioral analogue of pretending. In playing Monopoly, for example, we may describe what I do as pretending that I've ac- quired property; imagining that others owe me rent; and so on. But this may mark no difference in behavioral, inferential, and affective respects from my merely believing that, according to the rules of the game, points represented by fake money are distributed according to rolls of the dice. Likewise, in trying to explain, e.g., how a burglar entered the premises, my imagining his climbing over the fence and sneaking through the garden may be reducible to a set of beliefs with various levels of credence about what path he took. However, globally trying to reduce all invocations of the imagination to beliefs would have implausible consequences.[8]

One problem is such reduction would conflict with the phenomenology of affective states based on imaginings. For example, my imagining Anna Karenina suffering will tend to affect me powerfully, while merely my believing that it is part of Tolstoy's story that the character suffers would hardly lead to such a response. Likewise, there is a difference between the phenomenology of my pretending to, or actually coming to, desire that p as part of a game, and my believing that the rules of the game prescribe that I desire p. Indeed, it is not clear how merely *believing* that it is true in a fic- tion or game of pretense that some state of affairs holds can cause us to have any semblance of the feelings that the reliance on concepts of imagining or pretending have been introduced to explain. This is not to deny that having certain beliefs about what is represented in a fiction may be necessary for the fiction to cause us to feel an emotion. I will feel concern for Superman when imagining that he is exposed to kryptonite's radiation only if I believe that,

---

[8] For the argument against identifying the imagination as a distinct cognitive attitude, see Langland-Hassan (2012).

in stories featuring the superhero, that substance makes him weak. But this is a case of fictional import: in virtue of believing something about the sub-genre of Superman stories, I imagine some state of affairs to hold in one of its instances.

Treating imagining as reducible to believing also obscures the phenom-enology of iterated fictions, or stories within stories. For in a typical experi-ence of such a nested story (say, *Don Quixote* or *The Decameron*), the frame narratives lose their saliency as we experience the embedded representations as primary. That is, as we read the embedded story in which it is true that p, we imagine that p, not that someone within the main frame story is telling a story in which p is the case. If appeals to beliefs were substituted for imagin-ings, our experience would be construed as having the belief that A (the au-thor) tells a story according to which B (the narrator) tells a story according to which C (a character) tells a story according to which certain events occur. This seems too baroque a description of our mental state compared to the alternative description of our experience as our imagining some set of facts hold when focusing on the frame story, then imagining that another set of facts hold when following the nested story, then imagining that another set of facts hold when following the story embedded within the previous one.

A third consideration is that reducing all instances of imagining to beliefs would introduce an odd asymmetry between propositional and sensory imagining. One might propose that in all cases of putative imagining, "I be-lieve that, according to a fiction, p" could be substituted for "I imagine that p." But a parallel construction involving sensory imagining is elusive: e.g., "vis-ually perceives p in the fiction" cannot be substituted for "visually imagines p," just because sensory imagining does not entail any actual perception. My visualizing Achilles's shield does not imply my having any concurrent per-ceptual experience. A proponent of the view that imagining is reducible to other kinds of mental states might argue that propositional imagining should be understood as reducible to believing, while other modalities of imagining may not be reducible. But then an explanation is required for why there is this difference: Why can our propositional imaginings in relation to fictions be exchanged for propositional beliefs, but our sensory and other experien-tial forms of imagining cannot be substituted with perceptual or experiential beliefs?

Finally, the existence of a non-reducible attitude of imagining (and its behavioral analogue of pretending) seems especially salient in contexts in which one is asked to both imagine some content and believe it at the same time; or to pretend that something is true, while behaving in a way guided by one's belief that it is true. We can see an illustration in a seminal experiment by Alan Leslie. While young children (around two years old) watched, Leslie pretended to pour tea into two empty cups. He then picked up one of the cups, turned it over and shook it (as if to "empty" it), and placed it right side up next to the other cup. Although neither cup actually contained tea during the experiment, the children identified the "empty" cup as the one that Leslie turned over and the "full" cup as the one that remained upright.[9] According to the standard way of interpreting this, the child imagines that the cup that was overturned is empty while, of course, also believing that the cup is empty.

That the children in that experiment could identify a cup as both (really) empty and (in imagination) "empty" does not prove that the attitude of imagination is functionally distinct from that of belief. Perhaps the child's belief does not, contrary to appearances, have the same content as the child's imagination-like representation: the former is about the cup, while the latter might be about what description of the cup is called for by the rules of the experiment. However, such cases, where what is imagined as true corresponds to what is believed to be true make plain the implausible, albeit not dispositive, artificiality of reducing all instances of imagining to instances of belief.[10]

The preceding describes distinctions between the imagination and truth-apt attitudes such as belief. Let me now quickly survey what the cognitive theory of the imagination identifies as some of their interactions and parallels.

First, no counterfactual representation cites all the facts required for us to understand its contents. Instead, many of those facts are supplied by the beliefs that we import into the scenario we are asked to imagine.[11] Reading a detective story in which a coroner determines that a character died after unwittingly consuming tea laced with arsenic, I infer that she was likely murdered. For I implicitly introduce into the content of the story such beliefs as that arsenic is a deadly poison and that it's rarely accidentally ingested. These facts are then integrated seamlessly into an inference among my imaginative representations that leads from the coroner's discovery to the conclusion that there was probably foul play. Our beliefs supply implicit premises

---

[9] Leslie (1994).

[10] In a different context, but making a similar point, David Velleman (2000) worries that explaining what a child does in a given pretense by appeal to her knowledge of what behavior the pretense calls for "makes the child out to be depressingly unchildlike" (256).

[11] Harris (2000); Byrne (2007); Skolnick and Bloom (2006).

and background conditions for counterfactual imaginative representations in general, not just those elicited by fictions.[12] For example, in apportioning responsibility for an accident, an insurance claims-adjuster might imagine (counterfactually) that his client had not been speeding in order to determine whether, in those circumstances, the accident would still have occurred. There, his beliefs about braking distances, lines of sight, traffic flow, and the like enter into his imagining of the occurrence of the events without his client's contribution. These imaginings might then issue in certain conclusions about his client's actual causal responsibility.[13]

Finally, not only can beliefs be imported into imaginings and imaginings furnish propositions that can enter into our beliefs, but, as we saw in the arsenic case, there are parallels between the processes of making inferences among the propositions in each domain. Just as I would when reasoning among my beliefs, if I imagine that p and imagine that if p then q, I will conclude, ceteris paribus, in imagining that q.[14] Currie and Ravenscroft note that it is "this capacity of imaginings to mirror the inferential patterns of belief that makes fictional storytelling possible."[15] We see such inferential orderliness of the imagination in the behavior of the children in Leslie's experiment. They appear to make the same inferences among their imaginings (akin to "The 'full' cup was turned over; turning over a cup empties it; the 'once-full' cup is now empty") that they would make among analogous beliefs.

Previously I outlined some of the differences and parallels that exist between imagining and other mental attitudes directed, mainly, toward propositions. Let me now turn to a distinct kind of imagining, that directed toward experiences that are identified with those furnished by the senses. Just as propositional imagining involves adopting the attitude of imagination toward some content that is of the kind that could be the object of belief, sensory imagining involves adopting an imaginative attitude toward some content that is of the kind that could be the object of perception. As I might see some object in my environment, so I might "visualize" it in a way that is self-generated. This is true of other sense modalities as well, each of which permits ready parallels between endogenously and exogenously generated experiences.

---

[12] See Byrne (2007).
[13] See Williamson (2007).
[14] The "ceteris paribus" qualification will be explained in §2.3 as reflecting the constraints a fiction imposes on the scope of what is to be imagined in engaging with it.
[15] Currie and Ravenscroft (2002); see also Nichols (2006a, 7).

Another type of imagining that some theorists treat as a third kind, and others as a subset of sensory imagining, is *experiential imagining*, which can be illustrated in the following way: to propositionally imagine that a cat is in a tree is to hold only a belief-like imagining that such a state of affairs obtains. To engage in sensory imagining of a cat in a tree is to form a visual mental representation of the cat in a tree. However, to experientially imagine the cat in the tree is to imagine one's seeing it thus—to imagine what one visualizes as belonging to oneself gazing up at the cat ensconced among the branches. In effect, one imagines oneself having the experience of seeing the cat in the tree. Such experiential imagining requires sensory dimensions, but is not limited to such sensory dimensions, as it also involves, at least implicitly, a commitment to the sensory experience belonging to oneself as one imagines seeing, hearing, feeling, etc., whatever it is that is the content of one's representation.[16]

I want to introduce here one final feature of general theories of the imagination. Truth-apt representations such as beliefs and perceptions are typically insulated from imaginings. One can usually distinguish between one's mental states that are caused by standard external sources and those that are self-generated. But such quarantine is a normative ideal that is not always realized. Studies of reading comprehension find that in practice the barrier between beliefs and imaginings is sometimes illicitly breached. As I'll describe in a moment, these breakdowns in imaginative quarantine point to the possibility of belief- and imagination-representations being similarly implemented in both the mind and brain. I'll then turn to evidence in much more prevalent studies of sensory and experiential imagining that our experiences of endogenously and exogenously caused representations depend on shared psychological and neurological resources.

In one experiment, Markus Appel and Martina Mara found that readers' beliefs are sometimes affected by assertions made within what they know to be fictional stories. This alone would be unremarkable and not an obvious indication of a breach of imaginative quarantine, as fictional stories regularly make claims that are, in the right circumstances, appropriate sources of belief. Readers of Patrick O'Brian's *Master and Commander* novels of nineteenth-century seafaring are justified in assuming that their author aspires to accurately represent how ship-rigging and navigation were then performed. But

---

[16] Some philosophers argue that all imagining is experiential. Peacocke (1985), for example, claims that "to imagine something is always at least to imagine, from the inside, being in some conscious state" (21).

Appel and Mara's finding was conjoined with a demonstration that the degree of influence a story had on readers' beliefs was under some conditions proportionate to the level of trustworthiness that the story accords the *fictional character* who is the source of the story's fictional assertions. Thus, readers were more influenced by claims about fuel-efficient driving methods made by a fictional character who is represented in the fiction as an expert on the environment than by one presented as superficial and lacking integrity. This suggests that readers let the degree of reliability that they *imagine* a fictional speaker possesses illicitly influence their belief in what he says.[17]

Of course, disparate levels of trust accorded to two acknowledged fictional characters may reflect a reader's assumptions about the communicative intentions of the author—seeing the reliable character as offering information merits belief because that character is employed by the author to convey his or her own beliefs. Indeed, Appel and Mara found that readers highly absorbed in a fiction exhibited less varying levels of trust across different characters; perhaps this is because deep absorption in a fictional narrative prevents a high level of awareness of the work as the product of a communicative intention—such as to convey some truth about the real world.[18]

However, other studies suggest that readers sometimes acquire beliefs from the content presented in a fiction despite their explicitly being made aware that the content is false. In one case, reading false statements that were presented as true in a fictional text affected not only (as expected) readers' performance in answering questions about facts that they didn't know prior to reading the text, but also their performance in answering questions whose answers they previously knew.[19] Readers tended to endorse as true the facts that were presented in the fiction in place of what, prior to reading the text, they believed to be true. In another kind of study, readers were charged with identifying those sentences in a fictional story that contained false information about the real world. Yet, even though they successfully identified such misinformation in the text, they still tended to rely on it as if it were true during subsequent tests of their knowledge.[20] Such studies demonstrate that

---

[17] Appel and Mara (2013).

[18] On fiction as sometimes a source of justified belief via authorial testimony, see Stock (2017).

[19] Eslick, Fazio, and Marsh (2011) found that despite changing the color of the print to red in some fictional reading passages (leaving the others in black) and explicitly telling participants to attend to those rubricated passages as possibly containing false information about the real world, participants displayed no reduction in suggestibility—tending to identify those statements as true—when tested later on that information.

[20] Marsh and Fazio (2006).

people can be persuaded by false information when it is presented in narrative form, even if the unreliability of that information is made salient at an early stage of their exposure to the text.[21] That suggestibility persists even when readers are reminded that the source of the relevant beliefs is a fictional story.[22]

Related studies show a comparable failure of quarantine between what one visually imagines and what one believes oneself to have perceived. In one study, for example, Elizabeth Loftus and her colleagues found that participants were more likely to believe that they had experienced a given event in childhood, such as breaking a window with their hands, when they had been previously prompted to imagine the scenario.[23] Also, the more often people imagined performing a given action the more likely they were to believe they had performed it.[24] Other studies found that reading about some scenario disposed people to later mistakenly claim that they had seen pictures of the scenario. This may be explained as people taking the experience of the sensory images they formed while reading as corresponding to genuine experiences of external stimuli.[25] This effect obtains in predictions as well. People who were asked to imagine an event such as their winning a prize, committing a crime, contracting a disease, or giving blood, later reported a greater subjective probability that they would undergo that experience than did others who had not been given the assignment.[26] It also appears that the more emotionally arousing an imagining is, the greater effect it has in strengthening beliefs in its past or future occurrence.[27] Such studies suggest that in the absence of strong cues of veracity, people tend to take the interdependent dimensions of richness, emotional power, and ease of access or fluency of a given mental representation as an indication of its correctness, even when those features exist for reasons unrelated to the representation's accuracy.[28] Significantly for our purposes, those dimensions can be enhanced by merely having already imagined the representation's content.[29]

---

[21] Appel and Malečkar (2012).

[22] Green et al. (2006).

[23] Loftus (2003); Bernstein and Loftus (2009). See Koehler (1991) for a review of studies showing the influence of imagination on judgments of likelihood that some state of affairs obtained. See also Mazzoni and Memon (2003).

[24] Thomas, Bulevich, and Loftus (2003).

[25] Intraub and Hoffman (1992).

[26] Anderson (1983); Sherman et al. (1985); Gregory, Cialdini, and Carpenter (1982).

[27] Szpunar and Schacter (2013); Carroll (1978).

[28] See Shidlovski, Schul, and Mayo (2014).

[29] On the heuristics people employ in evaluating a representation's truth, see Johnson, Hashtroudi, and Lindsay (1993).

These empirical results can be interpreted in various ways. Recall from earlier both how our imaginings seem to exhibit the kind of inferential orderliness that is found among our beliefs and how imaginings and beliefs can enter into inferential relations with each other. One explanation of the suggestibility and source-monitoring errors illustrated in the studies I have mentioned is that they indicate a substantial overlap among the mechanisms that process beliefs, imaginings, and other representational states. In other words, what one imagines to be true can sometimes be plugged in in place of what one believes to be true because the mechanisms that handle such representations are similarly constituted from shared "parts." Perhaps these suggestibility effects are also enhanced by readers applying comparatively less scrutiny in verifying the statements that they encounter in fictions than they do with declarative statements of fact vying to be accepted as beliefs.

The determination of the extent to which there is such a descriptive continuity in the ways the mind and brain implement such propositional beliefs and imaginings waits upon further empirical study. However, analogous evidence that perceptions and sensory imaginings depend on shared neurological and psychological processes is comparatively strong.

Studies of visual imagery, for example, show that it can selectively interfere with visual perception, while, conversely, visual perception can interfere with visual imagining.[30] Cross-modal interactions occur as well, in which, e.g., where one imagines seeing an object located affects where one hears a sound originating.[31] Also, when people are asked to scan across the space separating two mentally visualized objects (holding constant their imagined position), they take more time when the distances between the objects are greater, just as they would if the scanning was performed between objects they perceived in the environment. Relatedly, when people's eye movements are tracked as they engage in visually imagining some scene, the paths and duration of their scanning are similar to those of their eye movements when they perceive analogous external stimuli.[32] Indeed, when people visually imagine something, they make saccadic eye movements similar to those they

---

[30] Hampson and Duffy (1984); Segal and Fusella (1970); Craver-Lemley and Reeves (1992).
[31] Berger and Ehrsson (2018).
[32] On duration of scanning analogous real and imagined scenes, see Denis and Kosslyn (1999); and Kosslyn (1973). On similar paths taken while scanning real and imagined scenes, see Laeng and Teodorescu (2002).

would perform if genuinely perceiving the thing, and that imagining is frustrated to the extent that such eye movement is deliberately restrained.[33]

Going beyond what is suggested about shared psychological mechanisms in those behavioral studies, a wide range of neuroanatomical research suggests that the experiences of internally generated imagery and externally caused perceptions are realized in similar states of the brain.[34]

Neuroimaging techniques show, for example, that when one alternately imagines some stimulus (e.g., an object, face, or place in the environment) and perceives an analogous one, a substantial degree of overlap appears in the activation patterns in the sensory cortices.[35] Relatedly, there is a substantial similarity between the neural representations of the topographical locations of objects when they are perceived and when imagined.[36] Stephen Kosslyn argues on the basis of such studies that the shared phenomenology of spatial awareness of objects in perception and imagining has an isomorphic physiological basis, like a schematic drawing composed in the medium of neurons: "numerous areas of cerebral cortex are topographically organised; patterns of activity within these areas make explicit and accessible the spatial organisation of the planar projection of a stimulus."[37]

Other studies have shown that some incapacities in sensory perception due to brain damage are associated with analogous incapacities in the sensory imagination. Edoardo Bisiach and Claudio Luzzatti found, for example, that patients with damage to the posterior right parietal lobe, who sometimes ignore or fail to see the left half of the visual field they are looking at, also had trouble imagining what is in the left half of their imagined visual field. Asked to visualize standing in a familiar location in the Piazza del Duomo in Milan, they could describe only landmarks that from their virtual vantage point were on the right side of the scene, and this omission of what they would have seen on their left was sustained when they were asked to imagine the piazza

---

[33] Brandt and Stark (1997); Demarais and Cohen (1998); Humphrey and Underwood (2008); Spivey et al. (2000); Bourlon et al. (2011). On impeding imagining, see Antrobus, Antrobus, and Singer (1964); Laeng and Teodorescu (2002).

[34] Farah (1984); Kosslyn, Ganis, and Thompson (2001); Ishai and Sagi (1995); and Cabeza and Nyberg (2000).

[35] Kreiman, Koch, and Fried (2000); O'Craven and Kanwisher (2000); Kosslyn, Ganis, and Thompson (2001); Stokes et al. (2009); Cichy, Heinzle, and Haynes (2011); and Reddy, Tsuchiya, and Serre (2010).

[36] Kosslyn et al. (1995); Slotnick, Thompson, and Kosslyn (2005); Thirion et al. (2006); Cichy, Heinzle, and Haynes (2011); and Stokes et al. (2009).

[37] (2005, 336). He adds that neuroanatomical studies of nonhuman primates show approximately half of the cortical areas serving vision are topographically organized.

from the alternative point of view that would be furnished by standing on the side opposite to their original position.[38]

Finally, in an fMRI study designed to determine the maximal degree of shared neural processing between analogous tasks of visual perception and visual imagining, Giorgio Ganis and his colleagues compared the brain regions that were activated when subjects perceived faint drawings of simple objects with those that were activated when they merely imagined the same image. The result was that approximately two-thirds of all the regions activated in these tasks were engaged by both tasks, with the regions engaged during visual imagery forming a subset of those engaged during visual perception. The researchers note that while the overlap is thus neither uniform nor complete, "visual imagery and visual perception draw on most of the same neural machinery."[39]

Although those studies addressed visual imagining, analogous findings exist for representations in other sensory modalities, such as in tactile,[40] auditory,[41] and motor imagery.[42] For example, a sharing of neuroanatomical processes between tactile perception and tactile imagining is suggested in studies showing that people who watched a film of a person's leg being touched with a stick exhibited activity in the same brain region (the secondary somatosensory cortex) that was activated when they felt their own bodies being touched in that way.[43]

While those experiments involving propositional and sensory imagining largely left the fictional status of their prompts unaddressed, their findings are borne out in studies of reading that employed several kinds of imagining (sensory, propositional, motor) that were specifically elicited by fictional stories. There, researchers find that the brain regions that are causally responsible for tracking activities in a fictional situation substantially overlap with those regions that play a role in seeing and engaging in analogous activities in the real world. Speer and her colleagues found, for example, close

---

[38] Bisiach and Luzzatti (1978).

[39] Ganis, Thompson, and Kosslyn (2004).

[40] Anema et al. (2012); Keysers et al. (2004).

[41] Zatorre et al. (1996); Halpern (2001).

[42] Roth et al. (1996); Ehrsson, Geyer, and Naito (2003). Jeannerod (1994) suggests that the neural mechanisms that subtend such motor images are inhibited at some stage of processing, preventing them from resulting in actual motor execution. See also Jeannerod (2001).

[43] That sensory imagining and perception share the same neural resources doesn't mean, of course, that they exhibit the same functions—i.e., relations to other elements in one's mental economy. What one perceives, for example, is under much less voluntary control than what one can visually imagine. This is true even though we do have a capacity to see one thing as (or in) another, like a face in the clouds, and the contents of our imaginings are often unbidden.

parallels between the changes in the brain that occur when one observes other people performing activities and the changes that arise when reading narratives about analogous activities: "regions involved in processing goal-directed human activity, navigating spatial environments, and manually manipulating objects in the real world increased in activation at points when those specific aspects of the narrated situation were changing."[44] In other words, understanding characters' goals and actions in literary texts involved activation in areas of the brain that serve the recognition and understanding of the goals and behavior of people in real life. Among those are areas of the brain involved in motor preparation and action execution.[45]

Those studies, and the cognitive theory of the imagination described earlier, suggest that, in psychological and neurological terms, there is a great deal of descriptive continuity between our experiences furnished by the imagination, and those supplied by beliefs and perceptions. There, fiction-directed imagining was treated as just one kind of counterfactual imagining among others. In the next section, I want to identify certain features of our imaginings prompted by fictions that call for a distinctive explanation.

2.2. Imagining with Fictions

Although made-up stories are readily employed alongside counterfactuals, hypotheticals, and other kinds of representations in illustrating the general cognitive theory of the imagination, there are certain dimensions of fictions that impose special constraints on what and how we imagine when we engage with them. The explanatory resources of the cognitive theory of imagining vis-à-vis fiction become salient only when we identify how the theory accommodates the conventions that determine our responses to fiction qua artistic representation, not just qua ordinary counterfactual representation. For example, my identification of a story's genre, my awareness of its author's communicative intentions, and my ends as a consumer of fiction shape which imaginings—of all those that a work might cause—would count as appropriate responses. As we'll see, this is typically not the case with the merely

---

[44] Speer et al. (2009). Using fMRI studies of the primary motor cortex, Roth et al. (1996) showed that about 30% of the pixels activated during the contraction of a group of muscles are also activated while imagining a movement involving the same muscles.

[45] Fischer and Zwaan (2008).

counterfactual representations that we might be prompted to imagine independent of our traffic with fictions.[46]

First let us observe that a foundational part of comprehending a literary fiction is to engage in a propositional imagining of its contents. That is, we adopt the mental attitude of imagination toward certain propositions that we take to hold true in the story. As noted in §2.1, that attitude of imagining is not distinguished from other attitudes such as belief or desire by its *content*. Rather, like all propositional attitudes, imagining is distinguished by the respective patterns of interactions it has with other elements of mind and behavior. For our purposes here, we may observe that while beliefs "aim at the true," propositional imaginings aim at what is true *in a fiction*.[47] In what follows, I will speak indiscriminately of a proposition being "true in a fiction," "true according to a fiction," and being a "fictional truth." What is true in a fiction can include prosaic facts such as details about events, locations, and characters that anyone following the story would recognize, as well as facts that are occasionally missed even in relatively competent readings. And what is true in the world of a fiction is often true of the real world, as when a novel tells us facts that hold both inside and outside what it represents. Note: here and throughout this volume, the familiar expression "the world of the story" (and its close cousins) is just a *façon de parler* referring to what is true according to the fiction.

But what makes something true in a fiction? That is, what dimensions of a story are our imaginings answerable to? We're usually not in doubt about what facts hold in a conventional fiction. But what principles or theories do we implicitly rely on in identifying those facts? Some theorists try to arrive at a general principle that determines how something becomes true in a fiction, aiming to systematize various elements of an unarticulated "folk theory" that

---

[46] I acknowledge that the general cognitive theory of the imagination is *consistent* with whatever dimensions we might identify as peculiar to our imaginative engagement with literary or artistic fictions. Because the general theory acknowledges that at least some kinds of our imaginings are subject to our will, it can allow that our imagining in relation to fictions is very different from imagining in other contexts because of how we *choose* to moderate our imaginings in accord with conventions constitutive of that engagement.

[47] See Walton (1990): "Imagining aims at the fictional as belief aims at the true" (41). The metaphorical characterization of beliefs as somehow specially tied to truth is from Williams (1976, 148). The precise relationship is philosophically controversial. Some philosophers argue that truth is an essential or constitutive norm of belief; others defend the view that truth norms apply to beliefs only descriptively, in virtue of, e.g., pragmatic considerations or biological design. See Chan (2014); Velleman (2000). One can identify analogous debates about fiction-directed imagining, e.g., whether it is essentially subject to the norm that it be a correct representation of what is true in a fictional text, or whether perhaps pragmatic or aesthetic considerations are what make that norm apply.

readers employ in discovering fictional states of affairs. In an influential account, David Lewis proposes that what is true in a fiction is what would be true in a (counterfactual) world, "where the fiction is told, but as known fact rather than fiction."[48] The relevant counterfactual world here is one that most resembles the one we believe our actual world to be, consistent with what is directly represented as true by the fiction. Call this principle the *Reality Principle*.[49] Kendall Walton represents it as follows:

If $p_1, \ldots, p_n$ are the propositions whose fictionality a representation generates directly, another proposition, q, is fictional in it if, and only if, were it the case that $p_1, \ldots, p_n$, it would be the case that q.[50]

Here what is true in a fiction is a function of both (1) what is explicitly stated to be true in the fiction and (2) what would be true in the actual world if the statements made in the fiction were true of the actual world. This approach is highly productive in that it offers an explanation of much of what is implied to be true in a fiction, but which is never stated. The narrator of *Pride and Prejudice* doesn't directly assert that Elizabeth and Darcy have functioning hearts and lungs, but we presume it to be part of the story that they do. This is because, counterfactually, if the states of affairs that are explicitly described in the novel were true, and the facts of the actual world consistent with such explicit descriptions were held constant, it would be true that Elizabeth and Darcy have functioning hearts and lungs. Facts about the real world are taken to be true in the fictional representation insofar as it does not appear to contradict them.

So far, the Reality Principle would appear to apply invariantly to imaginings generated specifically by fictions and to ordinary counterfactual imaginings characterized by the cognitive theory outlined in §2.1. This should be expected, as this account of what it is for something to be true in a fiction is an adaptation of the semantics of possible worlds developed to explain what it is for something to be true in a counterfactual state of affairs, simpliciter. However, as Lewis and other proponents of the theory acknowledge, there are problems in squaring his notion of fictional truth with the kind of content we associate with stories.

---

[48] Lewis (1978).
[49] Walton (1990). See also "the principle of minimal departure" advanced in Ryan (1991).
[50] Walton (1990, 145).

One concern is that the principle seems to over-predict what belongs to the contents of fictions, implausibly making them out to contain an indefinite number of facts that seem irrelevant to the stories they present. Austen's novel does not explicitly or implicitly contradict the truth of Gödel's incompleteness theorem or the germ explanation of disease, but it would be odd to conclude that they are therefore true in her story, as opposed to just having no place in it. Also, if we did assume that such irrelevant facts hold in the story, we would be forced to reach the counterintuitive conclusion that the fiction contains facts its author couldn't know about (e.g., those discovered after she wrote her novel) and which its contemporary readers would not have understood. These worries may follow from a more general assumption that, while any possible world, including our actual one, exhibits logical closure—any genuine proposition is either true or false in the world—fictional worlds are typically incomplete. Some propositions, such as that Emma Bovary has blue eyes, are neither true nor false in Flaubert's fiction, there being nothing in the narrative that gives us a reason to accept or deny that claim. What would have been true had the actual world been different is independent of what particular facts about that alternative world one might represent in a description. By contrast, what is true in or according to the counterfactual state of affairs represented by a work of fiction is partly determined by such contingencies as when, where, for whom, and by whom it was composed.

In an alternative analysis, Lewis proposes a principle that seeks to remedy the defects in the first. Call this the *Mutual Belief Principle*.[51] Here the implied facts in a story are those that follow from its explicit descriptions as matter of common knowledge in the circumstances in which the story originated. So even though the germ theory is not contradicted by anything explicitly stated in *Pride and Prejudice*, it is (rightly) not to be posited as true in the story because Austen's contemporaries wouldn't have thought any of the explicitly stated contents of the fiction entail it. This principle makes better sense of the intuition that what is true in a story is at least partly explained by what its community of origin thought was true of the actual world. However, the principle faces problems having to do with how to decide what belongs to a fiction when its author has idiosyncratic beliefs vis-à-vis her community. In asking what the implied facts are in a fiction, do we import what the author believed if it's inconsistent with what her community did?

---

[51] See Walton (1990, 151).

Furthermore, both principles, absent several ad hoc qualifications, lead to the imputation of bizarre propositions to many ordinary realist fictions. If *Madame Bovary* were told as known fact, we would be wrongly prompted to conclude that the narrator is someone who has a superhuman ability to reproduce the exact words uttered by denizens of Rouen. If *Hard Times* were told as known fact, we could mistakenly conclude that it is true in the fiction that people such as Gradgrind often suffer the misfortune of developing personalities associated with the surnames they were born with. Finally, the counterfactual approach wrongly ignores certain implied fictional truths, such as those that we discover via our understanding of symbols employed in the fiction.[52] The description of the wild boar's skull in *To the Lighthouse* foreshadows to readers that the family's affairs will be disrupted by death; but readers would not be justified in predicting that event if the description in the novel was treated as merely part of a counterfactual representation of the actual world. Also, as Lewis notes, assigning a given work to a genre may make certain things true in it (such that a story's dragon breathes fire) without that fact being indicated by any of the story's explicit propositions.[53]

Those and other difficulties with construing the content of a fiction as the content of any ordinary counterfactual have led many theorists to conclude that there may be no general principle that can systematically capture our pre-theoretic intuitions about what makes something true in a fiction. Walton suggests that the search for a single overarching principle betrays a confusion between analyzing the nature of fictional truth and explaining the means by which things come to be fictionally true.[54] Walton refers to those means as *principles of generation* and he denies that they reflect any systematic method by which a story's contents are constituted.

Instead, he proposes that the most general principles we can arrive at will function at best as heuristics.[55] Here, for example, the Reality Principle and the Mutual Belief Principle are indeed often relied on by authors to prescribe—and readers to discover—what is true in a story, but only defeasibly.[56] For a wide variety of means by which the contents of a story are constituted may trump those principles or narrow their application.

---

[52] Walton (1990, 165).

[53] Lewis (1978).

[54] Walton (1990, 161–69).

[55] Walton (1990, 139).

[56] Lamarque and Olsen (1996) agree. Despite being critics of Lewis's approach, they acknowledge that "fictional states of affairs . . . can be assumed to be like ordinary states of affairs . . . failing indication to the contrary" (95).

Walton proposes a very broad view of fictional truth that does not depend solely on the intentions of a fiction's author. Hence, he would count among items that have fictional content such things as naturally occurring cracks in a rock that happen to look like words. Other theorists adopt a narrower view: that for some proposition to be true in a fiction is for the proposition to be uttered or inscribed as part of a kind of communicative act in which an author intends to get an audience to pretend or imagine that the proposition is true.[57] Other propositions might be true in a work in a secondary sense because they form the background of those propositions that an author explicitly intends an audience to imagine to be true; follow from those propositions as inferences that are licensed by the work; or are inferred from such facts as those pertaining to the style, genre, conventions, or creator of the work. In what follows, I remain agnostic over which kind of theory best captures our identification of a story's contents. My only relevant commitments are (1) that there are some correctness constraints (whether derived from the author's intentions, conventions of literary practice, or some other source) on what we imagine to be true in engaging with a fiction; and (2) that any account of those constraints must be consistent with there being two kinds of sources of fictional truth, internal and external. I turn now to an explanation of those sources, which have already been informally appealed to.

2.3. Internal and External Sources of Fictional Truth

There are two perspectives that we may take on a fiction which are correlated with two kinds of sources from which we discover fictional truths. As we'll see, only one of those sources is recognized in the general cognitive theory of the imagination sketched in §2.1.

We adopt what can be referred to as the *internal* perspective on a fiction when we refer to facts in it that motivate us to imagine other propositions as true within the story; we adopt the complimentary *external* perspective when we refer to factors outside the fictional world that perform that imagination-generating function. The internal stance identifies the contents of that representation as if they were real or were being recounted by a real narrator. The

---

[57] This view is advanced in different forms, with different qualifications, in Currie (1990); Davies (2015). See also Stock (2017) for a defense of "extreme intentionalism," according to which the content of a fiction is supplied solely by what its author intended its readers to imagine.

external stance on the work, by contrast, describes it in terms of its identity as an artifact, with reference, e.g., to its characters, plot, style, medium, meter, tone, and other aspects of the vehicle of representation. From the internal stance, Othello's speech is rough ("rude am I in my speech"), but from the external it is refined, in the poetic diction Shakespeare employs.[58] Here we can see that it is only from the internal stance that the Reality Principle described earlier explains what is true in a fiction. It identifies what is true according to what would be the case if (counterfactually) the propositions of the fiction accurately represented the actual world. By contrast, the external stance identifies what is true in the fiction via reference to circumstances of its creation in the actual world.

These internal and external perspectives are correlated not only with two kinds of sources of what is true in a story, but two kinds of explanation of what occurs in it. Thus, an internal explanation of why Cordelia will not follow her sisters in their extravagant but formulaic expressions of filial piety to Lear will appeal to her sincerity or stubbornness; an external explanation will appeal to such factors as how her refusal sets the plot in motion and introduces the play's querying of the sources of a person's status and identity.[59]

No doubt, the generation of much of a fiction's contents can be described from an internal perspective. Reading "Mrs. Dalloway said she would buy the flowers herself," we take what the narrator says as a form of testimony of what is (in the fiction) true. When facing unreliable narrators, or characters with limited perspectives such as the dog in Virginia Woolf's *Flush*, we may discount the evidential value of what is stated, and find alternative avenues to working out what in the fiction occurs. However, this still instantiates an internal source of fictional truth because it mirrors how we would handle, if the story were told as known fact, an actual person's dubious assertion, assigning it a level of credence according to how much confidence we have in her sincerity and the means by which she arrived at her beliefs.

Furthermore, other truths are generated internally through inferences we are prompted to make from what is directly asserted. If I imagine of a fictional character that she was bitten by a poisonous snake, and that there is no antidote, then I'll imagine that she has a serious problem. Also, because we tend to monitor the consistency among our imaginings in relation to a given

---

[58] This way of describing the distinction is taken from Lamarque and Olsen (1996, 144–45). See also Walton (1978b, 21). An alternative internal reading is that Othello speaks such as to create a semblance of roughness.

[59] Kent: "I'll teach you differences" (Act I, scene 4).

fiction, we may give up what we thought was true in a fiction when information subsequently supplied by the narrative contradicts it.[60]

As the Reality Principle specifies, beliefs that saliently contradict what we are prescribed to imagine are not typically admitted into our inferences among those imaginings. For that would result in our imagining contradictions to exist in even the most quotidian naturalistic stories. When I'm asked to imagine that Elizabeth begins to see Darcy in an attractive light when she visits his estate at Pemberley, certain appropriate inferences about what else is true in the story follow from the beliefs that I have about country estates, their grandeur, tasteful landscaping, and so on, but not from the belief that there is no actual Pemberley in the area that Austen describes. Thus far, the generation of fictional truths from the internal perspective doesn't demonstrate anything distinctive about how the contents of what we imagine in response to fictions are generated. For the operations just described help us fill out the implied truths in the imagining of many (perhaps all?) kinds of counterfactuals.

However, we can see some of the distinctive ways in which fictional truths are generated when we describe them from a perspective that is external.

Consider, to begin, cases in which it seems appropriate to apply the Mutual Belief Principle—which recognizes the partial dependence of fictional truths on the circumstances of the fiction's creation—in determining what facts are imported into or withheld from a fictional representation. Here, what we know about a given fiction as an artifact shapes what we take to be true in what it represents. We might discover, for example, that the beliefs the author, audience, and community of origin shared are mistaken, without this occasioning those truths being withheld from the fiction. Recent discoveries suggest, for example, that the Battle of Agincourt may not have had such uneven odds. Yet an engagement with *Henry V* requires that we nonetheless continue to import that (now-disputable) belief into that story, if we assume that it was shared by Shakespeare's contemporaries.[61] Relatedly, we may abstain from importing certain facts into a fictional story if we believe that it represents a world highly dissimilar to our own. The long separation and uncertain reunion between Penelope and Odysseus (with test after test of his identity) may make us hesitant, for example, to see their mutual commitment

---

[60] This capacity to reason among the contents of a pretense just as we reason among the contents of our beliefs appears in children at least as young as two years old playing imaginary games, as shown, e.g., in Leslie's (1987) experiment. See also Harris (2000).

[61] Glanz (2009).

as expressive of our notion of romantic love. W. H. Auden complained of French classical tragedy that it is "impossible to imagine any of Racine's characters sneezing or wanting to go to the bathroom," which, if it were true, would restrict which of our ordinary beliefs about human bodies could be safely ascribed to those fictional worlds.[62]

It isn't always easy to determine, I should note, whether a feature of a work that we identify from the external stance makes a difference in the facts of the story considered solely from an internal one. Luis Buñuel's *That Obscure Object of Desire* uses two actresses, Carol Bouquet and Angela Molina, in the role of Conchita, alternating from one scene to another and sometimes switching places in the middle of a scene. Whether this is to be understood as generating or indicating a fact in the world the film presents, or is only a feature of the cinematic representation of that world, is uncertain. Perhaps audiences see the actors change, but within the fiction the person they play remains the same. Whatever we decide, only some of the sources of what is true in a fiction lie within the scope of the operator "it is make-believe that." Other grounds lie outside.

As Lewis noted, genre considerations alone can indicate that some proposition is true in a fiction. We can usually assume that in a gothic horror story a vampire cannot bear daylight, not because that's true of actual vampires among us, but because we know it is a convention of the genre. By the same token, if we assume that the dramatic principles attributed to Chekov are being followed in a staged narrative, then we can reasonably predict that when a gun hanging on the wall is mentioned in the first act, by the third it will go off.[63] And, recalling my earlier example, one need not actually believe that arsenic slipped into someone's tea causes immediate death in order to infer that that is what happens in a traditional mystery novel, given how common the plot device once was in that genre. Finally, we may also be justified in imagining certain facts to be true in one work by virtue of how it alludes to or is modeled on another. Walcott's *Omeros* is thus read in awareness of its relation to the *Iliad* and we encounter Fielding's ribald *Shamela* knowing of its heroine's doppelgänger in Richardson's earnest *Pamela*.

Finally, what is true in a fiction (from the internal stance) is conceptually prior to, and partly the grounds of, the sort of interpretive exercises that attribute a thematic, symbolic, allegorical, or other meaning to a story

---

[62] Auden (2012, 25).

[63] One version of which is "if in the first act you have hung a pistol on the wall, then in the following one it should be fired. Otherwise don't put it there" (Gurlyand 1904, 521).

(descriptions of it from an external perspective). However, in practice there may be a back-and-forth adjustment aiming at a reflective equilibrium between the two kinds of epistemic determinations. If, for example, we accept that Billy Budd's downfall is an allegory of Christ's Passion, we have a prima facie reason to attribute facts to the contents of Melville's narrative that are consistent with that interpretation, even if they are otherwise indeterminate in light of the novel's explicit descriptions.

In general, a fiction's overt descriptions of what is the case supply an opportunity to make an indefinite number of potential inferences about what else is true in the fiction. However, only a much smaller subset of mostly shared inferences is in practice activated in our engagement with the text. This is explained by how fictional descriptions manage our attention and interests, making only certain conjectures and conclusions *relevant* to us in the fictional context.[64]

Indeed, authorial sleight of hand may divert us from inferences that, if made, would reveal inconsistencies in a story or supply explanations of events that would compete with what the text mandates we imagine. We may thus admit a particular belief to enter into our imaginative representation of one dimension of a fiction but refrain from importing that belief into our imagining when it conflicts with another part of what is stipulated as true in the story. In a recurrent exchange in the original *Star Trek*, Captain Kirk's demand that more power be routed to the ship's engines is met by the engineer Scotty's protest: "I can't change the laws of physics!" Viewers are thus elicited to both import into the fiction their understanding that the laws of physics brook no exceptions and neglect to notice that the ship's capacity to enter "warp drive" and immediately translocate across vast regions of space is inconsistent with those laws.

In other cases, e.g., instances of meta- and self-referential fictions, inconsistencies are often foregrounded, but narrative techniques prevent them from undermining our absorption in the work. *The French Lieutenant's Woman* by John Fowles (1969) provides mutually inconsistent endings and the narrator appears as a character who flips a coin to choose among them. In Michael Almereyda's *Hamlet 2000*, Ethan Hawke plays the role of Hamlet while a videotaped performance of *Hamlet* is displayed on a television

---

[64] Nichols (2006a) cites some of the large empirical literature showing that differences among reader's goals (e.g., entertainment or knowledge) in engaging with a narrative entrain different kinds and degrees of the inferences they make as they read. See also Noordman and Vonk (1992); Zwaan, Magliano, and Graesser (1995).

behind him. It is thus true in the film that Hamlet is a real person, not a dramatic character, and yet also true in the film, according to the inclusion of the television broadcast, that Hamlet is a dramatic character, not a real person. In neither work does the self-referential paradox interrupt the story's unfolding.

Finally, in the case of a visual work of fiction such as a film, we may import elements of what we literally perceive on screen into the imagined visual representation that the film elicits. In some cases, for example, we imagine of an actor that he is a character with an appearance very much like that of the actor himself, inheriting, e.g., the latter's voice or physiognomy. In other cases, a fiction prescribes an imagining of perceptual features that depart from or are inconsistent with what we literally see represented. Dustin Hoffman was 29 years old and Anne Bancroft 35 at the time of the filming of *The Graduate* but audiences are not supposed to import that comparatively small difference in how old the actors appear into our imagining of the respective appearances of the characters they play.[65] A distinctive problem raised by works of fiction that essentially depend on the perceptual properties of their vehicles is deciding which features of what we see (or hear) belong solely to the work's vehicle of representation and which are (also) to be attributed to the content of what the work elicits us to represent in our imagination. Does black-and-white photography always represent a world of colors in the medium's available grays, or, as in some of Brassaï's images, do they sometimes present a world that itself is gray? Do performers in Broadway musicals always represent people engaging in ordinary speech? Or might some of those productions ask us to imagine people whose utterances in their world sound like song? Whatever the answers are in particular cases, they won't be supplied in an approach to fictions as merely one kind of counterfactual representation to be accommodated within a general theory of imagining. What is true in such fictions is determined in part by what is true (from an external standpoint) of such fictions as artifacts: e.g., the conventions they reflect, categories they belong to, symbols they employ, and themes they convey.

So far, I've focused mainly on how works of fiction generate prescriptions for us to imagine *that* certain facts hold. But, of course, such fictions shape the sensory and experiential dimensions of how we imagine what goes on in

---

[65] That selectivity of import should help alleviate the disquiet caused by a notorious episode of the sitcom *Friends* in which Bruce Willis appeared as the disapproving father of Ross's girlfriend. Despite Joey and Chandler having extensively discussed in earlier episodes their shared love for the action movie *Die Hard*, in which Willis starred, none of the characters remarked that the girlfriend's dad looked astonishingly like the film's hero.

them. Consider the kinds of mental representations we form in reading this passage from James Joyce's "Clay," in which Maria, a woman living in limited circumstances, plays a children's game in which an object one selects by chance while being blindfolded signifies one's fortune:

> They led her up to the table amid laughing and joking and she put her hand out in the air as she was told to do. She moved her hand about here and there in the air and descended on one of the saucers. She felt a soft wet substance with her fingers and was surprised that nobody spoke or took off her bandage. There was a pause for a few seconds; and then a great deal of scuffling and whispering.[66]

Here we are invited not only to entertain a proposition, that these events occur, but to undergo certain sensory and motor imaginings as well: we visualize Maria groping for an item, imagine grasping the soft clay, and hearing the disconcerting hush (the clay may be a symbol of death). Just as a fiction relies on our importing into its content some of our beliefs about the real world, so it may recruit our sensory, visceral, and experiential kinds of knowledge—knowledge of what things are like—in filling out the state of affairs it represents. While still subject to being guided by the fiction, such non-propositional imagining may be less constrained and exhibit greater variety than what we are elicited to propositionally imagine. Indeed, while we may have no motivation to contribute purely descriptive facts to a fiction when it leaves them indeterminate, certain sensory imaginings, even when not invited, are often unavoidable. For example, even without any authorial guidance, we usually can't avoid at least minimally imagining what a literary protagonist looks like.

That passage from Joyce's story points to a final significant feature of literary or artistic fictional representations that distinguishes them from non-artistic fictional representations (or representations for which the primary point of our engagement is not to experience their artistic values). Peter Lamarque dubs this feature *opacity*.[67] Opacity refers not to an essential feature of any kind of literary work, but to a manner of reading literature characterized by an interest in the way its form, style, language, plot, and other literary devices function in the service of conveying its contents: how "textual

---

[66] Joyce (1914/2006).
[67] Lamarque (2014).

nuances, implicit evaluations, narrator reliability, symbolic resonance, humour, irony, tone, allusions or figurative meanings in the textual content" give precise shape to the thoughts the content elicits.[68]

In other words, an approach to a work of fiction as opaque respects how the events, characters, and states of affairs of the narrative are constituted by the manner in which they are represented, i.e., how they are essentially connected to the descriptions used to characterize and refer to them. The nature of the objects, events, and states of affairs in a fiction are, at a fine-grained level of discrimination, constituted by how they are described. For Lamarque, this approach carries ontological commitments related to what counts as the creation of a fictional character, and to a character's numerical identity across different contexts (e.g., from one work of fiction to another).[69] But my interest here is only in our epistemic access to what characters are like. It is a constraint on any accurate description of Joyce's Maria that she is cheerily unsophisticated, narrow but tolerant in her understanding of others, the object of her co-workers' clichéd praise for her goodness, their condescending predictions that she'll marry, and so on. The attitude the narrative expresses toward her does not permit, for example, an alternative perspective on her from which she could be seen as resentful and cunning.

Here the content of a narrative is not just the set of propositions we are solicited to imagine as true when engaging with the work. Rather, that content is constituted by both the facts within a fictional world that are communicated *and* the modes of presentation through which those facts are conveyed. Usually, our access to what is true in a non-literary or non-artistically identified fiction, although achieved *through* whatever means by which its fictional states of affairs are represented, does not direct our attention to those means. By contrast, those means—dimensions of the vehicle of representation—are among the objects of our interest in the work as literature.[70]

To conclude, a general approach to fiction as merely a kind of counterfactual can explain the occurrence of some fictional event only by reference to a represented or implied fictional cause. But an approach defined by an interest in a counterfactual representation as literature, as a fiction that emerges out of our artistic practices, may be able to explain the occurrence of that event by reference to a wide variety of potential artistic functions it may serve.

---

[68] Lamarque (2014, 149).

[69] In a discussion of the individuation of fictional characters, for example, Lamarque (2014) notes that "character identity is indissolubly linked to character description" (70–71).

[70] Lamarque (2014, 71).

In the next chapter, we will turn to how our emotional responses to a fiction play a central role in the presentation of its contents. I will begin by considering a generally applicable theory of emotions and then turn to what qualifications are required for this account to serve as an adequate explanation of the emotions elicited specifically by fictions and imaginings.

3

Evaluative Emotions

This was the abyss into which he was afraid to look. To put himself in thought and feeling into another being was a mental exercise foreign to Karenin. He considered such mental exercise harmful and dangerous romancing.

—Tolstoy, *Anna Karenina*

Gloucester: I see it feelingly.

—*King Lear* 4.6

This study proceeds within two interrelated explanatory frameworks, broadly conceived. One is a cognitive theory of the imagination; the other is an evaluative theory of the emotions. In the last chapter I identified some of the major commitments of the imagination framework and then showed how it applies, with modification, to literary and other forms of artistic fictions. In this chapter I lay out the main elements of the emotion framework and show how it enters in theorizing about the experiences of emotion elicited by art.

3.1. Emotions as Evaluative Appraisals

The range of emotions that are elicited by the contents of fictions and imaginings is vast, likely including all those that can be elicited by experiences of the actual world. Some philosophers would add that there are also emotions afforded through the arts—particularly music—that are sui generis, having no analogies in everyday experience.[1] In light of that, any theory of emotions

---

[1] Thus, against mimetic theories of musical expression, William Hazlitt contended that music might express and elicit emotions but, if so, they are not appropriately identified, except by analogy, with those that are expressed in nature. For a contemporary discussion see Budd (1992, 134).

Apt Imaginings. Jonathan Gilmore, Oxford University Press (2020). © Oxford University Press.
DOI: 10.1093/oso/9780190096342.001.0001

that confines itself to addressing only their belief-based instantiations is incomplete. I begin this chapter by introducing and defending certain theoretical commitments about emotions based on truth-apt attitudes such as beliefs and perceptions. I then discuss to what extent, within the theoretical framework furnished by those commitments, there are relevant explanatory differences between reality-directed emotions and those prompted by fictions.

Broadly speaking, I adopt an approach that construes emotions as *evaluative representations*. Here an emotion is not merely identified with a bodily feeling or behavioral tendency caused by an encounter with some object (event, state of affairs, and so on) but has an intentionality, an "aboutness," vis-à-vis the thing that elicits it.[2] In particular, the emotion instantiates an appraisal of the value (to oneself or what one cares about) of that object.[3] Thus, my fear in seeing the snarling dog appraises it as dangerous; my disgust in anticipating the food that will emerge from an unsanitary restaurant kitchen evaluates it as a threat to my health; my gratitude in remembering my first teacher counts her as a benefactor; my pity for those fleeing their country's civil war is a recognition of their undeserved suffering; and, my hatred of Iago presents him as evil and conniving. We can see two features of emotions in these examples.

One is that even if all emotions instantiate evaluations, the mental state that connects them to their objects—that which supplies their intentionality—may be one of many different kinds. The subtending intentional state may be a perception, belief, imagining of fictional or real things, desire, memory, future-directed thought, or some other representational state. I will refer to this essential but variable element of any emotional episode as its *cognitive base*.[4]

Some kinds of emotions are routinely associated with particular kinds of cognitive bases. For example, nostalgia involves a memory of its object; anxiety depends on a future-directed thought; and, jealousy stems from a belief about some current or potential state of affairs. However, these relations are best thought of as only typical, rather than necessary, conditions

---

[2] On intentionality, see Tye (1995, 100).

[3] Representative appraisal theories include Arnold (1960); Lazarus (1984); Smith and Ellsworth (1985); Scherer, Schorr, and Johnstone (2001); Smith and Lazarus (1993); Schacter and Singer (1962).

[4] I borrow this term from Deonna and Teroni (2012). That emotions have a cognitive base, some way of connecting the mind to the emotion's object, should be distinguished from the claim of cognitive theories of emotions, in which that base, or the emotion as a whole, is sometimes construed exclusively as a belief-like judgment.

of the application of those emotion concepts. One can feel nostalgia (oddly, no doubt) in thinking of a past one didn't experience. Anxiety is often provoked when one merely remembers some event that made one anxious at the time. Fervid jealousy over a lover can be elicited by visual imaginings that one knows are irrelevant to one's relationship, as when the protagonist of Julian Barnes's *Before She Met Me* obsesses over his wife's long-ago romantic partners. It is important here that at least some kind of intentional state be present in an emotional episode; without that, an emotion would not be an evaluation of some particular object, event, state of affairs, and so on. Instead, the experience would be better classified as a mood, or as having just the bodily feeling or phenomenology of a given emotion without fully instantiating it (see §5.3 for more on moods).

The second feature is that, even though all emotions instantiate evaluations, different instances of emotions can be type-identified according to the evaluative properties they respectively attribute to their objects. Thus, my anger, which may be elicited by many very dissimilar kinds of things (your speaking over me while in conversation, a bigoted remark), attributes to all of them the quality of being an insult to me or those I care about. I will refer to these evaluative properties held in common by what might be otherwise different targets of an emotion as its *criterial qualities*.[5] Different explanatory contexts call for lesser or greater fine-grained specification of such qualities. Aristotle's *Rhetoric*, for example, aims to explain how to elicit certain highly precise categories of responses among audiences for political speech and accordingly offers an unusually nuanced specification of just which kinds of insults, from which kinds of people, carry anger's criterial qualities. Formally speaking, appealing to these qualities allows us to identify what renders my reactions to many different things as episodes of the same kind of emotion, and what renders emotions experienced by other people to be the same kind of emotion as mine. I'm angered by someone cutting in line ahead of me at the coffee shop; and the line-jumper is angered by the exaggerated umbrage I express over his minor transgression. Although the causes of our emotions are different, we experience an emotion of the same kind in virtue of each affective state presenting its cause as some sort of insult to one's dignity.[6]

---

[5] Lazarus (1991) introduces the notion of an emotion's *core relational theme* as a theoretically generic concept that captures the particular contextually specific harm or benefit to a person that each emotion expresses. I employ the related idea of criterial qualities to refer to the evaluative properties that an emotion presents its objects as possessing.

[6] The view that emotions present the world to us as having criterial value-laden features is defended in different forms in Greenspan (1988); de Sousa (1987); Roberts (1988).

Theorists of emotions largely agree that the existence of such criterial features of emotions is a function of how our emotions construe objects, or properties of objects, in light of their bearing on our well-being, interests, desires, and what we care about. That is, although we speak of fear presenting an object as dangerous, envy as presenting an object as desirable, and so on, these are claims that apply only against a background set of values specific to the person undergoing the emotion. You may only envy something that I am only disgusted by, without either of us being wrong in our judgments, just because those judgments may be underwritten by differences between us.[7] However, the nature of that representational relation between an emotion and its object is much disputed. Some theorists, call them *strict cognitivists*, hold that the relation—the cognitive base I referred to earlier—is always constituted by, or dependent on, a *judgment* that its object has the emotion-indexed criterial qualities.[8] Here, a judgment is typically seen as the act of forming a belief or committing in some other way to the truth of a proposition.[9]

As a characterization of all types of emotions, rather than just some particularly higher-order ones, this approach has fallen out of favor. One reason is that it appears to require, counterintuitively, that if infants and non-human animals are to experience an emotion, they must possess the concepts required for committing to the propositions that constitute the emotion's associated judgment.[10] But it is implausible to attribute to an infant or non-human animal a belief or belief-like representation that the object of its emotion bears evaluative qualities. Infants feel fear but they don't believe *that* its cause is dangerous. A dog may feel ashamed for creating a mess on the rug but he doesn't have the belief *that* his action was beneath his canine dignity. The objection here is not that the dog and baby cannot form beliefs, but that animals and infants don't possess the specific concepts whose exercise would

---

[7] Differences between the emotional experiences elicited by the same object may, of course, reflect differences in which features of the object are found salient. Thus, Roberts (2003, 81) speaks of emotions as "concern-based construals" in which the "concern" refers to how we see the emotion's object as related to what we care about, and the "construal" refers to the particular selection of the object's properties that are salient considerations in our evaluation of it.

[8] Cognitivist theories are developed in Nussbaum (2001); Solomon (1993); Lyons (1980); Kenny (1963); Gordon (1990); Lazarus (1984); Lazarus (1991).

[9] Solomon (1976) writes, "an emotion is an evaluative (or a 'normative') judgment . . . [for example] my shame is my judgment to the effect that I am responsible for an untoward situation or incident" (185). Similarly, Nussbaum (2004) treats an emotion as a judgment that assents to a value-laden appearance of things.

[10] Deigh (1994).

be required for them to have the beliefs allegedly constitutive of the emotions attributed to them.[11]

Another problem with characterizing all emotions as involving judgments is that at least some emotions seem to be triggered by stimuli with a speed and automaticity that is inconsistent with the deliberate and consciously accessible nature of judgments. Robert Zajonc observes that if a rabbit encountering a snake is to escape, "the action must be undertaken long before the completion of even a simple cognitive process—before, in fact, the rabbit has fully established and verified that a nearby movement might reveal a snake in all its coiled glory."[12] Thus, he concludes, judgments of the sort the appraisal theorists focus on could not play a role in the emotion the rabbit experiences.

Indeed, there is substantial support for the existence of unconscious emotions: emotional responses that affect a person's behavior and physiology yet remain inaccessible to the consciousness, and thus conscious deliberation.[13]

A further reason to resist treating judgments as essential to emotions is that one can fully embrace each of two or more conflicting emotions without this evincing emotional dysfunction or irrationality. By contrast, one's judgments are typically thought of as being normatively constrained to be consistent with one's other judgments, at least when the potentially inconsistent judgments are both consciously entertained. Indeed, one can have a non-phobic (i.e., non-pathological) emotion while holding a belief that is contrary to the judgment the emotion would putatively comprise. One can feel envy while at the same time acknowledging that its target doesn't exemplify the qualities the emotion attributes to it. Indeed, a strict cognitivist approach counterintuitively excludes episodes of emotions whose cognitive bases are representational states that do not have belief's essential mind-to-world direction of fit, such as the familiar examples of imaginings cited previously.

Of course, just because beliefs or belief-like judgments are not essential to all emotions does not mean they may not be present in many instances. It is plausible that emotions may fall into different kinds, some involving slower, deliberate, conscious, belief-like evaluations and others quickly triggered

---

[11] Stich (1979).

[12] Zajonc (1980, 156).

[13] Berridge and Winkielman (2003); Winkielman and Berridge (2004); Kovács, Téglás, and Endress (2010). For research that suggests that unconscious and conscious processing of fear may rely on respectively different neurophysiological systems, see Williams et al. (2006).

ones, which are perhaps modifiable after the fact. Alternatively, a cognitive appraisal and automatic response may be two parts of the same emotion, neither alone explaining the emotional experience in all its essential dimensions. *Moderate cognitivist* theories accordingly allow that the evaluative judgments that emotions instantiate need not be identified with beliefs. Thus, Patricia Greenspan stresses that feelings, or affective dimensions, are central to emotions in their operation as evaluative judgments, and she proposes that these judgments may involve "propositional attitudes that are weaker than strict belief: states of mind, like *imagining* that danger looms, that involve a predicative thought without assent."[14]

Still, there is a general worry expressed by Peter Goldie over both the strict and more moderate cognitive construals of emotions as judgments: both views threaten to mischaracterize the phenomenological dimension of the appraisal that is instantiated in an emotion. That phenomenology—what it feels like to have an emotion—is not an extra, inessential part of the emotional appraisal of an object, but inflects the very representation of the thing. Disputing what he refers to as "add-on" theories of emotions that provide only an explanatorily irrelevant role for their phenomenology as they instantiate appraisals, Goldie argues that emotions exhibit a non-reducible integration of their phenomenology and intentionality, what he calls "feeling towards."[15] Your exasperation can share with my "cold" response the judgment that a given state of affairs is intolerably annoying, but, if Goldie is right, your evaluation, qua evaluation, is not reducible to mine (they do not, e.g., convey the same information about their object). Here, it should be stressed, an appraisal is not an independent consequence of an emotion; it is partly constitutive of the emotion.

Thus, according to Goldie, if we are to explain the particular kind of evaluative response essential to emotions, we must make sense of both how the particular bodily feeling one has in an episode of an emotion is "infused" with the emotion's representation of its object, and how that intentionality of the emotion is "infused with a bodily characterization."[16] In a less metaphorical way of making his point, the experience of an emotion involves a family of peripheral, autonomic, endocrine, and motor responses, as well as the conscious feeling we associate with the emotion, and those dimensions

[14] Greenspan (1988, 3).
[15] Goldie (2000, 72–73); see also Goldie (2009, 237–38) on emotions as a distinctive kind of evaluative mental state.
[16] Goldie (2000, 57).

combine to give the emotional evaluation its particular character and content qua appraisal. Thus, for example, when we fear something we not only evaluate that thing as a threat, but that evaluation is inflected by a characteristic feeling of arousal, a mode of narrowed attention, and such bodily changes as increased heart rate and breathing, dryness of the mouth, tensing of muscles, and sweating palms.

Via such illustrations, we can make a distinction between forms of evaluation that exhibit no *essential* phenomenology, such as monetary measures, and those, such as the kinds of evaluations implicit in love, aesthetic experiences, and the emotions, for which the phenomenology of the evaluation enters into an explanation of the particular value we accord to the object. The feeling of annoyance expresses a significant qualitative dimension of the disvalue of its cause in a way that a cold appraisal does not. In this picture, one may be able to fully understand the content of someone else's emotional evaluation only if one has had, and can recall, an emotional experience of a similar kind.

One can find an alternative construal of emotions that seems to heed Goldie's admonition in a family of theories that identify affective states as assimilable or akin to perceptions, specifically perceptions of value.[17] A virtue of this approach is its capacity to capture the intrinsic phenomenology of emotions—that there is something it is like to have the experience of shame, just as there is something it is like to taste a lemon. Such intrinsic phenomenology is not usually attributed to the experience, as such, of making a judgment. Although forming a belief might have some sort of phenomenology, the particular phenomenology is not systematically related to the content of the belief. By contrast, the phenomenology of sensory representations does systematically vary with their contents. Perceptual theories of emotions thus better account for the fact stressed by Goldie that the feeling of an emotion is not some contingent dimension, but a constitutive factor in what makes the emotion the particular emotion it is.[18] Furthermore, the immediacy of perceptual experiences—which is not shared by judgments—seems to better characterize emotional appraisals. My anger at you for speaking over me in conversation isn't an evaluative judgment that I reach via a chain of inference. Rather, your behavior just *strikes* me as insulting.

---

[17] Wedgwood (2001); Tappolet (2016); Döring (2003); Johnston (2001); Prinz (2004).
[18] On how the phenomenology and representational dimensions of an emotion are part of the same experience, see Döring (2003, 226).

Indeed, if emotions instantiate such immediate and non-deliberative modes of appraisal, we can better explain how certain kinds of emotional dysfunctions, such as phobias, are possible. Just as optical illusions instantiate cases in which our perceptual experience conflicts with our beliefs, so a phobic experience might instantiate a case in which one's emotion, as a perception of a thing's value, conflicts with, and is inferentially insulated from, one's beliefs about its value. The same can be said for ordinary cases in which our feelings are immune to cognitive correction, as in Montaigne's—and later Hume's—description of one's fear, while suspended over a precipice in an iron cage, being wholly resistant to amelioration through one's knowledge that one is safe.[19] Theories of emotions that see them as akin to judgments have much more trouble explaining why one's emotions sometimes resist correction by one's beliefs.

Finally, despite moderate cognitivism's denial that emotions are necessarily based on or identical to judgments, the theory still reflects a commitment to emotions being about a proposition. One feels an emotion via imagining, desiring, thinking, etc., *that* some state of affairs holds. Perception theories of emotions, by contrast, point out that, unlike propositional attitudes, perceptions do not in all cases entail that one can employ the concepts involved in what one mentally represents. Hearing and recognizing a repeated high-pitched sound does not require me to exercise the concepts of *pitch* or *sound*. Analogously, a dog can be angered by your unceremonious appropriation of his toy, without that implying he has the concept of an insult or, per Aristotle, being treated as of no account.

As noted earlier among the objections to strict cognitivism, some findings point to emotions being elicited in a manner that seems to bypass cognitive processing, and the associated availability to conscious awareness, altogether. In one study, for example, Arne Öhman exposed people who had been conditioned to respond to pictures of angry faces, to those pictures for durations too short (30 milliseconds) to be consciously registered. Although they were only aware of being shown a succession of pictures of emotionally neutral faces (within which pictures of angry faces were periodically placed), they responded as if they had seen the angry faces, indicating the possibility of unconscious causes of emotions.[20] Other backward-masking experiments show

---

[19] "Put a philosopher into a cage of small thin set bars of iron, hang him on the top of the high tower of Notre Dame at Paris; he will see, by manifest reason, that he cannot possibly fall, and yet he will find (unless he has been used to the plumber's trade) that he cannot help but the sight of the excessive height will fright and astound him" Montaigne (1580/2004, 449).

[20] Morris, Öhman, and Dolan (1998); Öhman (2002); LeDoux (1996, 154–58).

that the initiation of an emotional fear response can begin before any conceptual engagement.[21] There one's perception of a frightened face causes the symptoms of fear before there is a cognitive classification of the perception, or an inference as to what response is required in one's current circumstances. Likewise, drawing on studies of rats, Joseph LeDoux has proposed that fear can sometimes be associated with activation of the amygdala without any necessary input from the cortex, where the refined recognition of stimuli and reasoning that are typically ascribed to higher cognition take place.[22] There, rudimentary information about a stimulus is carried along a subcortical, thus subdoxastic, route to the areas of the brain that produce emotions. In such cases, an emotional experience is like a sensory experience of some stimulus that occurs outside of the cognitive determination of what kind of thing the stimulus is, what properties it possesses, and so on. Such automatic processes may explain why some kinds of emotions on some occasions are highly resistant to cognitive control. As Jesse Prinz suggests, "bottom-up inputs *trump* top-down inputs when the two come into conflict."[23]

Those considerations suggest why it is plausible to think of episodes of emotions as *like* perceptual experiences. However, some theorists argue for a stronger position: that emotional experiences *are* perceptual experiences.[24] To feel fear, according to this theory, is to perceive some object as a threat; to feel sadness is to perceive oneself as experiencing a significant loss. In some approaches descending from William James, the perceptual theory holds that a particular kind of perception associated with bodily awareness plays an essential role in the activation of an emotion. In Prinz's account, for example, an emotion is a perception of the bodily changes, including their valence, that one undergoes when confronting some state of affairs. Other dimensions, such as the beliefs this experience gives rise to, may be part of the episode of the emotion but don't play an essential explanatory role in its initiation. Comparably, Jenefer Robinson describes emotions as embodied appraisals that are initiated before, but subject to modification by, subsequent cognitive monitoring.

Prinz and Robinson are clear in their identification of what modality of perception—a somatosensory one—is implicated in emotions. However,

---

[21] Williams et al. (2006).

[22] For philosophical accounts of how even such wholly subdoxastic processes can instantiate representations (and thus serve as evaluative representations) see Millikan (1984); Dretske (1997).

[23] Prinz (2006, 140).

[24] For a defense of an exclusively perceptual theory of the nature of emotions, see Tappolet (2016).

other theories that conceive of emotions literally as perceptions are less perspicuous.[25] The worry is not that all perceptions seem to essentially involve discrete sensory organs and there is no such proprietary organ for emotions. For the perceptual theorist of emotions might argue that such a constraint on the concept of perception is unwarranted. Christine Tappolet notes, for example, that speech perception involves both vision and audition but isn't enabled by a dedicated sense organ.[26] Rather, the objection is that, however broadly construed, perceptions occupy a place within our mental economy very different from that of emotions.

For example, genuine perceptions are caused by their objects and are systematically related to the sensation-causing properties of their object. One is, e.g., hallucinating, imagining, dreaming, or in some other way not really perceiving x if x does not exist. One says of a person who hallucinates the presence of an oasis in the desert that he doesn't really see it. However, it is implausible to say of a person feeling, e.g., indignant over something that (unknown to him) does not exist, that he is *not really* indignant. His emotion may be unjustified in how it presents its object, but this is different from saying that he only *apparently* feels the emotion he expresses.

Relatedly, it isn't clear that the temporal experiences of emotions and perceptions match up in the way perceptual theories seem to hold. Emotions can be long-lived, as resentment can simmer over weeks or months. But it seems awkward to describe that feeling as a continuous perception of its object. Furthermore, although this claim does not go wholly unopposed, perceptual experiences are plausibly characterized as "transparent": one's introspection of a given perceptual experience "reveals only the mind-independent objects, qualities and relations that one learns about through perception."[27] When one attends to features of one's own visual, auditory, or other perceptual experience, one inevitably attends solely to the world—its qualities, relations, etc.—that the experience is of. Emotions tend to lack this transparency: introspecting my emotional experience does not involve focusing only on what in the world that experience is *of*—what the emotion is about. I can focus on the quality of the emotion itself, e.g., its burning intensity, as well as its cause.

---

[25] See Brady (2013) for a thoroughgoing critique of the emotion-as-perception theory.
[26] Tappolet (2016, 28).
[27] Martin (2002); Gupta (2012).

Of course, an emotion can depend on or be partially constituted by a sensory perception—the cognitive base that connects the mind to an object. But that contingent relationship is different from emotions being metaphysically identified with perceptions. It is one thing to claim that a perception of an object might make salient those features of the object that are relevant to an evaluation; it is a more controversial claim that the perception constitutes the evaluation of the object.

Strict forms of the cognitivist and perceptual accounts of emotions are mutually exclusive. However, moderate approaches from each camp are consistent when they are shown to apply to either different kinds of emotions (e.g., basic versus sophisticated), or different components that may come into play in any given emotional episode.

We can see the application to *different* emotions in how perceptual accounts are particularly suitable for capturing the nature of so-called basic emotions, each of which has been identified—not uncontroversially—with a distinctive set of biologically fixed and coordinated motor action plans, facial or bodily expressions, and physiological responses (serving biological functions, e.g., self-preservation and homeostasis) that are homologous across human beings and many other animals. By contrast, cognitivist accounts make better sense of higher-order emotions, e.g., nostalgia, tristesse, wistfulness, love, spite, schadenfreude, and benign and malicious forms of envy, that are too fine-grained and too dependent on the internalization of certain culturally specific and historically contingent concepts and behavioral scripts to be accommodated by perceptions. Some theorists, such as Antonio Damasio, hypothesize that the higher-order emotions exploit mental machinery initially developed to serve the more basic ones: "euphoria and ecstasy are variations of happiness; melancholy and wistfulness are variations of sadness."[28]

We can see the application to different components of the *same* kind of emotion in how perceptual accounts may stress the automatic, unconscious trigger of an emotional episode, such as jealousy when one sees one's lover

---

[28] For Damasio, there are both a primary and developmentally early emotional system that works as posited by perceptual theories, and a secondary and later-developing system that depends on the presence of propositional representations as posited by cognitive theories. The primary emotional system is largely innate, shared with other species, and serves basic biological functions. It encodes features of our environment in light of the satisfaction of our basic needs. By contrast, the secondary emotions come into play as we form "systematic connections between categories of objects and situations, on the one hand, and the primary emotions, on the other" (1994, 116–17, 134, 137, 140). For discussion, see Charland (1997).

with another person, while cognitive monitoring and deliberative judgment may enhance or diminish the strength of that initial perceptual evaluation of that person as a romantic threat.[29]

Indeed, many recent neuroscientific accounts of the emotions stress the "dual processes," both automatic and conscious or deliberative, that can subtend the experience of an emotion, particularly when the emotion's representational relation to a stimulus instantiates a form of appraisal, developed via natural selection and conditioning, of the value of the stimulus for the subject (or the larger evolutionary group to which the subject belongs).[30]

In encountering what appears to be a rodent in one's garden, for example, one may feel disgust arising out of two simultaneous processes: (1) a fast, subcortical one wherein information from the sensory perception is sent to those areas of the brain that encode emotional responses (such as the sensory thalamus, affective division of the striatum, orbitofrontal cortex, and the amygdala); and (2) a slower, higher-order one in which the sensory information is sent to cortical regions of the brain, where it is cognitively assessed.[31] In the latter process, a person's beliefs influence how the stimulus is appraised. My feeling of disgust expresses the fact that I take its object to be unclean, impure, etc., even though only subsequent to having that feeling might I realize that what I perceived (e.g., the rodent's wet fur, a strange odor) and believe (rodents carry disease) explains and justifies that feeling. LeDoux calls the quick and automatic response the "low road" of emotional elicitation, and the latter slower and deliberative response the "high road."[32]

Some theorists would object to describing this as a dual process and propose, instead, to identify a basic emotion such as disgust with only the lower, largely modular, mechanism.[33] At the center of this debate is the question of which feature or features of an emotional response play the most central explanatory role in accounting for its unfolding. Non-cognitivists about emotion argue that, because the coordinated syndrome of physiological responses identified with an emotion can be elicited without a subject forming any interpretation of its source, cognition is not essential to emotions. However,

---

[29] Robinson (2005) addresses this process at the psychological level in describing the ways in which cognitive appraisal of the feeling constitutive of an emotion comes after an affective appraisal and physiological response, but, in a feedback mechanism, the conceptual awareness may then modify those other dimensions.

[30] See LeDoux (2000).

[31] LeDoux (1996); Rolls (2000).

[32] LeDoux (2000); Teasdale et al. (1999).

[33] Tamietto and De Gelder (2010).

cognitivists respond that it is question-begging to assume that the emotion proper should be identified with that coordinated physical response, as opposed to, say, the complex of the physical response and the subsequent cognition about its causes.[34] Non-cognitivists often look for support to Ledoux's demonstration of fear responses being activated without any input from the cortex.[35] However, as Ledoux acknowledges, even when certain "low road" emotional processes are automatically triggered by some stimulus, signals from the cortex can determine whether or not the emotional processes are permitted to occur.[36]

However we identify what is essential to an emotion, such empirical data suggest that higher and lower processes in combination tend to comprise both those instantiations of an emotion that are automatically elicited and those "sophisticated" ones in which a cognitive component is especially salient. For when the cortical brain structures that are central to cognition process the information furnished by a given sensory stimulus—e.g., by identifying and categorizing it—that information may be signaled to the lower subcortical areas, such as the amygdala, and thereby affect the initial response to the stimulus, e.g., making the response more intense, or dampening or halting it—as, say, one recognizes that what appeared to be a rat was only a squirrel.[37] And, in the other direction, brain structures such as the amygdala that play a key role in the automatic elicitation of emotions affect higher cognitive processes such as how attention is allocated.[38] The degree of such attention given to some stimulus partly determines the intensity of other dimension of the emotion that it triggers.

Similar interdependencies emerge at a psychological level of description as well. For example, experiencing an emotion has an effect on what are putatively purely cognitive tasks, such as making an economic decision or estimating the statistical likelihood of some event. Specifically, undergoing a given emotional experience tends to lead one to inflate the likelihood of emotion-congruent events—those that typically cause the emotion in question.[39] Feeling physical disgust, for example, causes one to raise one's estimate of the chance that one will encounter contaminated food.

---

[34] See, for example, Barrett (2006); Frijda (2007).
[35] LeDoux (1996, 154–58).
[36] LeDoux (1996, 161). See Robinson (2005) on cognitive monitoring of automatic responses.
[37] See Damasio (1994); Smith and Lazarus (1990); Robinson (2005).
[38] Holland and Gallagher (1999).
[39] Loewenstein and Lerner (2003); DeSteno et al. (2000).

Furthermore, experiencing an emotion may affect one's perception of its object. Speaking generally, fear tends to narrow one's attention, while positively valenced emotions such as joy tend to broaden one's focus.[40] Also, beyond factors explained by attention, the very input to our perceptual processes can be affected by emotion-related physiological changes. The aperture of the eyes varies in a predictable fashion along with the characteristic changes in the physiognomy of the face (such as widening the eyes when expressing fear or narrowing them when expressing disgust). Such changes affect the acuity and sensitivity of the registration of information that is visually taken in.[41]

Finally, despite perceptual processing being highly modular, it is not immune to the top-down influence of emotional experience.[42] The interdependence of such physiological and cognitive features in many, if not all, paradigmatic episodes of emotions supports the point made by Goldie noted earlier that emotions instantiate "thinking with feeling," a way of engaging with some state of affairs that is not reducible to a representation and a bodily affect. The phenomenology, physiology, and representational dimensions of emotions are, from an explanatory standpoint, intertwined.

3.2. Evaluative Emotions for Fictions and Imaginings

I have so far addressed emotions as evaluative representations of things in the real world. Emotions, of course, also appraise the contents of our imaginings caused by fictions. We feel shock and revulsion over Medea's murder of her children; bereavement over the death of a character in a novel; disdain for the scheming Don Juan; anger at having been unceremoniously shot down in a role-playing video game; stimulation from sexual portrayals; discomfort over an awkward suitor's attempted seduction in a television comedy; admiration for a plucky heroine; despair over a drama of unrelenting oppression;

---

[40] See Fredrickson and Branigan (2005). On the effects of emotion on attention, see Damasio (1994, 197–98); Derryberry and Tucker (1994).

[41] See Lee et al. (2014).

[42] For example, some studies show that negative thoughts cause one to see one's environment as darker. Banerjee, Chatterjee, and Sinha (2012); Meier et al. (2007). Other studies found that scary music causes us to attribute to ambiguous images the scarier of two or more interpretations. Seidel and Prinz (2013); Zadra and Clore (2011). For a recent critique of findings that cognition influences perception, see Firestone and Scholl (2016).

and anticipated loss as a character exits from a long-running series. These are not mere responses triggered by our confrontations with those works; they instantiate evaluations of the fictional states of affairs therein.

Historically, the presumption that our affective responses to fictions are of a piece with what we feel for real things was a source of concern. For Plato, poetic drama, as exemplified in Homer and the great tragedies, leads audiences to identify with, and consequently risk emulating, figures such as Clytemnestra as she takes revenge against Agamemnon, where the judgments of value endorsed in these works are not those that a self-sufficient, properly rational being ought to share. "When even the best of us hear Homer or some other tragedian imitating one of the heroes sorrowing . . . you know that we enjoy it, give ourselves up to following it, sympathize with the hero, take his sufferings seriously, and praise as a good poet the one who affects us most in this way."[43] The problem, Socrates warns, is that "when one has nurtured and strengthened one's capacity for pity on the lives of others, it is difficult to suppress it in one's own sufferings."[44] It is because the theater calls on the same affective dispositions and capacities with which we operate in response to the real world that they can have, in Plato's view, such a baneful influence on real-world emotions.[45]

That concern based on a putative continuity across our responses to art and life became especially pronounced in subsequent eras with the popularization of the novel and the ascendancy of silent, solitary reading practices.[46] For the private imaginative experience of readers could no longer be easily monitored for whether it conformed to principles of virtue and appropriateness, as was assumed to be the case within communal practices of reading before the expansion of literacy. Samuel Johnson complained that realistic novels thus have a malign effect on readers' moral makeup through combining an "accurate observation of the living world" that matches such readers' experiences with a lack of indication of which characters and personal qualities should be emulated.[47] More extreme, and more typical of the gendered assumptions about the dangers of reading, is Rousseau's caution

---

[43] *Republic* X, 605d–e.

[44] *Republic* X, 600b7–8. See also *Republic* III, 395d1–3 and *Laws* II, 655b–56b. More specifically, in *Republic*, Book III, it is a performer's identification with the character, while in Book X, it is the audience's less-direct but still psychologically deleterious feeling for the character that affects their own virtue. For this distinction see Halliwell (2002, 78–79).

[45] The part of our soul that "hungers for the satisfaction of weeping and wailing . . . is the very part that receives satisfaction and enjoyment from poets." *Republic* X, 606b.

[46] Saenger (1997).

[47] Johnson (1751).

in his *Julie* that when a woman "dares to read but one page" of a novel, she becomes a "fallen girl."[48] Later, Flaubert's Emma is led astray by taking as a model for her life what she reads in romance novels, "full of love affairs, lovers, mistresses, . . . gloomy forests, broken hearts, vows, sobs, tears," and Pushkin's Tatyana falls in love with Eugene Onegin because he seems like the fascinating men of her novels, "[s]eeing herself as a creation . . . by writers of her admiration."[49]

A contemporary, more optimistic, attitude toward the intimate connection between our emotional responses to fictions and what we take to be real can be found in theories that construe such continuity as enabling moral education and a fostering of empathetic capacities. Martha Nussbaum, for example, proposes that "the literary imagination" is an "essential ingredient of an ethical stance that asks us to concern ourselves with the good of other people whose lives are distant from our own."[50] Robert Musil echoes Nussbaum's stance in describing his work as akin to a "moral laboratory." And, recently, Hilary Mantel described herself as a novelist aspiring, like George Eliot, to "expand our sympathies," countering harm that "stems from our failure to imagine other people as fully human."[51] Others note that such enhancements of our capacities for recognizing others' mental states may not be always so edifying: for the same abilities to understand how others feel that may enhance our concern for their well-being can also be deployed in manipulating people through identifying their vulnerabilities and predicting their behavior.[52]

In any case, my concern is not with the benefits or harms associated with our emotional engagements with literature. Rather, I want to address what support there is for the presupposition that those arguments about the edification of literature all share: our affective responses to fictions are of the same kind, and are to be explained in the same way, as those we have for things in the real world. I'll first survey some significant empirical findings supporting such continuity. Then I'll examine some arguments that aim to show that, despite such findings, our emotions for fictions and for the real world are

---

[48] Rousseau (1761).

[49] Flaubert (1992, 43); Pushkin (2003, Chapter 3, X, 62).

[50] Nussbaum (1995b). See also Nussbaum (2001, 35); Murdoch (2013); Eldridge (1989).

[51] Mantel (2005, 7). On the theory that fiction improves theory of mind, see Kidd and Castano (2013); Mar et al. (2006).

[52] On the use of such mindreading in social strategizing, see the essays collected in Byrne and Whiten (1988). Zunshine (2006) notes that the sort of roving empathy in which a reader serially drops in and out of the minds of multiple characters in a novel might be conducive to acquiring the skills operative in social dominance.

in relevant ways asymmetric. Here I address only *descriptive* continuity; whether the *norms* governing our emotions are invariant across fictional and real contexts will be discussed in the next chapter.

One kind of evidence of there being a descriptive continuity in our emotions across real-world and fictional contexts is that both the structures of the brain and psychological mechanisms of the mind responsible for emotional experiences appear to operative indifferently with respect to the sources of their stimuli.[53]

Specifically, studies of emotional responses to imaginings find that whether the representations that underlie our emotions are caused exogenously (as in perceiving) or endogenously (as in free imagining), they appear to follow the same neural pathways to the brain structures that are causally responsible for the emotions.[54] There are no neural pathways to the emotion centers reserved just for representations formed in the imagination, nor is there a proprietary affective mental mechanism for processing such imaginings.[55] Mikkel Wallentin and his colleagues found, accordingly, that when people read emotionally arousing fictional stories, the patterns of bodily responses and neural changes they exhibited tended to match those that occur when people experience ordinary conditioned responses to auditory stimuli known to reliably elicit affective reactions.[56] Comparable results emerged in other studies of emotional responses that were elicited by fictional video and auditory narratives.[57]

---

[53] Tamar Gendler (2010) writes, "certain features of our mental architecture are *source-indifferent* in the sense that they process internally and externally generated content in similar ways" (238). See also Harris's (2000) account of children's pretense giving rise to emotions because the content of the pretense is processed in a "default mode" that does not reflect whether the content is believed (82). Nichols (2004) argues that "the emotional systems will respond to pretense representations much as they do to parallel beliefs" (131). Compare Meskin and Weinberg (2003): "the affect systems are such that representations of the form SOMEONE IS IN DISTRESS triggers the pity-system, and *it does not matter whether that representation*" is a belief or an imagining (132).

[54] Wallentin et al. (2011); Sabatinelli et al. (2006).

[55] Schroeder and Matheson (2006).

[56] Wallentin et al. (2011). See also Lang (1984). Schwartz, Weinberger, and Singer (1981) conclude from a more limited study of the effects of emotionally arousing pictures that "there is no evidence to suggest that the patterns of physiological response to affective imagery differs qualitatively from those in the actual situation" (346).

[57] Decety and Chaminade (2003); Ferstl, Rinck, and Von Cramon (2005); Sabatinelli et al. (2006); Jabbi, Bastiaansen, and Keysers (2008). See also Damasio et al. (2000). Other studies that used only images, individual words, and short phrases to provoke emotions confirm such similarities of response across real-world and imagination-directed emotions. However, the nature of their prompts limit their usefulness in characterizing what goes on during the reading of full-fledged fictions. See, for example, Vrana, Cuthbert, and Lang (1989); Holmes and Mathews (2005); Lang (1984); Isenberg et al. (1999); Badgaiyan, Fischman, and Alpert (2009); Naccache et al. (2005).

Such subpersonal forms of continuity appear to enable person-level continuity in affective experiences, that is, a phenomenological similarity in emotions triggered by internal and external sources. Participants in studies that examine the comprehension of fictions report, for example, undergoing identical or substantially overlapping emotions in the way they think about both real people and imagined characters, and sometimes forming attachments with make-believe individuals that match those they have with actual ones.[58]

Those studies do not identify the degree to which formal features of the fictional representations may have contributed to eliciting affective responses (I will address such formal features in §5.3). Instead, they confine themselves to the emotional effects of two kinds of representations of what is internal to a story. One is the sensorimotor imagining of actions and sensory details—what we've already addressed as the imagining of what is true in the fiction. The other is the simulation of the thoughts of fictional characters.[59]

In the remainder of this section, I want to characterize the contribution to a reader's emotional responses of that latter dimension of understanding stories—our representation of the feelings of fictional characters. Such "affective mindreading" is an important focus in the study of continuity in our emotional engagements in part because the imaginative capacities that allow empathetic responses to fictional people appear to also make possible our empathetic responses to actual ones.[60] I will describe two distinct processes by which that identification with fictional characters occurs. The first is a process of simulation; the second involves processes of mirroring and affective contagion. In what follows I treat empathetic identification as a species of simulation, distinguished by its attention to, of all potential mental attitudes, the emotions, feelings, pains, or pleasures of its target.[61]

---

[58] For overviews, see Lang (1984); Harris (2000). For studies of this in children see Taylor (2001); Gleason (2013); Cohen (2004); Mar and Oatley (2008).

[59] Paul Harris (2000) notes the two sources: "As young children engaged in pretend play, and also as readers of a text, we can take up a vantage-point within an imagined spatio-temporal framework. . . . Once we enter that state of absorption, it is the events occurring within the imagined world that drive our emotional system. Indeed, our emotional response to those events is heightened by their being viewed alongside, or from the perspective of, the main protagonists. We share their aspirations and disappointments" (65–66). See also, Speer et al. (2009).

[60] Coplan (2004, 141–52). For an approach that assimilates mindreading to the kind of imagining that, inter alia, is involved in counterfactual representations and engagement with fictions, see Currie and Ravenscroft (2002). See also Alvin Goldman's (2006b) description of what he calls "E-imagination" (a species of ordinary imagining) as sharing functional similarities with cognition caused by ordinary (exogenous) sources.

[61] See Feagin (2011). Other accounts of empathy vis-à-vis fictions that adopt the simulationist model (at least implicitly) are Currie (1995a); Neill (1996); Murray Smith (1995); and Harold (2000).

Simulation theorists argue that our capacity to imagine counterfactual states of affairs plays an important role in our ability to understand other people's minds.[62] Specifically, understanding another person sometimes involves imagining of oneself that one has certain of the other's beliefs, desires, perceptions, and alternative mental states—that one is in the other's shoes. Although initially posited in explanations of our ability to predict and explain people's decisions and behavior, simulation now plays a significant role in accounts of our ability to discover and imaginatively experience people's emotions.

An alternative, more "intellectual" approach to explaining our knowledge of others' emotions appeals to our use of inferential reasoning. In this approach, our knowledge of another's emotions involves

(a) recognizing what a person's beliefs and desires are;
(b) appealing to one or more general psychological principles describing what emotion someone with those beliefs and desires in those circumstances would tend to feel; and
(c) thereby inferring at least some dimensions of what the person feels.

The psychological principles here are often described as one's "theory" of the relevant domain, leading this mode of explanation to be dubbed "theory-theory," but it is not a presumption in all accounts that one always has conscious access to the relevant theory entering into such explanations; it may remain a tacit form of knowledge.[63]

Simulation, by contrast, involves my imagining having another's beliefs, desires, and other mental states, which then serve as inputs to affective, cognitive, and behavioral mechanisms that I and the target of my simulation share. I don't need to know, not even tacitly, how these mechanisms work on their inputs in producing the relevant outputs. Rather, I just see what the outputs of these mechanisms are—e.g., how I feel as a result of imagining having such mental states—and I attribute them to the other person. In a common simulationist comparison, one's own mind can be used as a model in the prediction and understanding of another person's mind, akin to how

---

[62] For a survey of competing accounts of simulation theory, see Nichols et al. (1996). See also, Nichols and Stich (2003, 131–42).

[63] See the papers collected in Carruthers and Smith (1996). On tacit or subdoxastic knowledge, see, e.g., Stich (1978).

a model of an airplane in a wind tunnel can be used to predict how an actual airplane will behave under analogous but real conditions.[64]

Importantly, such simulation occurs "offline," or *quarantined* from my genuine beliefs and desires.[65] My actual beliefs and desires do not enter as inputs in the process if they would contaminate my imagining of the beliefs and desires of my target, and the decisions and behavioral tendencies that would follow from imagining having the beliefs and desires of the target are, in me, inhibited. Understanding how a small child feels and predicting how he will react when my friendly dog sniffs his hand requires me to keep what I know about my dog, but what the child does not, out of my imagining of how things seem to him. This does not mean that all outputs of the simulation process are contained; for, as we shall discuss, a familiar experience when empathizing with someone is not just to feel an emotion about her feelings (e.g., pity over another's sadness), but to feel to some degree the target's emotion oneself.

Unsurprisingly, simulation theories have been posited to explain how we attribute emotions to fictional characters.[66] In the simulationist model, our awareness of the affective state of a fictional character (say, of Emma Bovary's dissatisfaction with bourgeois domesticity) does not stem solely from inferential reasoning about what attitudes would likely follow from what the fiction represents as her beliefs and desires, but is arrived at more directly through imagining being her. I imagine having Emma's beliefs and desires and occupying her situation. Then, adjusting for other relevant differences between us, I attribute to her the emotions or other states that I discover this process generates in me. I can distinguish what she feels in the face of Charles's insipidness—his conversation "flat as a sidewalk"—from what I'm caused to feel when I imagine what it would be like to have her floridly romantic beliefs and desires.[67]

However, just as I don't confuse the initial mental states that I adopt in imagining the fictional scenario with my own mental states, so I don't confuse the emotions and other states generated in me as a consequence of that simulation with my own. Still, by imagining of myself that I am in Emma's circumstances, and discovering what feelings this imagining gives rise to, I can learn through non-inferential means something about her state of

---

[64] See Stich and Nichols (1992).
[65] On quarantine, see Goldman (1995, 190).
[66] See Feagin (1996). See also Currie (1995b); Goldman (2006a); Walton (1997/2015).
[67] Flaubert (1992, 48).

mind. More precisely, starting with what I take to be true in the fiction, true of the character, and so on, I can discover through simulation further facts about what state of mind the fiction attributes to the character.

An immediate worry about the very idea of extending a theory of simulation to explain our engagements with fictional characters is that, unlike a simulation's real-life targets, fictional creatures don't have mental mechanisms whose workings our own could mirror. Fictional people are only *represented* (by a text, film, etc.) as sharing mental processes with us, and thus we don't actually simulate anything when we imagine standing in a given character's shoes on our way to determining how she feels. As Susan Feagin notes, our simulation of fictional characters "is not a relationship holding between two persons."[68]

To respond to this worry, we should return to a point made in Chapter 1: psychology doesn't always respect ontology. Fictional characters are constituted by how they are represented, yet the psychological dispositions that underpin our responses to such representations are among those that explain our responses to real persons. Works of fiction exploit such dispositions to have us imagine not only that such and such a (fictional) person exists but that she has a mind like ours. If all goes well, when we imagine being in the character's shoes, we discover through the workings of our own mind offline what the text prescribes, or at least guides, us to imagine of the character's mental state or likely behavior.[69]

We can see how the foregoing process is a genuine form of simulation, albeit not one directed at a real person, in the way in which what a simulator discovers is not, in the first instance, how *she* would feel or behave if she were in the situation of the simulation's target, but how *anyone* suitably similar to the simulator and target would tend to feel or behave.[70] This generality is a reflection of a successful simulation being dependent on shared affective and reasoning processes between simulator and target. Simulation based on the representation of a fictional character thus issues in domain-general understandings and predictions that are also applicable to inhabitants of the real world. I imagine myself in what the fiction represents as Emma's

---

[68] Feagin (1996, 95).
[69] If the absence of actual psychological mechanisms in fictional characters prevents simulation theory from being an explanation of how we understand them, no theory that appeals to social-psychological explanations in our understanding of fictional characters would appear to be licit.
[70] Feagin (2011).

situation and discover from my resulting emotion or emotion-like state how (along with anyone possessed of a similar psychological profile) Emma feels.

Finally, note that there are theories of the nature of imaginative identification with fictional characters that may be construed as alternatives to simulation theory. One family of proposals holds that to identify with a character is to imagine occupying the character's situation, not in all respects, but only partially and aspectivally. Here to identify with a character may be to imagine sharing some part of how she represents the world: e.g., her perceptual experience but not necessarily her beliefs or her feelings.[71] A point-of-view shot, for example, invites us to perceptually identify with a fictional character, but that identification (as in shots from the killer's perspective in horror films) need not entail that we identify with the character in all other respects, such as in his desires.[72]

However, a theory of such aspectival identification does not so much offer an alternative to the simulationist's account, as just make more precise what the simulationist holds. For any imaginative representation is selective as to which dimensions of its object comprise its content. In this respect, no matter how richly I might imagine being in the situation of a fictional character or real-life individual, I won't imagine adopting *every* dimension of her mental state, only those relevant to the aim of my simulation, e.g., discovering how she feels or predicting how she'll act. My identification with any object of a simulation is partial and aspectival, just as the putatively alternative model of identification with fictional characters suggests. Note that our identification in at least a spatial-situational sense with protagonists of fictions is demonstrated in several studies showing that consumers of fictions read and understand more quickly those passages in which states of affairs are described from the protagonist's vantage point, and that they exhibit better recall of features of the fictional scenario in which the protagonist is described as being present.[73] Interestingly, in studies that used stories in which no point of view was specified, readers still tended to visually represent and recall its spatial details as they would be seen from the point of view of the story's protagonist.[74]

---

[71] Gaut (2010).

[72] For criticisms of point-of-view shots as constituting an identification with the relevant fictional character, see Currie (1995a).

[73] Black, Turner, and Bower (1979); Bower and Morrow (1990); Glenberg, Meyer, and Lindem (1987).

[74] Bryant, Tversky, and Franklin (1992).

Critics of simulation as an explanation of our affective response to fiction allow that it sometimes occurs, but argue that its scope is highly limited. First, we can often account for a substantial portion of what we know of a character's emotions from descriptive information a narrator provides about her thoughts and via inferences from what she says and does. We may also successfully attribute an emotion to a character because within the fiction the appropriate grounds for that emotion are made salient. We see this in the early twentieth-century Soviet filmmaker Lev Kuleshov's demonstration that an audience's assignment of thoughts and feelings to an actor based on facial expression can be manipulated by contextual cues—indications of what would be an appropriate emotion for the character to have. When, for example, identical clips of the screen star Ivan Mozzhukhin's face were juxtaposed with film sequences of either a funeral or a playing child, audiences attributed to Mozzhukhin the respective emotional states of being morose and joyful.[75]

Furthermore, our knowledge of how a character feels and behaves comes in part from our familiarity with the genre, or other relevant category to which the work belongs. One can typically predict that when a horror film features a babysitter hearing strange noises coming from the attic, she will (unaccountably) not be motivated to flee the house with her charge. One is able to attribute that lack of desire to her in virtue of one's familiarity with the conventions of the subgenre, not because one imagines occupying her situation. More generally, as noted in §2.3, dimensions of a fiction that can be described only from an external perspective—its kind, style, theme, and so on—may tell us facts beyond those available from the internal perspective.[76] Indeed, the mental state we attribute to a fictional character on the basis of a simulation from the inside may compete with those attributions elicited by features of the text identified from the outside. Why doesn't a character feel as we would expect her to? Sometimes because of the demands of the plot.

[75] Kawin (1992). Other studies confirming the Kuleshov Effect have demonstrated, e.g., that contextual framing can cause observers to perceive neutral faces as alternately happy and sad, and angry faces as not angry but fearful. See Wallbott (1988); Carroll and Russell (1996). Although it is widely used in film to communicate to audiences the mental states of characters, the phenomenon may exemplify a general disposition—not confined to artistic representations—to make social attributions based on how an observer takes it to be appropriate, rational, or stereotypical for a person to respond in a given situation.

[76] See Feagin (1996, 95–98) for a discussion of how approaches to understanding a fictional character from both a simulationist perspective and an interpretative perspective (one attentive to external dimensions of the fiction) combine.

Yet those alternative explanations of our knowledge of characters' emotions undermine only theories that claim an *exclusive* role for simulation in that process, not alternative hybrid models that recognize simulation's dependence on an information-rich, if sometimes only implicit, base of beliefs.[77] As an explanation of how we understand the emotions of a fictional character, simulation should be seen as operating—as hybrid theories propose—against a broad background of beliefs imported into, and about, the fiction. Our empathetic understanding of Emma Bovary depends on beliefs that we have about romance novels, psychological tendencies, domestic life, and so on. Such beliefs can help, for example, narrow the scope of the beliefs, desires, and other mental states that we posit as belonging to her and thus which serve as inputs to our simulation.

Of course, if the simulation of fictional characters leads us only to recognize what their feelings are, it would not explain how we, as readers of a fiction, are caused to experience those feelings ourselves. However, successfully simulating the point of view of another person or fictional character entails coming to feel what she feels as a result of imagining being in her situation. Indeed, to attribute an emotion to a character (or real person) is a secondary process parasitic on the recognition of the nature of the primary emotion one is caused to undergo "offline" in the simulation. (In §3.3, I discuss debates over how to conceptualize these imagination-provoked emotions.)

Brain studies suggest that the emotions evoked through the simulation of fictional characters are highly similar, with respect to their underlying neural patterns, to those that arise through our empathetic identification with real people. For example, in a 2011 meta-analysis, Raymond Mar found that neural networks involved in story comprehension substantially overlap with those that are activated in contexts in which we try to discover the thoughts of others.[78] Mar does not break out the different kinds of thoughts attributed to fictional characters or actual people in these studies, but emotions figured prominently among them. Complementary psychological studies show that readers form elaborate representations of the emotions of fictional characters akin to those they construct for real individuals; and readers readily identify the emotions that characters undergo as belonging to specific context-motivated kinds, just as they do for actual people.[79] Of course,

[77] Goldman (2006b); Sterleny (2003, 211–17).
[78] Mar (2011).
[79] See De Vega, Diaz, and León (1997); Gygax, Oakhill, and Garnham (2003).

in reading a fiction, the target of such reflection may be the actual *author's* thoughts, and thus not a person within a fiction but one who inhabits the reader's world (leave aside the question of whether that target can be reliably reached). However, an understanding of the author's thoughts via simulation is compatible with a successive or simultaneous understanding via simulation of a fictional character's mind as well.

The second mode of emotional recognition that occurs across both real and fictional contexts involves processes of mirroring and affective contagion: here, it's widely noted that perceiving another person's expression, such as a smile or frown, tends to activate—in a wholly causal manner—one's own corresponding facial muscles.[80] We take on the expression of cheer in seeing a cheerful face.[81]

Hume registers the phenomenon of affective contagion in mechanical terms drawn from musical instruments: "as in strings equally wound up, the motion of one communicates itself to the rest; so all the affections readily pass from one person to another, and beget correspondent movements in every human creature."[82] Although he adds that our ability to attribute emotions to another can also arise through inferences from a recognition of either their effects or causes, his mechanical account of the motor mimicry constituting contagion is similar to Plato's analogy between a performer's effects on an audience and magnetism passing through rings. For both philosophers, such mimicry is an *arational* conception of emotional elicitation.[83]

That form of emotional causation has also been demonstrated in cases where experimental participants are instructed to merely imagine such facial expressions. Francesco Foroni and Gün Semin found, for example, that reading or hearing a word that refers to an active emotional expression (e.g., "smiling") recruits to some degree the same neural substrates and muscles as

---

[80] Dimberg and Petterson (2000); Dimberg et al. (2000). This mirroring is hypothesized as a mode of understanding of other people's emotional states in Gallese (2001) and Rizzolatti and Craighero (2004). Winkielman, Niedenthal, and Oberman (2008) also hypothesized an effect on one's evaluative judgments.

[81] Charles Darwin (1872) notes the effect: "The free expression by outward signs of an emotion intensifies it. On the other hand, the repression, as far as this is possible, of all outward signs softens our emotions. He who gives way to violent gestures will increase his rage; he who does not control the signs of fear will experience fear in a greater degree; . . . Even the simulation of an emotion tends to arouse it in our minds" (366).

[82] Hume (1739–40/1978, 576).

[83] In Plato's *Ion*, the god, muse, poet, rhapsode, and audience constitute a causal chain (535e7–536b4), explaining how a rhapsode can recite Homer so beautifully yet still not have expertise in what he does.

seeing someone exhibit that expression.[84] Notably, our awareness of others' emotional states acquired through perception appears to be diminished when we are unable to engage in such mirroring, suggesting that such automatic emotional imitation might play a role in social cognition.[85] If subjects observe an emotionally expressive face but are prevented from automatically mirroring the muscle contractions of the observed face (e.g., because they hold a pencil in their mouth), they are less able to identify the emotion expressed.[86] That impairment in reading subtle facial expressions of others was also found to occur in studies in which a perceiver's own face was slightly paralyzed via an injection of Botox.[87]

As noted in the case of simulation, merely recognizing what another person feels does not entail having those feelings oneself (i.e., empathizing). Seeing someone squeeze his eyes closed as he rubs his temples allows one to infer that he has a headache, without suffering from that oneself. However, the process of emotional recognition instantiated by affective contagion and mirroring is hypothesized to operate through causing a subject's physiognomy to configure itself in such a way as to *cause* in the subject herself an experience of the target's emotions.[88] Indeed, whereas those studies cited earlier focus on how we match our facial expression to those of others undergoing emotions, other studies note that a substantial portion of the brain regions active in experiencing a given emotion are activated when we merely perceive another person exhibiting the emotion.[89] This has been shown for the neural coordinates associated with, inter alia, disgust, fear, happiness, and anger.[90] Similarly, when participants in several studies were shown pictures of people in painful poses, and asked to imagine themselves or others in

---

[84] Foroni and Semin (2009). For other studies suggesting that language comprehension involves simulation and recruitment of neural systems underlying behavior, perception, and emotion, see Buccino et al. (2005); Pulvermüller (2005); Zwaan and Taylor (2006).

[85] Niedenthal et al. (2001); Stel (2008). Contrary evidence appears in studies of disorders affecting facial expressivity that show no striking impairments of emotion recognition. See Keillor et al. (2002). On contagion's role in social cognition, see Preston and De Waal (2002).

[86] Niedenthal et al. (2005).

[87] Baumeister, Papa, and Foroni (2016). The obverse phenomenon was suggested in Botox procedures that seemed to diminish the intensity of certain emotions through preventing their typical facial expression. See Finzi and Rosenthal (2014).

[88] In Chapter 5, I suggest that the nature of mirroring and contagion ("relatively automatic, unintentional, uncontrollable, and largely inaccessible to conversant awareness") lends support to the thesis of normative discontinuity. Hatfield, Cacioppo, and Rapson (1994, 5).

[89] See Decety and Jackson (2006) on empathy.

[90] On disgust, see Jabbi, Swart, and Keysers (2007); Wicker et al. (2003). On happiness, see Jabbi, Swart, and Keysers (2007); Hennenlotter et al. (2005). On fear, see Adolphs et al. (1994). On anger, see Lawrence et al. (2002). And on combinations of different emotions, see Carr et al. (2003).

those positions, both perspectives activated regions of the brain that come into play (with much greater magnitude) during one's own experience of actual pain.[91] These forms of brain activation occur not only when we see people in pain, or pictures of them, directly, but when we merely read about and represent via the imagination their painful experiences.[92]

Such automatic elicitation of affect in an observer may remain unavailable to the observer's consciousness.[93] One may undergo such resonance processes without realizing that they are occurring. Thus, an instantiation of such automatic triggering of emotions should qualify as a form of empathetic identification with another only when it results in a recognition of the other's feelings. Of course, even in full-blown simulation and mirroring, one's feelings typically don't have the same intensity or duration as those of one's target. Factors such as coping strategies, distancing, affective history, and awareness of physical differences can limit the emotions one undergoes. Some brain studies have also found that imagining another person feeling pain tends to produce less personal distress than imagining oneself being in pain. This difference is associated with the first-person imagining recruiting neural areas involved in the actual experience of pain more extensively than the other-imagining.[94] An explanation might be simply that we are better at vividly representing our own experience of painful stimuli than representing the analogous experience of others.

These studies suggest that the processes of simulation, mirroring, and affective contagion by which we come to recognize and experience the feelings of fictional characters are not different in kind from how we come to emotionally identify with real people. Of course, it should be stressed, our emotions for fictional characters are not exclusively explained by such forms of identification.

Our feelings for a character, for example, may not match those that the character undergoes because we have access to facts within the story that the character does not: *she* may feel excitedly optimistic about her assignation

---

[91] Jackson et al. (2006); Botvinick et al. (2005). Singer et al. (2004) used fMRI to study brain activation both when people viewed their own hand and when they viewed the hand of their spouse receiving painful electrical stimulation. They found that the same pain-responsive brain structures were activated in both cases.

[92] Bastiaansen, Thioux, and Keysers (2009); Lamm et al. (2008); Jackson et al. (2006); Lamm, Batson, and Decety (2007).

[93] Bastiaansen, Thioux, and Keysers (2009).

[94] Specifically, in the case of imagining oneself in pain, there was greater activation in the main structures that code the affective and motivational aspects of painful experiences. Lamm et al. (2008); Jackson et al. (2006).

with a stranger, but we, privy to things that she hasn't seen, feel wary of that encounter.[95] Indeed, in many cases the emotions we may feel for characters in a fictional scenario don't correspond to the emotions of any of its characters. Because of Flaubert's framing, we find the events of *Bouvard and Pecuchet* amusingly grim; however, the unlucky duo's feelings are always optimistic. Finally, we may recognize what the feelings of a given character are but, instead of sharing them, feel contrary emotions. A malevolent but reliable narrator, such as Montresor in Poe's "Cask of Amontillado" or Bateman in Ellis's *American Psycho* might be such that we don't empathize with his perspective, and yet still respond with the correct story-prescribed emotions to the events he recounts.

3.3. Asymmetries between Emotions Generated by Fictions and the Real World

The previous section addressed some of the empirical literature supporting a continuity of explanation between fiction- and imagination-directed emotions and those felt for actual states of affairs. Here I want to address arguments that claim that, notwithstanding that research, we have conceptual or metaphysical reasons to hold that such emotions are not, descriptively, of the same kind across fictions and the real world.

One potential asymmetry pertains to the explanatory concept of an emotion. Those, call them *realists*, who adopt a widely shared pre-theoretical stance, take it for granted that both emotions elicited by our experiences of fictions and those caused by our experiences in the actual world are genuine and of the same explanatory kind. Indeed, as noted, fictional films and stories are a substantial source of emotional elicitation in studies designed to probe real-world emotions.[96] However, some philosophers, call them *irrealists*, argue against that assimilation of fiction-directed emotions to those based on beliefs, perceptions, and other fact-oriented attitudes. They note that there are certain significant differences between our emotions elicited by beliefs

---

[95] "When the heroine is splashing about with abandon as, unbeknownst to her, a killer shark is zooming in for the kill, we feel concern for her. But that's not what she is feeling. She's feeling delighted" Carroll (2003b, 90). He refers to this as the "asymmetry of affect" (2008a, 168).

[96] The putative similarity in relevant respects between the effects of fictional and nonfictional representations is assumed by many researchers to be sufficient to allow fiction-generated emotions in experimental conditions to exemplify emotions in general. See Coan and Allen (2007); Amodio, Zinner, and Harmon-Jones (2007).

and imaginings that should provoke skepticism about whether they belong to the same explanatory kind. The question here is not a terminological one about what kinds of feelings should be called "emotions." It is what concept of an emotion (if there is a univocal one) best fits with the myriad explanations in which the concept is employed.

All parties to this debate acknowledge that there are typically qualitative differences between the emotion-like responses we have to what we take to be real and those elicited by fictional representations. Fear evoked by the refined techniques of a horror film may be more extreme than that which is typically evoked by ordinary experiences. Grief over the death of someone one cares for in a fiction isn't typically as profound or long standing as sadness over the loss of a real friend.[97] And, by contrast, we may regulate or tamp down our emotions according to social norms and practical expediency in real-life contexts while giving full vent to those feelings when such social and practical demands are suspended in the theater (when reading a novel, listening to a sad song, and so on).

Irrealists about fiction-directed emotions go further to argue that our respective behaviors in response to fictional and actual situations are not just different in quality or degree, but different in kind. For example, our knowing that the monster in the movie who provokes our fear is a fictional creature doesn't merely diminish our tendency to flee, it forecloses the possibility of our appropriately having any such motivation. And whereas our grief over the loss of a real person seems to suffuse our thoughts and feelings about unconnected states of affairs, our feeling grief over the death of a beloved protagonist in a novel is compatible with being full of cheer once our absorption is interrupted and our attention diverted from its fictional world.

To explain these differences, irrealists argue that we must posit that the relevant feelings we have for fictions are, as a class, distinct from ordinary or *genuine* emotions, despite often being accompanied by the standard physiological and phenomenological dimensions of emotions prompted by the real world.[98] Such theorists would not deny the genuineness of emotions elicited

---

[97] For a finding that the intensity of feelings subjects had for similar video clips alternatively identified as fictional and factual was less for those presented as fictional, see Sperduti (2016).

[98] The case for such pretend, or "quasi," emotions was introduced in Walton (1978a) and later defended as part of a general theory of fiction and representation in Walton (1990). In Walton (2015a) he specifies that the emotions elicited in make-believe contexts are genuine emotions, just not emotions that are literally felt about their (fictional) targets: "Appreciators do not literally pity Will Loman, grieve for Anna Karenina, and admire Superman" (281). On the debate between realists and irrealists see Gaut (2003).

by a fiction or character considered as an artifact, e.g., anger over the anti-Semitic stereotypes used in some fictional characterization. For an immoral attitude expressed by a work of art toward fictional characters is not itself fictional (although we may be unsure whether to attribute the attitude to the work's author or the work itself). Nor would they deny that genuine emotions can be primed by a work of fiction, as when reading a ghost story causes one to feel apprehension over one's house's creaking floorboards. The irrealist's target is the class of emotions that are about what is acknowledged to be only fictional or pretend.

Irrealists situate our experience of such fiction-directed emotions *within* the pretense that fictions elicit from us. In other words, it is not that we pity the fictional character in a story; rather, we engage in a form of pretense in which we pretend that we pity him or her. It is part of our imaginative engagement with the contents of a fiction that we experience such emotion-like states, dubbed "quasi-emotions" in Kendall Walton's influential version of irrealism. One's pretending or imagining of oneself that one experiences an emotion might recruit many of the same neural and psychological processes that produce real emotions (as discussed in §3.2), but this would not entail that the emotion is literally about its (imagined) cause. Nor does the fact that the feelings we experience as part of a pretense or imagining are often involuntary count against their being only virtual counterparts of real emotions. For many dimensions of an exercise of pretense can be unintentional without that entailing that they are not themselves constitutive of the pretense. In the midst of absorption in a story, for example, we often find ourselves being caused to imagine what is prescribed by the fiction, without consciously deciding to do so.

Realists about fiction-directed emotions need not hold that all the emotions we feel for the contents of fictions are genuine. They can acknowledge that sometimes we do just pretend, e.g., to be scared when playing with children, or offended when engaging in banter. Rather realists need hold only that the emotions elicited by fictions that do feel real can lie outside of the scope of the operator "it is fictional that" and be appropriately directed at what is within.

A background commitment in at least some irrealist approaches to emotions is the strict cognitive conception of an affective state described in §3.1, according to which an emotion is constituted by, or dependent on, a belief about its object. To genuinely fear something requires that I judge it to pose a threat. Pitying someone depends on my believing that she suffers misfortune. The objects of fictions do not support the requisite beliefs that real emotions require; therefore, these irrealists hold, any putative emotions felt for fictions are either irrational (flouting the cognitive requirement) or, in their preferred interpretation, not really genuine. If the defense of irrealism depends on that theory that emotions are necessarily constituted or underwritten by beliefs or other truth-apt mental representations, it is infected by the problems associated with the strict form of cognitivism. Because of those problems, realists about fiction-directed emotions typically allow that emotions can be constituted by or dependent on a variety of intentional states beyond just that of belief: these include memories, hopes, counterfactual imaginings, purposefully distorting perceptions, free imaginings, and, of course, the prescribed imaginings of fictional works of art.[99]

However, there are alternative arguments in favor of irrealism that don't depend on the disfavored strict cognitivist approach. One, as noted earlier, is the observation of significant differences between fiction-directed emotions and those based on beliefs or perceptions with respect to such features as their motivational potential and behavioral effects. The irrealist may hold that the emotions we find elicited in relation to fictions are sufficiently distinct in such behavioral consequences from those elicited by real-world sources that they should be identified as belonging to a distinct explanatory kind. Pity felt for a person who is hurt in the real world tends to be accompanied by a motivation to help alleviate her suffering, even if other motivations forestall that concern from being acted on. Pity felt for a character in analogous circumstances within a play appears to carry no such motivation.

One problem with this distinction is that if the motivation in question is a conscious desire, the distinction between the presence of such motivation in the real-world case and its absence in the fictional case can be explained by the fact that conscious desires depend on relevant beliefs to be acted on, and there is no such belief in the fictional case.[100] That is, we don't need to posit a different kind of affective state operative in the fictional and real cases in order to explain their different motivational character; we can instead appeal to a difference in the accompanying beliefs about the emotion's object.

More generally, the imaginative representations responsible for causing a fiction-directed emotion may arise along with other factors that can dispose us to ignore, tamp down, counter, or modify the emotion's typical behavioral

---

[99] E.g., Roberts (2003).

[100] For the point that acting on desires depends on accompanying beliefs, see Carruthers (2006).

effects: these include other kinds of representations (e.g., beliefs), other emotions, and motor routines and behavioral scripts.[101]

The representations associated with one's imagining that Lear holds Cordelia's lifeless body are tokened along with representations corresponding to one's belief that the characters are represented by actors on a stage. Thus, there may be no difference between the nature of emotions based on beliefs and those elicited by fictions: rather, the differences may be found in contextual features governing their expression and associated actions.

Goldie notes that with fictions we "allow ourselves to a considerable degree to *indulge* our profound feelings for humankind, and let our sentiments run away with us without concerns about their connection to action."[102] The implication is that with respect to fictional representations we experience emotions that we would restrain, because of their behavioral consequences, if the representations were of real things. But that doesn't describe a distinction between emotional responses to fictions and to real life but between instances of emotions that, respectively, would and would not justify related behaviors.

For example, if there are no behavioral consequences to our emotions, it may not be because they are part of a pretense but because acting from those emotions can serve no point. One might be appalled by the treatment of enslaved people one reads about in a historical representation, but that feeling, even though directed at real individuals, can no more motivate behavior to alleviate their condition than can emotions felt for fictional characters lead to interventions that would help them.

Likewise, differences in the cognitive base of an emotion may enjoin differences in expected behavior. If my representational relation to a snarling dog is a perception, this will typically motivate me to flee; if that representational relation is, say, a memory or anticipation, this will typically have different motivational consequences.

Realists thus point out that there is something unsatisfyingly ad hoc about treating emotions that are fiction-directed as only pretend, in virtue of their

---

[101] And emotions themselves can be regulated, both effortfully or consciously and automatically at a subpersonal level. Such regulative processes include: suppressing one's emotion-expressive behavior; generating new emotions; and altering components of ongoing emotional experiences, e.g., through redirecting one's attention (as when one "distances" oneself from a painful or distressing state of affairs). Bargh and Williams (2007).

[102] Goldie (2003, 62). Lillard (2013) suggests that our purposes in engaging with works of art, such as entertainment and absorption, might encourage a reduction in our inhibitions over taking on alternative perspectives.

lack of behavioral effects, given that emotions directed at the contents of a wide range of other sorts of representations that also don't have any motivational potential are uncontroversially counted as genuine.[103]

The irrealist may then adopt a more modest position: perhaps it is in the nature of only *some* emotions that their attribution depends on behavioral effects or a belief in their objects. Only in those cases would our feelings for something we know to be make-believe not be literally felt about its object. Other emotions, if not subject to requirements of belief or behavior, could be literally felt for things that are only imagined.[104] The debate, then, may not be about whether realists or irrealists are right about fiction-directed emotions, but about which types of emotions belong to the category of requiring behavior, or belief in their object, and which do not.

In any case, spectators who are absorbed in experiencing fictions may indeed feel motivated to act by the emotions those fictions elicit. In his *Theory of Moral Sentiments*, Adam Smith notes this effect:

> When we see a stroke aimed and just ready to fall upon the leg or arm of another person, we naturally shrink and draw back our own leg or our own arm; and when it does fall, we feel it in some measure, and are hurt by it as well as the sufferer. The mob, when they are gazing at a dancer on the slack rope, naturally writhe and twist and balance their own bodies, as they see him do, and as they feel that they themselves must do if in his situation.[105]

If a film or play represents characters in a fix, we don't intervene to help them, but we may scan the scene presented to see where they might take shelter, find escape, and so on. No doubt, such behavior may be classified as part of the activity of understanding the fiction—responding according to the work's solicitation to discover its content. Yet the process of making such judgments is a kind of helping behavior, the only sort available to audiences excluded from the fictional world.

Alternatively, although we may not overtly carry out behaviors in response to what we take to be only fictional or imagined, there is evidence that we

---

[103] Moran (1994).

[104] This is suggested in Walton (2015a): "Whether one's fear or jealousy or annoyance are actual or merely imagined, when one engages in a simulation, depends on whether fear or jealousy or annoyance of the relevant kinds require either the usual links to behavior . . . , or the belief that the situation is actual" (280).

[105] Smith (1759/2010, I.i.1). See Hurley (2008) on the familiar phenomenon of "moviegoers or sports fans in their seats mak[ing] movements they would like to see" (31).

sometimes exhibit motor readiness or a primed tendency to act in a certain way due to what we merely represent in the imagination. Researchers find, for example, that subjects' neural activity while they engage in emotionally affecting imagining, compared to when imagining more neutral contents, exhibits greater physiological activity in motor systems, as well as in aspects of the autonomic nervous system involved in readying behavior (e.g., in the sweat glands, heart rate, and blood pressure).[106] In a study prompting subjects to imagine specifically themselves in emotionally charged situations, Sabatinelli found that the "act of imagining oneself engaged in a narrative recruits areas of the brain involved in planning and executing action—supplementary motor area, prefrontal cortex, and cerebellum. These effects are consistent with fMRI studies of explicit motor imagery."[107] Why we don't follow through with the behavior is hypothesized to be a result of distinct inhibitory mechanisms that are generated in parallel with the preparation for action.[108]

One might ask at this point why the debate between realists and irrealists hasn't been decided by the demonstration in many studies, such as those already cited, that the emotions we feel on the basis of imaginings are associated with many of the same brain states as emotions based on truth-apt states such as beliefs and perceptions. If the respective neural bases of our fiction-directed and reality-directed emotions are very similar, why not see those emotions as belonging to the same explanatory kind? The problem is twofold.

First, while those experiments were designed to record affective responses based on beliefs and perceptions, they do not exclude the possibility of the participants' imaginative activity having served as their emotion's source as well, or instead.

For obvious reasons relating to the difficulty of supplying the typical causes of certain kinds of emotions in a laboratory setting, researchers use visual

---

[106] Munzert, Lorey, and Zentgraf (2009). A general review is Cuthbert, Vrana, and Bradley (1991).

[107] In Sabatinelli et al. (2006) participants were instructed to imagine themselves in various situations (in bed with a lover; watching a game; being approached by a vagrant; in a filthy room; etc.). These self-involved representations do not conform to the typical third-person-perspective imaginings that consumers of fictions engage in. See also Hanakawa et al. (2003).

[108] Lotze et al. (1999) write that the high concordance of executed and imagined movements "with respect to activation in the secondary and primary motor areas, support[s] the notion that motor preparation and imagery share common neural substrates" (498). They add that the data also suggest "that motor preparation may have to be inhibited when motor imagery is performed." See also Ehrsson, Geyer, and Naito (2003); Jeannerod (1994). For a strong objection to this interpretation of the fMRI data, see Dietrich (2008).

images—photographs and films—to provoke emotions in study participants as fMRI and PET scans record the associated neural patterns in their brain. Much work has been done to establish the experimental validity of such imagery, and its introduction into studies of the emotions allows a greater degree of control, consistency, and replicability in generating responses than such alternative techniques as using confederates, hypnosis, scripts, not to mention a former practice of eliciting emotions with buckets of live frogs.[109]

Still, as Kathleen Stock notes, even the standardized pictures used as stimuli in typical studies of emotions can evoke imaginings about their contents (as any image can). Unfortunately, this means that the emotions they elicit do not serve as a secure comparison class of solely reality-directed emotions to be measured against cases of imagination-generated ones.[110] Even factual vignettes described to subjects as representing real-world states of affairs may evoke imagining, if only because verbal descriptions underdetermine even the most faithful sensory imaginings that they are designed to elicit. Thus, the studies cited do not unequivocally show that one and the same neural structures implement perception- and belief-representations and imagination-representations, for the former real-world-directed states may have included elements of imagining too.

It is true that, in some kinds of studies, emotion-inducing stimuli have been employed that do not require, in the first instance, visual or verbal representations—as when pain in the laboratory is elicited via shocks and pinpricks and negative moods evoked through unpleasant odors and sounds. Yet the range of responses that can be thereby elicited without employing verbal or visual representations is quite narrow if the stimulus must be delivered to a person staying immobile in an fMRI scanner. In any case, such emotion elicitors may introduce imagining (e.g., about the source of the odor) as well.

Second, if (as indicated in the studies surveyed in §2.1) the mental representations of beliefs and imaginings (and perceptions and visualizations) share underlying neural and psychological bases, it should be no surprise that the emotions we experience in response to such representations are similar. Such similarity in fiction-directed and reality-based emotional responses is what we would expect given the similarity in

---

[109] See Coan and Allen (2007).
[110] Stock (2014, 217).

the representations of their objects; it is not a proof that the emotions belong to the same explanatory kind.

Given the equivocal contribution of the experimental data to the question, I suggest we address what explanatory goals are at stake in the debate.

When using our folk psychological conception of emotions, we tend to identify a person's experience as exemplifying a genuine emotion by appeal to several different factors: inter alia, the antecedent causes of the experience, its causal consequences, what that experience allows us to explain, and the facial or bodily expression associated with the emotion. Also, normative considerations may influence whether we attribute an emotion to someone. If, for example, we think a person is rational and largely sensitive to the value of things, we may conclude that his otherwise apparent grief over losing a button cannot be genuine. Such different considerations in the attribution of emotion may be individually graded, and have different weights in different contexts.

We might be able to ignore the diversity of such diagnostic criteria of emotional experiences as pre-theoretical intuitions or "folk" platitudes that should give way to scientific understanding. However, psychological theories of emotions also disagree over when a token response by a person constitutes an emotion.

Theorists who subscribe to a model of "basic emotions" classify emotions as belonging to a small set of discrete and biologically fixed activations of evolved brain networks: affect programs or motor action plans involved in self-preservation and homeostasis that are homologous across human beings and many other animals.[111] By contrast, constructionist theories say that a given emotion is constituted in part from the interpretation of the person undergoing the emotion. In other words, one does not discover what one is (and has been) feeling; rather one's feeling is only an inchoate experience until transformed into a proper emotion via one's identification of it—using perhaps highly culturally variably concepts and categories.[112] Behaviorist theories of emotions tend to identify them with certain typical behaviors,

---

[111] Ekman (1992) writes, "There must be unique physiological [central nervous system] patterns for each emotion" (182).

[112] Barrett (2006; 2012). An early motivation for this approach was Schacter and Singer's (1962) experiment in which they gave subjects adrenaline injections, presumably generating similar bodily feelings in each subject, and found that what the subjects identified as the emotion expressed or constituted by the feelings could be independently manipulated through cues supplied by the researchers. For an overview of anthropological studies of the cultural specificity of emotions, see Lutz and White (1986).

including changes in one's face, body, stance, and vocal pitch. They thus exclude from the relevant scientific data in classifying and explaining emotions the first-personal phenomenology of what it feels like to undergo them.[113] By contrast, theorists who think that the most fundamental role of emotions is a social one, e.g., to communicate, will stress distinctive facial, somatic, and behavioral forms of meaningful expression associated with emotions. Appraisal theories argue that there is a fixed set of dimensions along which each emotion can be measured, such as degree of arousal, valence, avoidance or approach tendency, personal relevance, certainty, control, and stability. The particular cluster of measures on each of these scales distinguishes one kind of emotion from another.[114] Finally, those who identify emotions with changes in such somatic dimensions as heart rate, blood pressure, and skin conductance try to individuate different emotions via reference to distinct autonomic signatures. For example, anger and fear involve greater heart rate than disgust, and greater perspiration accompanies disgust compared to happiness, but reviews of such research suggest that these correlations are limited in their scope.[115]

Faced with the plurality of such candidates for the explanatorily central components of an emotion, it is also worth noting that empirical studies suggest that the different dimensions of discrete kinds of emotions—dimensions by which token emotions are putatively type-identified—are not consistently exhibited.[116] As the constructionists about emotions point out, an animal in fright might flee in one context but freeze in another. Even the expression of smiling, which might seem to be a sine qua non of an episode of feeling happiness, has been found to be only loosely correlated with experience of that emotion.[117]

This lack of consensus over the concepts of an emotion and particular emotion types suggests that, despite the debate between the realists and irrealists

---

[113] LeDoux (2000).

[114] For such appraisal theories, see §3.1.

[115] For a review, see Cacioppo et al. (2000).

[116] In a large review, Lindquist et al. (2012) write, "Since the beginning of psychology, researchers have questioned the idea that discrete emotion categories are each associated with a single, diagnostic pattern of response in the brain and body.... More recently, a number of empirical reviews ... have highlighted the disconfirming evidence: Different discrete emotion categories are not distinguished by distinct patterns of peripheral physiology ..., facial muscle movements ..., vocal acoustics ..., or by subcortical circuits in the mammalian brain" (141, references to relevant studies removed in ellipses).

[117] Gross and Canteras (2012). On smiling, see studies by Fernández-Dols et al. (1997), who found that people experiencing intense happiness in real-world situations, e.g., winning some sports competition, tended not to smile except during social exchanges.

about the status of fiction-directed emotions being organized around the presence or absence of one or two factors that are taken to be dispositive (e.g., beliefs and motivations), it is unlikely that any narrow set of determinative features respects the prevailing empirical findings.[118]

Fortunately, those differences over the concept of an emotion and what indicates the occurrence of a particular emotion don't undermine the different explanatory uses of appeals to emotions. We can explain why, e.g., in watching a scary film, an audience member's heart races and his attention narrows, whether or not we countenance calling it a genuine emotion of fear. And knowing that particular feeling's causes, and current state, we can predict what sorts of behaviors it will lead to, and which ones, in context, it is unlikely to bring about (such as fleeing from the theater). Differences between the realist and irrealist accounts of fiction-directed emotions may thus be merely verbal, at least with respect to our explanatory interests in them. For the differences in such concepts of emotions don't correspond to systematic differences in the kinds of explanations they would offer of emotion and emotion-like expression and behavior.

Two other kinds of apparent asymmetries between emotions elicited by imaginings and by factive attitudes such as beliefs and perceptions may be better sustained.

One asymmetry is that the emotions we feel for a fiction tend to be dependent on its content's mode of presentation. For example, how we feel about a character within a fiction getting knocked on the head may differ according to what genre—slapstick, children's animation, or police drama—the representation belongs to. One way of representing that content may provoke distress, while another way of representing it provokes pleasure. However, this dependence is not peculiar to fictions. It is common, as well, for different *factual* representations of relevantly similar states of affairs to have different results in the emotions they elicit. In *Swann's Way* Proust gently mocks Françoise, the family's cook, for being coldly dismissive of the unhappy conditions of the young servant girls around her, while being driven to paroxysms of grief when reading of strangers in similar situations in the newspaper. No doubt one can find people behaving similarly in the real world. The asymmetry between emotions elicited by fictional and factual representations' content is not that one kind is mediated by its mode of

---

[118] For the suggestion that the category of emotion is protypical, see Ben-Ze'ev (2010). A similar suggestion is made by John Elster (1999), who thinks that the category is open-ended (241).

presentation and the other not—for both are—but that in the former case, we are standardly aware of and endorse such a dependency. We are, as it were, complicit in our pleasure being caused by a farcical representation of some state of affairs. We don't, by contrast, typically choose to be exposed to representations of factual states of affairs so as to feel the emotion that the representation's mode of presentation is designed to provoke.

The other asymmetry, related to the first, can be illustrated via appeal to our experiences of tragic dramas. Tragedies present states of affairs that distress us and that make us wish, or imagine that we wish, things could be otherwise. We want a character to survive, but it is true in the fiction that she does not. In this respect, our feelings of grief over the loss of a fictional character seem to be analogous to and the same kind as our feelings for the loss of an actual person we care about; they just depend on different kinds of cognitive bases. However, a significant disanalogy emerges when we consider that one's experience of a fictional representation of a tragic event has another dimension that is not usually part of one's experience of tragedy in real life: one's sadness over the death of the fictional character is bound up with happiness or pleasure.[119] This is the pleasure we take in the fictional story, of which that death is an essential part.

By contrast, one's sadness over the death of a friend is not typically internally related to a desire that the world be such that it contains the deaths of friends, even if valuing some things depends upon an awareness of their vulnerability. Our sadness in response to a fictional loss is in conflict with our pleasure in the fiction; they are aimed at the same object under different descriptions: one that refers to a character's death from an internal perspective as an event that one imagines to be real; and one that refers to the death from an external perspective, as an element within the artistic design of the work.[120] When faced with a real loss, however, our sadness involves no such (systematically) conflicting desire: unlike our attitude toward the fictional work, we typically want the world to have been different, if not cosmically, then locally, so that the particular cause of the sadness would not have occurred.

More generally, while some people do respond to events from the perspective of how things were "meant" to be, or how it was "God's will," the emotions we feel for things in the actual world are not typically modulated by emotions

---

[119] See Chapter 7, where I address the question of what mental states are implicated in our experience of tragedies.

[120] Lamarque and Olsen (1996).

elicited from the recognition of those things belonging to some overarching design, one that directs not only the tragic event but our response to it as well.

Those two asymmetries don't demonstrate that the emotions elicited by fictions are different in kind from everyday emotions; however, they do show how the explanatory power of a theory of the emotions as evaluative representations depends on recognizing how phenomena such as the modes of presentation, genres, and formal or aesthetic features of a fictional representation play a prominent role in determining what emotions our engagements with fictions, qua works of art, bring about.

One could, in principle, feel conflicting emotions directed at, respectively, the non-aesthetic and aesthetic dimensions of some real state of affairs. Monet castigated himself for focusing on the aesthetic qualities of his wife's complexion while she was dying of tuberculosis beside him: "I caught myself, my eyes fixed on her tragic forehead, in the act of mechanically analyzing the succession of appropriate color gradations which death was imposing on her immobile face. Tones of blue, of yellow, of grey."[121] The difference between the fictional and real case is that fictions, unlike real states of affairs, are *designed* to elicit such dual perspectives. The experience of such conflicting emotions evinces a proper comprehension of such works. There is no comparable norm that says that, on pain of failing to properly engage with a real situation, one ought to respond to its aesthetic or formal mode of presentation. My exasperation over a political administration's corrupt practices may be paired with a kind of pleasurable astonishment over their baroque excesses, but any such "aesthetic" response need not be part of properly comprehending them.

I began this chapter adumbrating an account of emotions that are dependent upon or constituted by the contents of perceptual and propositional representations of stimuli drawn from the real world. I then showed why we should think of fiction- or imagination-elicited emotions as no different in kind, despite some important asymmetries, from those prompted by representations of the actual world. The main reason, I noted, is that both kinds of representations are registered and processed in the mind in similar ways. There is a *descriptive* or *empirical* continuity between our emotional responses based on veridical representations and those based on representations that may be only fictional, pretend, or imagined.

---

[121] In a letter to George Clemenceau written several years after the death in 1870 of his wife, Camille Doncieux.

In subsequent chapters I address the core question of this book, whether, given that descriptive continuity, there is *normative* continuity between these kinds of emotions as well. I ask, that is, Do the norms governing the aptness, fit, or rationality of emotions apply invariantly across those elicited by fictions and those caused by the real world?

4

Apt Emotions and Normative Continuity

> And it was not a tragedy. I had not even the consolation of that way of
> picturing the matter. Tragedy belongs in art. Life has no tragedies.
> —Iris Murdoch, *A Word Child*

In the last chapter I addressed some of the empirical evidence demonstrating that our affective mechanisms process the contents of our imaginings in ways that are parallel to how they process the contents of our
beliefs and other veridical representations. With respect to their neural,
psychological, and phenomenological dimensions, our emotions are substantially continuous across the real and imagined contexts in which they
are elicited. In this chapter, I ask whether there is also a continuity in the
norms governing those emotions. Do the criteria relevant to the justification of our emotions hold invariantly across our engagements with real
and imagined domains?

As we saw in Chapter 3, an assumption shared by many otherwise different contemporary philosophical treatments of the emotions is that our
affective responses are susceptible to assessments of rationality, fittingness, or some other notion of aptness. Here one's emotional response to
some object (an event, person, state of affairs, etc.) can properly be held
to such evaluations as that it is misdirected, unjustified, abnormal, or
somehow an emotion one ought not to have, in general or in the particular case. Accordingly, fear is inappropriate if directed at what is harmless; sadness shouldn't be felt if its object is only a trivial loss; and spite
(per Aristotle) is always wrong in invariably misrepresenting the relevant
qualities of whatever it is directed toward. No doubt there are dissenting
voices, and much rests in how one construes the nature of that aptness
condition, but the current consensus is that at least paradigm instances

Apt Imaginings. Jonathan Gilmore, Oxford University Press (2020). © Oxford University Press.
DOI: 10.1093/oso/9780190096342.001.0001

of emotions bear essential *normative*, not just causal or explanatory, relations to their objects.[1]

Analogous assumptions concerning the normativity of emotions apply to those directed at what is only *fictional*, or what is only *imagined* to be the case. One who pities the bloodthirsty monster of a horror film because its innocent victim has escaped would usually be under some misapprehension of the film's content. If one would feel shame in being discovered in some compromising position—say, stealing from one's employer—then shame, not delight, seems to be a fitting response to vividly imagining oneself exposed in those circumstances.

My primary question in this chapter and the next is whether the criteria governing the aptness (fittingness, rationality, appropriateness) of the emotions we have toward what we take to be real things apply invariantly to emotions we have toward what we take to be only imagined or fictional. In other words, are the conditions that ground the relation of being *warranted* or *merited* that holds between an emotion and its object the same, *modulo* the different cognitive bases, when that object is (1) real, (2) only imagined, and (3) only imagined in connection with a fictional work of art? If pity is an apt response to one who undergoes undeserved suffering, are the same kinds of reasons relevant in the justification and criticism of a feeling of pity regardless of which of those domains its object belongs to? Or can an emotion be criticized as inappropriate if felt toward a state of affairs that is taken to be real but defended when—and in virtue of being—felt toward that state of affairs as represented in fiction?

4.1. Aptness

What I will refer to as the *continuity thesis* is that the criteria for appropriateness of emotions are identical across real and imagined domains. Of course, those criteria cannot include requiring of an apt emotion that its object

---

[1] Outside of the theory of emotions proper, this normative approach occupies the center of major sentimentalist accounts of value defended both by cognitivists such as John McDowell (1998) and David Wiggins (1998) and by noncognitivists such as Simon Blackburn (1998) and Allan Gibbard (1992). These philosophers share the view, roughly stated, that certain evaluative qualities of an action or person (such as being morally blameworthy) are to be analyzed solely in terms of what sentiments or emotions it is merited for one to feel toward those actions or qualities. For other accounts that feature normative views of emotions, see Elster (1999); Mulligan (1998); Lyons (1980); Warnock (1957).

exist in the real world, independent of one's imaginative or fictional stance. However, allowing for the differences in the kinds of intentional states connecting emotions to their objects (the cognitive bases described in §3.1), the continuity proponent sees the considerations that can justify or criticize an emotion with respect to its fit to a real object as identical to those that can justify or criticize an emotional response to what is taken to be only fictional or imagined.

What I will call the *discontinuity thesis*, by contrast, is that there are differences between the criteria governing the aptness of reality-directed emotions and the criteria governing the aptness of fiction- or imagination-directed ones. We should not assume—this is the disputed claim in the debate—that an emotion is justified when experienced in response to an object of some kind in a fiction if and only if the emotion is justified in response to an object of that kind in the real world. It may be appropriate, e.g., to feel amused by something in a fiction while it is not appropriate to be amused by a suitably analogous event in real life. In what follows I introduce and assess some considerations in favor of these two theses of continuity and discontinuity, both of which have a prima facie plausibility.

My aim in this and the next chapter is to demonstrate which account of the norms governing our affective responses has the best descriptive fit and explanatory power. Thus, I don't ask whether there *should* be an invariance of such norms across our engagements with fiction and real life. I ask only whether it is an internal feature of our practices involving affective responses to imaginings that such invariance obtains.

Certainly, as we saw in §2.1 and §3.2, much recent work in cognitive psychology, neuroscience, and philosophy of the imagination supports the idea that there is a significant degree of descriptive or empirical continuity in the causal mechanisms that explain our affective responses to the contents of imaginings (including fiction-directed imaginings) and the contents of mental representations of the real world.

My question in what follows is, assuming that those forms of empirical continuity exist, is there also a continuity in the *norms* associated with our responses? Thus, although I will sometimes refer to dimensions of our experience at a subpersonal level of description (e.g., in terms referring to brain states, perceptual mechanisms, and physiological responses), my focus is on the processes and products of the imagination characterized at the person level. It is at that level of description where rational and other norms can apply to mental states and intentional behavior.

To anticipate, I argue (this is defended in Chapter 5) that, while certain prom-inent defenses of discontinuity fail, there is at least one significant consideration in its favor: there are, as I will demonstrate, a wide variety of differences across the real/imagined divide in what considerations we accept as potential reasons for an emotion, reasons that justify its fit to its object. But before assessing those arguments, I will need to characterize a relevant notion of aptness that both parties to this debate can employ.

Although philosophical and psychological treatments of the emotions regularly inquire into the grounds of their appropriateness, this question is less often assumed to apply to emotions based on fictions and imaginings. When acknowledged by researchers, those kinds of emotions, along with phobias, are typically treated as outliers that do not put much pressure on a theory of fittingness of garden-variety emotions.[2] My strategy in what follows is to begin by offering a characterization of aptness that would be amenable to theories that take reality-directed emotions as their primary explananda. However, this account will be posed in terms that are suffi-ciently formal to avoid making any commitment to beliefs and perceptions having any essential role in determining aptness. For that would too quickly exclude emotions that depend on other intentional states, including those that are not veridical, from being apt in the same sense as those that de-pend on mental attitudes that constitutively aim at what is true. With that generic account of aptness in hand, we will see whether the reasons that *in principle* can enter into the justification of an emotion's aptness differ just because of a difference in the emotion's source in, respectively, imagining and belief.

Let me introduce some caveats that will help narrow the question of conti-nuity into a tractable form.

As we saw in §3.3, different theories of emotions offer different accounts of the dimensions (e.g., representational, etiological, physiological, motivational, phenomenological, communicative) along which affective states are to be characterized. Accordingly, theories of aptness may differ over which of those dimensions of emotions they take to be central.

---

[2] Representative treatments of the appropriateness of emotions are Roberts (2003); Nussbaum (2001); de Sousa (1987); Greenspan (1988); Helm (2007). Some accounts that build moral or aes-thetic considerations into the concept of an apt emotion directed at works of art are Livingston and Mele (1997); Choi (2003); Robinson (2005). For considerations entering into the appropriateness of emotions and desires directed toward fictions that represent real-life individuals, see Friend (2003).

In what follows I focus mainly on the aspect of emotions associated with their intentional or, more specifically, representational content.[3] Such content presents the world as being in a certain way. Contra the view of some strict cognitivists, that representational aspect doesn't exhaust the nature of emotions. However, it can be plausibly construed as more central than, and in some cases conceptually prior to, other important aspects. For example, the physiological expression of fear is no doubt an important feature of the emotion, but one in the throes of fear would not experience its characteristic effects on respiration, attention, blood pressure, and so on, in the absence of some sort of representational relation connecting one's mind and physiology to the object of one's fear.[4]

Relatedly, there is a broader, multidimensional notion of emotion justification that I will not address: what sort of emotion it is rational for a person to have all things considered. There might be, for example, overwhelming prudential reasons to find the jokes told by one's boss amusing. And I might have sufficient reason to feel calm before the mangy dog showing its teeth, assuming it can "smell my fear." But those sorts of reasons don't speak to whether or not the emotions would be justified in their representational dimension. In some sense, it is right to feel amusement at the boss's jokes and to feel calm before the snarling dog, but not in the sense that makes intelligible *what it is* for something to be amusing or calming.[5] Indeed, reasons why an emotion is apt in a representational sense may be trumped by reasons showing a failure of fit according to its other dimensions. So I explore the fit between an emotion and its object only in a contributory or pro tanto, not all-things-considered, sense.

Some theorists would accept the above distinctions but still hold that reasons of a specifically moral sort can make an emotion apt or inapt in the limited representational sense employed here. I suggest that moral reasons count in favor of or against the aptness of an emotion only when that emotion is of a kind that is essentially concerned with the morally evaluable qualities of its object, e.g., emotions such as remorse, compassion, and indignation. In

---

[3] For the notion of "representational content, see Peacocke (1992). On the content of a perception having correctness conditions, see Crane (1992, 136–57).

[4] Thinking of emotions as assessable with respect to their representational content does not exclude assessing them as actions, specifically, intended judgments of certain sorts over which we have some control, and hence responsibility; see, e.g., Sartre (1948). However, it is the former notion of epistemic rationality that I address here, not a practical rationality that might also apply.

[5] On the problem of individuating the "right kind of reasons" in favor of an evaluative attitude, see Rabinowicz and Ronnow-Rasmussen (2004).

other cases, we may have a moral reason not to respond with a given emotion without that reason entering at all into the aptness (in the limited representational sense) of the emotion. It might be always morally wrong to feel schadenfreude, without that entailing that its objects cannot have the qualities that merit (in the representational sense) that kind of pleasure.[6] In any case, my question is whether continuity or discontinuity holds in standards of aptness. So, here, my concern with moral constraints on aptness extends only to the question, *If* moral reasons make a difference in the aptness of reality-directed emotions (in the representational sense), must they make a difference in the aptness of fiction- or imagination-directed emotions?

Finally, the rationality of emotions has been frequently addressed in solutions to the paradox of fiction. We feel emotions for fictional states of affairs, yet we tend not to, and assume we ought not to, feel emotions for what we take not to exist. One family of solutions proposes that such responses can be revealed as appropriate in virtue of instantiating a broadly exhibited disposition to respond behaviorally, cognitively, and affectively toward some kinds of stimuli in a way that is indifferent to their sources.[7] Such a disposition is justified in light of its tendency to promote (or at least not conflict with) an individual's well-being in virtue of delivering such benefits as the pleasure offered by engagement with fictions; the ability to plan for the future by consulting one's emotional responses to imagining the adoption of differing options; and the capacity to learn of another's point of view through empathetic modeling of her emotions.[8]

However, that approach to the paradox offers a strong defense of fiction- and imagination-directed emotions being rational, or not systematically irrational, as a class. It does not solve the problem to be addressed here of what makes any particular emotional response to the contents of a counterfactual thought or imagining rational. For, even if the categorical rationality of fiction-directed emotions (or of the disposition to feel those emotions) is secured, we still need to ask under what conditions any token emotional response is rational, fitting, or apt. And are those conditions identical in relevant respects to those pertaining to rational emotions felt about the real world? Let us now turn to that question of aptness.

---

[6] For this point and a subtle discussion of the aptness of sentiments in general, see D'Arms and Jacobson (2000).

[7] Damasio (1994); Gendler and Kovakovich (2006); Robinson (2005, 145–46).

[8] See Lamarque (1981); Matravers (2001); Joyce (2000); Gaut (2007); Gendler and Kovakovich (2006). For a more formal account of the rationality of emotions see de Sousa (1987).

Recall from the last chapter the framework in which emotions are explained as affective appraisals. There emotions depend on some mental state directed at an object identified under a generic evaluative description. The generic description brings out the evaluative property that is shared by otherwise different kinds of objects of any one type of emotion. So, for example, fear is directed at what are often very different kinds of objects that have the evaluative quality of being a threat; pity is directed at people who exhibit the property of unjustified suffering; anger is directed at what is seen as insulting. I refer to these generic evaluative properties associated with each emotion type as the *criterial qualities* of the emotion.

In line with that approach, a generally applicable way of characterizing the relation between an emotion and its object is to say that an emotion *presents* its objects as having a certain kind of evaluative quality that individuates that type of emotion.[9] This is analogous to how other kinds of mental states present their objects as having a certain kind of property: a belief presents its contents as true, a desire presents its object as meriting being wanted, a perception of x presents an x-experience as occurrent, a remembering presents its content as having occurred in the past and been directly experienced. We can evaluate any token emotion according to the adequacy of that intentional representation. If I resent someone's actions, my emotion is not only directed at that person's actions but presents those actions as instantiating a culpable offense toward me. Here the particular cognitive base upon which an emotion depends, e.g., a belief, can be faulty, and thus be a source of error or inaptness in an emotion. The envy I feel in thinking that my colleague cruises around town on a vintage Vespa *motorino* is inapt if he does no such thing. However, if we recall Goldie's earlier admonition that any theory of emotions must allow for their intrinsic phenomenology, other dimensions of an emotion can also contribute to how it presents its object, and thus be a source of errors in that presentation. For we are asking about the aptness of how the emotional episode or experience as a whole presents its object, not just how its subtending cognitive base (perception, memory, belief, intention) presents its object.[10]

---

[9] The view that emotions present the world to us as having criteria value-laden features is defended in different forms in Greenspan (1988); de Sousa (1987); Roberts (1988).

[10] This multidimensional makeup of an emotion's mode of representing is conveyed by Goldie's (2000, chap. 2) characterization of emotions as "feeling towards"; Döring's (2007) "affective perceptions"; Roberts's (1988) notion of "concern-based construals"; and Helm's (2002) "felt evaluations."

For example, my clenched fists, dilated pupils, and motor readiness to strike, can together present someone's behavior toward me as threatening violence, even if I haven't (yet) formed the belief that it does. We can thus inquire into whether that presentation is apt, without attending solely to whether I have beliefs about the action, and whether they are true. Indeed, I may continue to experience an emotion that presents something you said as insulting, even after I realize that it was only an innocuous remark. Of course, an emotion can be the right kind of response to an object, yet its intensity or duration miscalibrated. Ire may be an appropriate response to the meandering driver ahead, but road rage is not. Both emotions are species of anger, but few situations that call for the one would also merit the other.

We can identify two ways of characterizing that aptness, in terms either of *justification* or of *correctness*. When we ask of an emotion whether in its capacity as an evaluative judgment it is justified, we are asking whether there are sufficient subjective reasons supporting its presentation of its object as having the evaluative qualities that it is the emotion's function to detect. These reasons may be that the object appears to have the evaluative qualities or that it appears to have non-evaluative qualities upon which those evaluative qualities supervene.[11] This way of characterizing the aptness relation makes aptness depend only on whether the emotion's representation is *reasonable*.[12] We can make intuitive sense of this proposal if we consider that there is nothing abnormal about a person feeling fear over a credible but nonetheless false report. By contrast, when we ask whether the emotion in its capacity as an evaluative judgment is correct, we are asking whether the evaluative quality it presents its object as having really belongs to that object— whether how it presents things is how they are.

Reasonableness and correctness correspond to two different kinds of norms, and their joint application to the same emotional episode can deliver different verdicts of aptness, without inconsistency.[13] However, the notion of aptness I adopt here employs only the second and more stringent approach that stresses correctness. For reasonableness expresses in an indirect fashion

---

[11] See Korsgaard (2009).

[12] See Greenspan (1980).

[13] The distinction between a correct and a reasonable emotion is analogous to that between an attitude, such as a belief, that is justified by objective reasons and one that is justified by only subjective or apparent reasons. Objective reasons are considerations that count in favor of the attitude. Subjective or apparent reasons count in favor of the rationality of the attitude; it is rational to treat them as objective reasons even though they are not. For an early statement of the distinction, see Williams (1981).

what correctness identifies directly. The reasons that justify an emotion in its representational dimension apply only because they are posited (sometimes mistakenly) as tracking how things are.

A quick way to express this stricter condition of fit would be to say that an apt emotion must present its object as the object is. More precisely, an emotion is apt only if its representation of its object is true (veridical, or correct in whatever way that its subtending intentional representation can be correct) *and* the emotion is experienced in virtue of the fact that the representation is true (veridical, correct, etc.). Here, if I feel anxiety in virtue of believing that the car I'm driving is about to run out of gasoline, that emotion is apt only if it is felt in virtue of the fact that my belief is true. A minor adjustment to this view should be made, however, in that it seems too strict in failing to isolate the *relevant* ways in which an emotion's presentation of its object and the nature of the object may depart. Not every fact about an object that an emotion commits to is relevant to whether that emotion is apt (my anxiety would still properly hold if it is diesel that my car is about to run out of). It seems that an apt emotion should be required to present an object correctly only in light of facts that make a difference in the *evaluative* qualities of the object that are criterial for the emotion.[14]

Thus, I propose, there are two necessary and jointly sufficient conditions of an emotion being apt (rational, fitting, or otherwise warranted, in the narrow representational sense): that it (1) correctly presents its object as having the value-relevant properties that are criterial for that emotion; and (2) is experienced in virtue of that presentation being correct. My fear presents the bear as dangerous. Whether that fear is apt depends on whether, in fact, the bear is dangerous, and whether I undergo the emotion because the bear has that (relational) property.

We can thus identify certain kinds of justifying reasons for an emotion— reasons that speak to its aptness. These include whether the object possesses the criterial property, or properties that are consistently correlated with the presence of the criterial property, or properties upon which the criterial property directly supervenes. My feeling of admiration for a person is apt even if I don't identify her as admirable but only as having a combination of qualities—say, courage, wisdom, and kindness—in virtue of which one is admirable.

---

[14] For a related approach to aptness of emotions see Owens (2012).

It is important here to stress that the process of justifying an emotion may not mirror the process by which the emotion is explained.[15] Recall from §3.1 that the criterial qualities of an emotion may be imputed to the object of the emotion without the subject who undergoes that emotion employing the concept of that quality. Here one's emotion may fit its object even if one does not possess concepts of the object's properties in virtue of which that fit is justified. A person can exhibit an emotion without being able to represent to herself that she feels the emotion. An infant can fear something without having the concept of fear. What matters in the attribution of the emotion is that the agent's response tracks directly or indirectly the evaluative qualities the emotion has the function of identifying.[16]

I should also stress that this account of aptness provides only a formal characterization of when an emotion is warranted; substantive accounts of what particular qualities in an object merit a given emotion are often contested, and may change with changes in our culture and values (as occurred with feeling "awe," which seems to have once applied only to the supernatural). My aim is only to provide a descriptive and explanatory account of the structure of our justifications of emotions across real and imagined contexts.

Finally, let me acknowledge a potential resistance to the very idea of there being standards of aptness for the emotions we feel for art. One might object that a significant source of what is valuable to us in art is the *diversity* of responses it evokes—how art allows us to form and discover ourselves through our individual responses, not through our conforming to a universally applicable standard. I register that point, but also note that another value of art that has prima facie plausibility is its capacity to foster a community of sentiment—the kind of community formed when individuals argue for the merits of their respective responses and find echoes of those responses in others. This dimension of artistic value wouldn't be available if all responses were potentially radically particular.[17]

---

[15] See Goldie (2004).

[16] For the indirect route, see Prinz (2004).

[17] No doubt, one of the central problems of aesthetics is the question of whether and how grounds for generally shared norms of response can be established. See Gilmore (2013).

4.2. Continuity

At first glance, it might appear that adopting the preceding notion of aptness would render the criteria governing emotions' fit to their objects discontinuous across fictional and real-world domains. An emotion is apt if and only if it correctly presents its object as having the criterial qualities relevant to that emotion. Yet, at least according to mainstream theories of fictional entities, sui generis objects of fictions do not exist, and thus are not the kinds of things that *could* bear the properties that are criterial for the emotions we feel toward them.[18] Rather, such objects can only be represented or imagined as existing and bearing such qualities. Of course, real things, e.g., New York City, can be represented in a fiction. However, both in cases in which a fiction represents a non-existent object and cases in which it represents an object that exists independent of the fiction, our emotions are about the object *as represented by* the fiction or the object as imagined. This contrasts with our emotions about things in the real world. There our emotions are not only about how things are represented, e.g., via descriptions, but about how they are.[19] My amusement in seeing a character in a film fall into an open manhole may be apt if the event is successfully represented in the film as amusing; but my amusement would not be apt (assuming I care for the person's welfare) if I saw an analogous event occur in front of me.

However, is this difference in the kinds of things that our emotions are about sufficient to show that there is a difference in the norms governing the aptness (as characterized earlier) of those emotions? A proponent of continuity would say no. For she would hold that in both the real-world and fictional cases, the emotions in question are held to the same standard: in the former, the amusement is apt only if its object has the criterial qualities of that emotion; in the latter case, it is apt only if its object is *represented as having* those qualities.

That is, the proponent of continuity will acknowledge that the kinds of things that our emotions are about differ metaphysically across real and fictional or imagined domains; on the one side, we respond to what is true, on the other, we respond to what is true in the fiction. However, it is consistent

---

[18] Arguments to the effect that fictional objects do exist largely acknowledge that they don't exist in the same metaphysical sense as their real-world counterparts do. See Brock and Everett (2015).

[19] See Currie (2014).

with that difference in the objects of our emotions that the relevant reasons that can justify the emotions are the same.

More generally, the proponent of continuity can help herself to the observation that emotional responses depend variously on many kinds of cognitive bases (beliefs, imaginings, desires, fantasies) via which their objects are represented. These different forms of mental representation bear different metaphysical commitments to their objects (wishes, unlike desires, for example, are plausibly not constrained to represent their contents as physically or metaphysically possible). But it is not clear why we should conclude that they must also introduce different justifying reasons for the emotions they underlie. For the continuity theorist, my pity for someone is justified if she is a victim of undeserved hardship; that holds whether she suffers in the real world or is only represented as such by a fiction. More specifically, my pity for someone in real life is apt only if I feel that pity in virtue of my accurately believing that she unjustifiably suffers; analogously, my pity for a character in a fiction is apt only if I feel that pity in virtue of my correctly imagining that she so suffers. It must be, indeed, part of, or true in, the story that she suffers unjustifiably, and I imagine her as deserving of pity accordingly.[20]

The question of whether an emotion is warranted in response to its object is a question of whether the emotion's presentation of its object's emotion-relevant evaluative qualities is correct. If the intentional state is a belief, then it is a constraint on the aptness of the emotion that the object has the qualities in fact that the emotion presents it as having. If the intentional state is an imagining, the qualities the emotion presents the object as possessing must be possessed by it as-correctly-*imagined* for the emotion to be apt.

The problem of what it is to correctly imagine something is too open-ended to be adequately addressed here (viz., can one *incorrectly* imagine x if x has no counterpart in the real world? Can one correctly imagine a metaphysical impossibility?). Many philosophers, noting that imaginings are subject to the will, adopt a stipulative account of the identity of what one imagines, such that there is little room to mistakenly identify the imagination's contents. Jerry Fodor, for example, writes, "What makes my stick figure an image of a tiger is not that it looks much like one . . . but rather that it's *my* image, so I'm the one who gets to say what it's an image of." And Colin McGinn asserts that "I cannot misidentify the object of my imagining" because "the

---

[20] Jenefer Robinson (2005) relatedly calls attention to the ways in which "our emotional experience of the novel or play is itself a form of *understanding*, even if it is an inarticulate or relatively inarticulate understanding" (123).

identity of my imagined object is fixed by my intentions."[21] One should object that it is hardly uncontroversial to assume the intentions or stipulations
described in such accounts are always realized. If an artist working from the
wrong photographs intends to produce a picture of Queen Elizabeth, but
ends up depicting a person that looks just like the Queen Mother, then why
should his intention trump the character of the work itself in deciding what it
depicts? One can ask an analogous question of a person who imagines a mule
when intending to visualize a donkey. What the stipulative approach gets
right is the observation that *if* there are no criteria external to one's imaginative activity that constrain the correctness of the representation that results,
its identity is up to oneself.

Fortunately, for our purposes, there are such correctness criteria external
to the imaginative activity that causes emotions. For one's emotions purport
to represent the presence of qualities in their objects which hold independently of one's imaginative representation of the objects—namely, those relational qualities that pertain to what one cares about. We can address the
correctness of an emotion based on an imagining by asking whether the
qualities that the emotion attributes to an imagined object are possessed by
the object. For example, when imagining that I am playing with what is stipulated to be a harmless puppy, I might come to feel a rush of agitation and
apprehension (say, because I was once bitten by a full-grown dog). My fear
presents the imagined state of affairs as posing a threat even though that state
of affairs is, as specified, harmless. The emotion inaptly presents the scenario
as instantiating an evaluative quality that in the imagined representation it
does not have.

Of course, some imaginative activity—free imagining—proceeds with no
directives as to its contents.[22] However, a central element in the experience of
engaging with a fictional work of art is to have our imagining guided or prescribed by the work. Specifically, a fictional work of art solicits us to imagine
what is true in, or according to, the story. *Don Quixote* directs us to imagine
that, via an absorption in tales of chivalry, a threadbare noble is deluded into
believing that he is a knight errant. *Emma* asks us to imagine that Emma
Woodhouse fancies herself to be a good matchmaker.

---

[21] Fodor (1975, 191); McGinn (2004, 31).

[22] Wittgenstein (1934/1958) remarks: "Someone says, he imagines King's College on fire. We ask
him: 'How do you know that it's *King's College* you imagine on fire? Couldn't it be a different building,
very much like it? . . . And still you say: 'There's no doubt I imagine King's College and no other
building.' But can't saying this be making the very connection we want? For saying it is like writing
the words 'Portrait of Mr. So-and-so' under a picture."

All but the most relativist theories of what constitutes a fiction—what is true in it, what point of view it takes on its contents, and so on—are committed to some constraints on which of a reader's potential imaginings can count as correct comprehensions of the work. A thoroughgoing intentionalist theory holds that an author is solely responsible for the contents of her work.[23] A more moderate intentionalism treats the meaning of a work as what the author intended, insofar as that meaning is consistent with the text's conventional sentence-meaning.[24] Hypothetical intentionalism allows only certain kinds of evidence into what counts as an author's intention and posits a work's meaning as what, given those restrictions, "an appropriately informed, sympathetic, and discriminating reader" would attribute to the text.[25] Finally, a value-maximizing theory takes it to be an internal feature of our very engagement with works of art qua works of art that we seek in them, or in an experience of them, a maximal degree of artistic value consistent with what we know about the works.[26] Accordingly, it is a reason for preferring one interpretation over another, when each is consistent with the known facts of the work, that the first interpretation lends the work greater artistic value or makes possible a greater artistic experience.

Fortunately, the continuity proponent does not have to be burdened with committing to the adequacy of any particular theory of fictional content. For she can say that *whatever it is* for it to be true within or according to a fiction that something (an event, person, state of affairs) has the properties that merit a given emotional response, the potential reasons that justify that aptness are the same across real and fictional domains. That is, the debate over continuity of affective norms is not how some state of affairs is made to hold within a fiction. Rather the debate concerns the norms that govern affective responses to whatever fictional states of affairs are thereby established.

One important argument in favor of continuity is that it would seem to be mysterious how we could so naturally and unreflectively respond emotionally to many works in a way that reflects an adequate comprehension of their contents if we were not bringing to them our schemata for appropriate affective responses to real things. It is rarely the case that a work explicitly tells us how to feel toward the states of affairs that it represents. (And even when a work does carry such instructions, we still need to determine how to

[23] Stock (2017).
[24] Carroll (1992); Stecker (2006).
[25] Levinson (2006, 302).
[26] Davies (1991, 181–206); Lamarque (2002b).

respond to the represented content and instructions.) For the continuity theorist, sad states of affairs make us sad, disgusting objects disgust us, whether those states of affairs and objects are real or only represented in a story.[27]

Jenefer Robinson thus appears to endorse the continuity thesis in suggesting that the proper understanding of a novel involves emotions supported by the same reasons as those involved in ordinary nonfictional or non-literary understanding: "It seems that in real life we *need* emotional understanding and fellow-feeling if we are to understand other people properly, and that cognition without emotion simply does not do as good a job. If this is true for our understanding of people in real life, it is likely to be true of fictional characters as well."[28] It is consistent with Robinson's observation that emotional understanding obeys different rules or functions between fictions and the real world. However, a continuity proponent would say that if Robinson is right, it is much more parsimonious to conclude that emotional responses to fiction follow the same norms as emotional understanding in real life.[29]

Comparably, Susan Feagin proposes a continuity of norms (although for more than just emotions) in what she dubs "the real-life principle": the warrant for responses to events in fictional literature is transferred from "the warrant one has for responding in such ways to actual events of that type." Specifically, "If a reader S is warranted in responding in way R to an actual event of a certain sort, then S is warranted in responding in way R to the description of that sort of event in the work."[30] Feagin doesn't specify what dimensions of the real-life response pertain to its warrant, but she allows

---

[27] Nussbaum (2001) thus explains the instance of pity we feel in response to a given fictional representation of unjustified suffering in virtue of its belonging to a kind of thing—unjustified suffering in general—that also exists in the real world. "Pity has the content, 'Someone who is (right now) important to me is suffering undeserved misfortune.' This content is deployed at two levels: at a concrete level these thoughts take Philoctetes, the fictional character, as their intentional object. . . . At a more general level, however, pity takes as its intentional object the unjustified suffering that is really in the world. . . . If the work were not held to life in this way, by threads of plausibility, it could not engross us emotionally as it does" (245).

[28] Robinson (2005, 128).

[29] Robinson (2005) appears to endorse both descriptive and normative versions of the continuity thesis. Indeed, the substantial theory of the emotions that she develops seems intended to apply invariantly across emotions elicited by real-life experiences and those caused by fictions. However, as she notes, it is consistent with different readers being held to the same norms of fit or correctness in their emotional responses to a fiction, that those responses can disagree: "because interpretations are the result of cognitive monitoring of our non-cognitive affective appraisals, and because those non-cognitive appraisals are likely to be different for different people with different goals, wants, and interests, there is likely to be disagreement about the resulting cognitive overview of plot, character, and theme" (141–42).

[30] Feagin (1996, 216–17).

that, in the literary case, the warrant can be outweighed or undermined by other factors of a work such as its formal features.[31]

Aside from its role in describing such relations between our emotions for fictions and real states of affairs, continuity is assumed in a prominent solution to the question of how we *can*, and why we sometimes do, have feelings for what we believe not to exist. There, our feelings for fiction are explained as the manifestation of a general-purpose capacity to respond emotionally toward what we know to be counterfactual representations. This capacity is proposed to play a significant role in practical rationality, in allowing us to richly imagine and emotionally evaluate various courses of potential action at a lower cost than would be incurred in actually trying out each alternative.[32] For this solution to work, the operative norms governing our emotions must be invariant across fictional and real-world contexts. Otherwise, one's emotional evaluation of the counterfactual scenario would be no guide to how to properly assign an evaluation to the scenario if it were actual.

The preceding point can be generalized beyond our engagements with fictions. For there are a significant number of non-artistic counterfactual contexts (thought experiments, hypotheticals, the creation of living wills, and so on) in which the operative assumption is that how we emotionally respond to the contents of an imagined situation tracks how we would respond, and what evaluations those responses would express, if that situation were real. *Affective forecasting*, for example, permits us to assess the value of potential events to our future selves in order to decide how to act in the present.[33] But for such simulation to be effective, the correspondence between how we feel in the future and how our imagining of the future makes us feel in the present cannot be a happy accident, but would exist because the same norms for responses that fit their objects are being observed. In other words, if my response to the imagined scenario is not to be suspected of being systematically aberrant—inappropriate in ways that would make it a poor basis of prediction for how I would feel about that state of affairs should it come to pass—it must be because I abide by the same criteria of fit for those emotions in the imagined case as I do in reality.

---

[31] Feagin (1996, 216).

[32] See Currie (1995b, 157). Gordon (1995) likewise argues that in the process of simulation we employ the same "perceptual, cognitive, motivational, and emotive resources" involved in ordinary practical reasoning, to understand others and to engage in reasoning about hypothetical states of affairs (732–33).

[33] On affective forecasting, see Gilbert and Wilson (2007). Note that while studies of such assessment through the imagination of potential events demonstrate its function in shaping our current decisions, they also show how such prospective evaluation can be systematically misleading. Gilbert et al. (1998).

Indeed, a continuity theorist might propose the *reductio* argument: if a commitment to discontinuity entails that the reliance on such ordinary counterfactual thinking is systematically unjustified, discontinuity must be false.

The challenge for the discontinuity proponent is to show that our affective responses to fictions are sufficiently and appropriately *unlike* our affective responses to other prescriptions to counterfactually imagine, such that different criteria of aptness for those emotions for fictions may apply. Let us now turn to that case for discontinuity.

5

Defending Discontinuity

> Theatrical as well as every other poetical illusion is a waking dream,
> to which we voluntarily surrender ourselves.
>
> —Schlegel, 1849

> We . . . become . . . aware of the way we have been turned into emo-
> tional and aesthetic imbeciles when we hear ourselves humming the
> sickly, goody-goody songs.
>
> —Pauline Kael, review of *The Sound of Music*

In the last chapter I introduced the question of whether the criteria relevant to justifying our emotions and related affective states hold invariantly
across our responses to representations of real and imagined domains. In
this chapter I argue against such invariance in favor of the discontinuity
thesis: the norms that apply to our emotions for fictional representations
can be inconsistent with those that govern our emotions for what we take to
be true.

5.1. The Threat of Discontinuity

The continuity thesis holds that an emotion is justified when experienced
in response to an object (event, person, state of affairs, etc.) in a fiction if
and only if the emotion is justified in response to an analogous object (event,
person, state of affairs, etc.) in the actual world.[1] Here, the aptness, in the

---

[1] It is difficult to offer general conditions under which we should say that fictional and real objects
of an emotion belong to the same kind. In some cases, we can compare our emotional responses to
the fact that *p* with those responses to the fictional representation that *p*. However, descriptions of the
real and fictional objects of an emotion may also refer to distinct individuals that, from the standpoint of the emotion, belong to the same relevant kind. Although no real individual is identical in
all respects to how Anna Karenina is represented as being, we can make intuitive sense of an actual

Apt Imaginings. Jonathan Gilmore, Oxford University Press (2020). © Oxford University Press.
DOI: 10.1093/oso/9780190096342.001.0001

limited representational sense, of an emotion felt for some kind of thing in a fiction is either inherited from, or of a piece with, the aptness of that emotion felt for an analogous kind of real thing. Conversely, if an emotion would not fit a given object in the real world, it would not fit an object of the same relevant kind as represented in a fiction. Continuity thus characterizes both our responses to fictions and our responses elicited in nonfictional or belief-based engagements as guided by the same norms. The shifting emotions I feel in, e.g., reading a novel reflect a domain-general capacity to track the evaluative properties of states of affairs, independent of the particular attitude (belief, imagining, memory, desire) by which they are represented.

That thesis may sound innocuous. However, in one form or another it is a foundational assumption in some significant accounts of the relation between art and life. If continuity fails to hold, that should raise serious concerns about how to reform those theories. Let me identify the consequences of discontinuity for three such theories.

5.1.1. First Theory

According to one kind of theory, when we try to identify a person's evaluative dispositions—what she tends to judge to be morally good, meritorious, admirable, beautiful, desirable, and so on—the evidence furnished by her affective responses to what is fictional or only imagined does not differ in kind from the evidence furnished by her responses to what she takes to be actual. More precisely, when we are confident that one is affectively responding to what is fictional or imagined in a way that is apt—in a way that correctly represents the relevant evaluative properties of what one imagines—that response is assumed to be a reliable guide to how one is disposed to respond to analogous states of affairs in the actual world.

Relying on that theory, Richard Moran points to the inconsistency between (1) the thesis that our emotions felt for fictions are only the sort of "quasi-emotions" that are solely internal to a pretense, and (2) the assumption that one may make discoveries about oneself through examining how one responds to fictions. The latter exercise would be hard to understand, Moran notes, if what a person felt for some fictional scenario "was as remote

person and Anna being of the same relevant kind of, say, those who suffer from the social exclusion of a moralizing society.

from his real temperament as the events on the screen are remote from his real beliefs about the world."[2]

However, it would not be sufficient, as Moran seems to suggest in that passage, that the emotions that we feel for fictions be genuine for them to serve as guides to our real-life temperament. They must also be guided by the same norms. What we feel in response to some fictional state of affairs does not tell us how we feel about analogous real states of affairs, unless those feelings across the fictional/real divide are guided by roughly invariant criteria governing what counts as an appropriate response to their objects. If we abided by different norms across fictions and the real world in feeling, e.g., pity, experiencing that sentiment in the former context would not predict its occurrence in the latter.

It is true, as Moran argues, that the "ordinary practice of eliciting, sharing, and criticizing such emotional responses to fictions would be a quite bizarre and pointless exercise if these responses and the attitudes they express were not located on this side of the counterfactual divide."[3] However, that ordinary practice in which people share and dispute their emotional responses to a fiction is consistent with those responses being governed by different norms of aptness or fit from people's emotional responses to real things. We're enthralled as Charlie Chaplin's Little Tramp is swallowed by the cogs of a factory machine, but would rightly feel a very different kind of emotion, such as dread, if that scenario were to unfold in real life. Thus, if the discontinuity thesis is true, it should motivate skepticism about the assumption that our engagements with fictions and the stuff of real life express the same evaluative dispositions. Diderot points to that skepticism about moral character in his rueful remarks on reading Richardson's *Clarissa*: "How good I was! How just I was! How satisfied I was with myself."[4] The sympathetic, great-souled persona the novel prescribes for adoption by its reader need not correspond to the moral temperament the reader evinces in everyday life.

A parallel theory is assumed in some defenses of "response moralism," the proposal that our mental representations of fictional states of affairs can be morally defective on grounds independent of any practical or motivational effects they may have. Berys Gaut, for example, argues that our responses to fiction can be subject to moral evaluation because "the attitudes people . . . manifest toward imagined scenarios have implications for their attitudes toward their real-life counterparts, for the attitudes are partly directed toward kinds, not just individuals."[5] A misogynist may pleasurably imagine the sexual exploitation of some wholly fictional female character. Even though the character does not exist, and thus cannot be hurt, the imagining may nonetheless be morally criticized insofar as it gives pleasure to the misogynist in virtue of presenting the fictional woman as belonging to the same relevant kind as women in real life. That is, insofar as a fictional woman's (putative) membership in that kind plays a determining role in the generation of the misogynist's response, his response to the character reveals—indeed exemplifies—his morally defective attitude toward real women as well. Such membership need not be metaphysically defensible; all the response moralist needs to show is that it is in virtue of seeing the fictional woman as exemplifying the kind that includes real women, that the misogynist takes pleasure in her being harmed.

Here, however, it is important to identify where the threat of discontinuity lies. If, per Gaut, our responses to a fictional character are to that character *as* a member of a kind that includes real individuals, then our response is not, *in that respect*, interestingly identified as an engagement with a fiction. For our response is directed at something we take to be real.

The defense of discontinuity has greater relevance for versions of response moralism that ethically scrutinize attitudes toward fictional characters even when the characters are not assumed to belong to the same morally relevant kind as actual beings. If one holds that we can learn of a person's defective character through the pleasure she takes in imagining the torture of such beings, one is likely implicitly committed to the continuity thesis. One is likely committed, that is, to the proposition that a given attitude toward a fictional character is morally permissible if and only if that attitude is morally permissible when held toward an actually existing counterpart of that character. Again, the attitude at issue here is not experienced *in virtue of* the fictional being belonging to the same kind as a real being (even though they may in fact do so).

I hedge the preceding to allow that we might see, e.g., the pleasure a person takes in imagining the torture of fictional characters only as an indirect clue to her defective character, without that inference depending on a commitment to continuity. We might worry about someone who devotes his or her media consumption exclusively to literature and film that prescribe sadistic

---

[5] Gaut (1998, 186); Hazlett (2009, 251).

fantasies, even if we don't believe one's responses to any one such work reveals how one would be disposed to feel about its represented scenario taking place in real life.[6] For one's desire to have certain real experiences can no doubt sometimes be reflected in one's pursuit of opportunities to imagine virtual versions of them.

5.1.2. Second Theory

A second kind of theory that relies on a continuity thesis is that emotions and other states we experience in response to fictions often serve as rehearsals, training, or some sort of useful proxy for feelings of the same kind elicited by real states of affairs. For example, according to the continuity thesis, because the norms governing my feeling of sympathy are the same across fictional and real contexts, undergoing a sympathetic response to a fictional character can serve as a mode of low-cost, low-risk cultivation of my sensitivity to the proper grounds of sympathy in case the sentiment is called for in real life. Conversely, one may worry that violent films and video games have a deleterious effect on consumers' attitudes and behavior by normalizing aggressive thoughts in real circumstances in virtue of cultivating them in response to imaginings (more on this in Chapter 8).[7] Or, with Plato, one might be concerned about the habituation effects of artistic consumption: the "enjoyment of other people's sufferings is necessarily transferred to our own," and the pity that is provoked in response to the sufferings of fictional characters "won't be easily held in check when we ourselves suffer."[8] A related assumption, referred to in §3.2, is the familiar idea that fiction-guided imagination can aid us in honing our moral sensibilities through exposing us to richly imagined moral dilemmas and placing us in the shoes of those with alternative outlooks on life.[9]

For the proponent of discontinuity, the problem with these appeals to the edifying effects of engaging with fictions is that if the available justifications and criticisms of our responses to two events of the same kind can appropriately diverge because one belongs to the content of an imagining and the other to the content of a belief, then there may not be any straightforward

---

[6] See Walton (1997/2015).
[7] Bushman and Anderson (2009); Anderson et al. (2010).
[8] Plato (1975, Book X).
[9] As in Nussbaum (1992); Putnam (2013); Beardsmore (1971).

transfer of those capacities of evaluation from one domain to the other. In his *Lettre à d'Alembert*, Rousseau proposes that, far from nurturing in us a genuine capacity for sympathy outside aesthetic contexts, the best tragedies only function to "reduce all the duties of man to some passing and sterile emotions that have no consequences, [except] to make us applaud . . . our humanity in pitying the ills that we could have cured."[10]

A related account of the epistemic value of such imagination-based emotions holds that we can discover how we will likely feel if some counterfactual state of affairs involving us were to become actual, by vividly imagining that such a state of affairs has come to pass. Such counterfactual imagining is employed in a wide range of scenarios, inter alia, suppositions in which we discover which of several options we might take would give us the greatest satisfaction. In such contexts, the presumption is that our affective responses to, respectively, a counterfactual state of affairs and an analogous actual state of affairs are guided by the same norms governing their fit to their objects. In other words, ceteris paribus, the emotional responses dependent on the two kinds of mental states can be predicted to be reliably similar in virtue of being subject to the same norms of fit to their objects. If the discontinuity thesis is defensible, substantial confidence in such predictions is misplaced.

5.1.3. Third Theory

Finally, a third kind of theory is assumed in the widely adopted scientific methodology (noted in Chapter 3) of using fictional narratives and films to ascertain the nature—the physiological, phenomenological, and behavioral dimensions—of affective responses *in general*.[11] In other words, it is a methodological commitment in many studies of the emotions that our affective responses across analogous fictional and real-world scenarios are invariant in explanatorily relevant respects.

---

[10] "In the final accounting, when a man has gone to admire fine actions in stories and cry for imaginary miseries, what more can be asked of him? . . . Has he not acquitted himself of all that he owes to virtue by the homage which he has just rendered it? What more could one want of him: That he practice it himself?" (1758/1968, 25).

[11] For illustrations, see Gross and Levenson (1995) and Izard (1991, 172). Adelmann and Zajonc (1989) describe the use of film representations in experiments on facial expression and emotion. For a favorable discussion of this method see Oatley, Mar, and Djikic (2012).

However, the ecological validity of those studies' findings is threatened if their participants have internalized different criteria of warrant or justification—different norms—for their responses to what is true in the fiction and what is true outside of it. For then their responses may differ according to whether they construe the represented events as real or as merely the contents of a fictional story. Perhaps audiences allow themselves to be affected by formal and stylistic aspects of a representation when they construe it as fictional, but try to limit those effects on their responses insofar as they believe that the description is a representation of the real world.

Those three theories exemplify some of what is at stake if the discontinuity thesis is true. Let me now turn to arguments in its favor.

5.2. Discontinuity and Framing Effects

The endorsement of discontinuity often rests on a strong intuition: it is a hall-mark of our ordinary traffic with fictional and other imagined things that we can respond to them in ways that radically depart from how we respond to their real-life counterparts. And, correlatively, such departures are not only possible but often mandated according to the norms that constitute many artistic and other pretense-based practices. We can find a kind of person contemptible in real life but likable when represented in a narrative.[12] We often respond to the contents of daydreams, to sexual and other kinds of fantasies, in ways that we recognize are contrary to how we would, and would want to, respond if their events really transpired. In watching a film we might worry that the gang of safecrackers in the basement will be heard by the cops on the street above but, in real life, we would welcome their being discovered.

Such observations motivate the discontinuity thesis that, under certain conditions, for some proposition p, emotions (and other affective responses) that would not be apt when elicited in believing that p, may be apt when elicited in only imagining that p. In other words, there can be an inconsistency between the feelings that fit what is fictional and what is taken to be real.[13]

---

[12] This asymmetry is discussed in Currie (1997): "We frequently like and take the part of people in fiction whom we would not like or take the part of in real life. The desires we seem to have concerning fictional things can be very unlike the desires we have concerning real life" (65).

[13] Note: it is difficult to explain how any two emotions could be inconsistent. Some kinds of emotions exclude others in an empirical sense, such as disgust and joy, because the physiological and psychological constituents of the two states are incompatible. The relevant inconsistency in the

Of course, sometimes what appears to be an inconsistency between our feelings for a fiction and an analogous real state of affairs can be explained away as only apparent. I can feel approval and disapproval of the same scenario without any rational tension if my feelings are only pro tanto: I can admire the ingenuity in the assassin's technique, but feel contempt for his aims. Likewise, there is no genuine inconsistency in feeling an emotion for an object under one aspect or description and feeling a contrary emotion when considering the object under a different aspect or description. There is no interesting conflict between Lois Lane's adoration of Superman and her mere affectionate tolerance of Clark Kent. Finally, sometimes our emotions felt in imagining p are different from what would be elicited by an experience of p, simply because our imagining is limited in the vividness, accuracy, duration, or other respects that the real experience is not.

Furthermore, even when we do have genuinely *inconsistent* emotional responses to an object when it is, respectively, part of the actual world and represented in a fiction or imagining, that does not entail that such distinct responses have an equal claim to being endorsed at a higher level of reflection. Perhaps, as Plato charged, works of art corrupt the proper attunement of our feelings.

A discontinuity theorist will acknowledge that, indeed, *some* instances of disparate responses to the analogous states of affairs within and outside a fiction create no problem for the continuity thesis. Even when the same norms do apply, our responses do not always abide by them. However, the discontinuity theorist will point out that it is intuitively problematic to classify all responses to fictions that run contrary to our responses to real life as instantiating failures of fit. Such disparate responses are ubiquitous, and it would be odd to say that they always fall short of the relevant governing norms, or that they fail to realize their proper function (in, e.g., registering the value of their targets). When a child takes satisfaction in the pretense of slaying a battalion of soldiers represented by his stuffed animals, it would be churlish to suggest that his enthusiasm for winning the battle should be tempered with regret for the loss of furry lifeforms the victory entailed. We would miss out on much of what makes imagining and pretending valuable if our emotional responses in those activities were always constrained to respect the norms governing our emotions for what is real.

debate over normative continuity would be found between the sets of reasons that respectively can justify two token emotions.

The discontinuity theorist thus proposes that, if we can respond with apt yet contrary emotions to, respectively, an object in the real world and the object as part of what is fictional, we ought to be persuaded that there are different criteria governing aptness in those different domains. If the continuity thesis forces us to decide that only one of two contrary emotions for, respectively, a fictional and real object can be apt, this presents a strong intuitive challenge to that thesis's plausibility.

However, for that challenge to continuity to hold, a discontinuity theorist needs to explain how it is possible that we can have such responses that are both apt but mutually inconsistent across our beliefs and fiction-guided imaginings. If our emotions felt for the contents of what we imagine are of the same explanatory kind as the emotions felt for the contents of our beliefs, we need some explanation of why their different cognitive bases introduce different standards for their appropriateness. For without such an explanation, one who wants to preserve the continuity thesis might (1) accept the counterintuitive result described previously; (2) revert to the irrealist's proposal that fiction- and imagination-directed emotions are not "genuine" emotions and so can't furnish counterexamples to continuity; or (3) propose that if an object in a fiction and the object in real life can provoke such different responses, perhaps we are wrong to identify those objects as belonging to the same relevant kind.

I want to consider an explanation that is widely subscribed to, but which, I will argue, ultimately fails. The explanation states that our response to a fictional object is not just to the object in itself but to the object *as presented* in a fictional representation. Flint Schier, for example, writes, "Our reaction to fictional characters is not just a reaction to fictional people, it is a reaction to them *as represented* in the text. . . . Therefore, our reaction is necessarily governed by *how* they are represented, and the kind of emotion that it is appropriate to feel is determined by the quality of the representation."[14]

In the previous chapter, I noted that our emotions are directed at different kinds of objects across real and fictional domains, but denied that this difference suffices to show that the norms governing those emotions differ across those domains. Here, however, the relevant difference that is proposed to explain the application of putatively different norms is not metaphysical (real vs. merely fictional objects) but, rather, a difference in the (epistemic) ways these objects are presented to us. The difference is seen in how the manner in

[14] Schier (1983).

which the contents of a fiction are described can impose a frame or point of view on the content, such that we respond to it with emotions that are potentially different from and contrary to those we would feel for its instantiation in the real world.[15]

Framing effects occur when the same content—e.g., a state of affairs, problem, or choice—is presented in different ways such that correspondingly different cognitive, explanatory, and evaluative attitudes toward that content are privileged. A decision between, for example, drilling for oil on land or at sea can be presented in a way that highlights considerations of economic efficiency or a way that stresses environmental protection. Each way of framing the question renders salient alternative aspects of the same decision. Framing effects are not necessarily distorting, although they show that an agent can be caused to express inconsistent preferences across different representations of the same choice—such as when it is framed, alternatively, as one in which gains are maximized or losses are minimized.[16] If, as in the preceding example, different ways of framing a problem merely make salient different relevant features of it, there may be no fact of the matter determining which set of features should play a determinative role in the choice at hand. However, some framing effects have less innocent results, where through the framing of some scenario factors that are *irrelevant* to how a given choice or evaluation should be made are illicitly permitted to have an influence in it. Critics of the reliance on intuitions in moral theorizing, for example, point to how the framing of a moral problem can cause us to unwittingly allow extraneous considerations to determine our moral judgments.[17]

Under the proposal considered here, a work of fiction does not merely represent persons, events, states of affairs as possessing whatever properties they would have, or consequences to which they would lead, were they to exist in real life. Rather, it represents those objects in a way—via a framework or point of view—that makes some of those properties or consequences more salient to us than others as the basis of our response. The style in which an

---

[15] For an account that casts a point of view as an operator that identifies only certain features of a given context as relevant to one's judgment or deliberation, see Brandom (1982). Discussions of framing and point of view in relation to fictions include Gendler (2000); Currie (2010); Dadlez (1997); Goldie (2003); Moran (1994).

[16] Framing approaches include, inter alia, risky choice framing (e.g., the risk that 10 out of 100 lives will be lost versus the opportunity to save 90 out of 100 lives); attribute framing (e.g., describing ice cream as 90% fat-free vs. 10% fat); and goal framing (e.g., a desire to gain some benefit versus a desire not to suffer a penalty of that amount). See Tversky and Kahneman (1981, 453); Levin, Schneider, and Gaeth (1998).

[17] See, e.g., Sinnott-Armstrong (2008); Horowitz (1998).

event is represented might, for example, make certain properties especially vivid, elicit only certain inferences while blocking others, direct our attention toward some of its effects and away from others, or emphasize some explanatory lines when alternatives are just as plausible. To fictionally represent a car chase as pleasurably thrilling, for example, might require diminishing the saliency of the collateral destruction and injury it causes, and other likely costs we would infer, in favor of maintaining our focus on a desire we share with fictional protagonists that they elude capture.

As we can see in that example, among the properties that such framing effects can steer our attention to are evaluative properties that are criterial for a given emotion. Through presenting an object (event, state of affairs, and so on) so as to foreground such properties, a work can express an emotional attitude toward what it represents and may succeed in inducing us to adopt that attitude as well. *The Great Dictator* depicts Chaplin's Hynkel, a stand-in for Hitler, as risibly grandiose by emphasizing his on-screen antics over the off-screen carnage the film also attributes to him. Renoir's portrayal of the café society of *Le Moulin de la Galette* evokes a cheerfulness through showing its polite and carefree atmosphere; Picasso's moody portrayal in his own *Moulin de la Galette* generates a contrary evaluation of the outdoor dancehall-restaurant by highlighting its sordid and seamy allure.

That structure of framing devices and the associated points of view they are marshalled to express offer a good explanation of how we can have contrary responses to an object when represented in a fiction and when taken to be real; however, that explanation does not support an argument against continuity.

For the presence of framing effects suggests that the comparison made between emotions directed at what we take to be fictional and take to be real is not like with like, and so does not furnish a genuine *test* of continuity. The question should not be

- Can we have contrary but apt responses to a scenario of some kind in real life and a scenario of the same kind as presented in a fiction?

Rather it should be

- Can we have contrary but apt responses to a scenario as presented in a fiction and that scenario presented in the same manner—that is, identically framed—in real life?

Events in real life don't typically occur in a given style (although one may perform a given action in a style), but we can see and describe them from comic, tragic, ironic, and other points of view. We might engage in gallows humor, construing some situation as comical, even though we believe, all told, that it hardly merits amusement. And the same facts may be described using different forms of figurative language and rhetoric, thereby eliciting different evaluations and emotional responses. Framing effects, as noted, occur in real life as well as fictions, disposing us to treat certain features of a situation, among all those elements we are aware of, as more significant factors in our deliberations and evaluations than others.

Thus, the argument that there are different norms governing responses to fictions and real life is not advanced via the observation that our access to the objects of a fiction is distinctively affected by a framework or point of view. For our response to objects in real life is often shaped in that manner as well.

Let me offer a rejoinder on behalf of the discontinuity proponent that, while intuitively appealing, should also be rejected: while an emotional response to a real object on the basis of properties made salient by one point of view is susceptible to being challenged by properties potentially made salient by other points of view, the evaluation-relevant qualities of a fictional object are *only those* that the fiction's point of view presents the object as having.[18] The evaluative qualities do not, i.e., belong to a larger class that are de-emphasized; rather, they are *constitutive* of the object represented by a fiction. The features of shallowness and ostentation that Dickens invokes in the name of the Veneerings in *Our Mutual Friend* are intrinsic qualities of those characters themselves. The evaluation we are elicited to make of them via that name and other descriptions is part of their very identity as characters. As Peter Lamarque notes, it is not "as if there is some other perspective on the Veneerings under which they subsist as decent, honest, kindly, altruistic folk who have somehow been falsely captured by the mocking tone of the narrator."[19]

The proposal here is that my emotional response to a real object is committed to presenting it in light of all considerations available to me and, in

---

[18] Dadlez (1997) makes this point in saying that a fiction "manipulates our attention in such a way that making certain construals is virtually a foregone conclusion . . . those are the only situations we get, and there is little else to attend to" (95).

[19] Lamarque (2007, 121). Compare Peter Van Inwagen's (1977) remark that "if someone had been looking over Dickens' shoulder when Dickens was writing [*Martin Chuzzlewit*], and said to him, 'No, no, you've got her [Mrs. Gamp] all wrong. She is quite thin, about twenty-four, and her voice is melodious,' this would simply have made no sense" (301).

that respect, is committed to diminishing any recognized distortion that framing effects may impose. Yet, by contrast, my emotional response to an object in a fiction is committed to presenting it as the artwork presents it, not to getting the content of the depiction right somehow independent of how it is shown or described.[20]

That important distinction, however, shows only that the sets of potentially determinate facts (real and fictional) about the objects of our emotions can differ across reality and fiction, not that there is any difference in the criteria governing what emotional responses are apt in light of those facts.

It is true that, in one case, the fit of an emotion is constrained by the way the world is; in the other case, the fit is constrained by the way a fiction or instance of imagining represents the world. However, when we ask *which features* of those objects count in justifying (or criticizing) the emotions, we may find that the features are indeed the same. The continuity proponent can sensibly claim that, e.g., fear of an object that we take to be real is justified only if it is true that object is a threat to what one cares about; and fear of an object in a fiction is justified only if it is true *in the fiction* that the object is a threat to what one cares about. Modulo the differences in metaphysical status of their objects, affective responses are governed by norms that appear to be the same across how a fiction represents the world, and how beliefs and other veridical attitudes do.

5.3. Discontinuity, Reasons, and Causes

Where I propose the discontinuity thesis gains more traction is in identifying what kinds of considerations can count as reasons in justifying (or criticizing) a given emotional response to the content of a fiction or imagination. Recall that, according to the account of aptness in the limited representational sense offered in §4.1, an emotion felt for a real thing is apt only if it is experienced in virtue of correctly presenting its object as having the properties criterial for the emotion. And thus the only reasons that can justify that aptness are those that speak to the object's possession of those qualities. In arguing for discontinuity, I want to suggest that sometimes, in the fictional case, there are also reasons that can justify the aptness of an emotion which do not speak to the object's possession of the emotion's criterial qualities.

[20] See also Currie (2014).

I will argue, specifically, that if a fictional work of art or exercise of the imagination is designed to evoke an emotion toward some object it represents, and succeeds in doing so by virtue of that design, that is a reason counting in favor of the emotion's aptness. That reason counts in favor of the emotion's aptness even when its object does not bear the emotion's criterial qualities.[21]

It is true that works of art standardly evoke a given emotion through supplying reasons that point to its object's possession of the relevant features. When we feel contempt for Iago because of his malign intentions, our emotion is justified for the same reasons that would justify feeling contempt for a similar kind of person with those motivations outside of a fiction.

However, we can see how works of art also sometimes represent people, events, states of affairs, and so on in ways designed to elicit certain emotions *without* supplying what would count as reasons for those emotions if they were felt toward analogous things in real life. I will first introduce a few illustrations and then offer a general explanation of this dimension of our affective engagements with fictions.

In one familiar experience, the soundtrack of a film or play causes and mediates an emotional response without offering any reasons internal to the fiction for that response. Music that sounds menacing can trigger fear of some scenario, while a cheerful score can bring about delight. That effect on our emotions can take many forms. Sometimes music primes us to feel an emotion but justifying facts must be found within the fiction for those emotions to be fully elicited. Other times, music may cause us to feel an emotion without there being any obvious facts conveyed by what we see on screen that would count in the affective experience's favor. Finally, music may modulate an emotion we form for other reasons, say by exposing the emotion's core, reversing or tempering it, or causing us to be aware of it in ways that do not leave it unchanged.[22]

For example, in Francis Ford Coppola's *Apocalypse Now*, Lieutenant Bill Kilgore blasts "Ride of the Valkyries" from helicopter-mounted speakers during his squadron's assault on an area controlled by the Vietcong. Although used within the narrative as a device to motivate the American soldiers and unsettle their enemies, the music's soaring, triumphal content and rarified

---

[21] The qualifier "in virtue of that design" is meant to exclude cases in which the work elicits an emotion it was designed to elicit, but not because of how it was designed. One might find a Borscht Belt joke funny in spite of, rather than as a realization of, its attempt at humor.

[22] On the effects of music on emotions achieved through automatic processes of affective contagion and mirroring, see Davies (2011).

status initially prompt in audiences a mordant fascination with the military's absurdly grandiose self-image. However, just after that feeling takes hold, a Vietnamese woman lobs a grenade into one of the US helicopters, killing all onboard. The same music that moments earlier elicited enjoyment in the rollicking violent spectacle now evokes horror and dread, feelings that we now see were merited in relation to the fiction all along. This is a "surprised by sin" moment, where the unserious and freewheeling attitude implied in our and the soldiers' pleasure is shown up for the grievous misapprehension it is. Contrast that with the role of the score of Wagner's *Lohengrin* played during the sequence of *The Great Dictator* in which Hynkel floats and bobs an inflated globe as he dreams of worldwide domination. There his acrobatic grace, mirrored by the beauty of the score, leaves us unconcerned that in the fiction it is the fate of the world with which he is literally "toying"—that is, until we are brought back from complacency when the balloon pops in his hands. In each case, the music does not offer information relevant to evaluating the scenes it accompanies, but causes us to see those situations under one aspect at the expense (we soon learn) of others.

Another familiar effect is our being induced to see characters as morally contemptible or threatening through a film's presentation of them as physically ugly or deformed—exploiting thereby our disposition to associate virtue with beauty along the lines of the ancient conception of "beauty of soul."

Defending that theory, the Earl of Shaftesbury writes:

No sooner are Actions view'd, no sooner the human Affections and Passions discern'd ... then straight an inward Eye distinguishes, and sees the Fair and Shapely, the Amiable and Admirable, apart from the Deform'd, the Foul, The Odious, or the Despicable.[23]

Although, reflectively, we would not subscribe to such a connection, it is a trope of popular movies that sinister characters are physically repulsive in both face and bearing, while innocent protagonists are possessed of both beauty and refinement. This is partially a convention of certain styles and genres—we know that Roald Dahl's hideous Mr. and Mrs. Twit are sinister because ugliness like theirs is, in most of his works, exclusively attributed to

---

[23] Shaftsbury (1714, 414–15). For the connection of this idea to Enlightenment moral theory, see Norton (1997). See also McGinn (1997). Representative studies of the psychological tendency are Dion, Berscheid, and Walster (1972); Nisbett and Wilson (1977).

morally deviant characters. But even children without mastery of fictional genres and conventions discriminate via visual appearances between those in a film or television show who are "good" and those who are not to be trusted.

Despite its adoption as a cheap means of establishing character identity, the exploitation of that bias is not confined to popular entertainment. It is a shorthand device among novelists as well. In the opening pages of *Crime and Punishment*, Dostoevsky's narrator describes, irrelevantly it seems, our protagonist as "remarkably good-looking, taller than average, slender and trim, with beautiful dark eyes and dark blond hair" and, two pages later, the pawnbroker as "a tiny, dried-up old crone, about sixty, with sharp, spiteful little eyes and a small, sharp nose" and with a long thin neck that "resembled a chicken's leg."[24] Here, at least at this point in the novel, the contrast between attractive and repulsive features does not so much let us know where our allegiances *should* lie, as cause those allegiances to form. Of course, subverting the expectation that beauty expresses virtue can be a source of dramatic value, where the lovely character with whom we align turns out to be the villain, or, by contrast, when we discover, just as Beauty does, that the Beast is good of heart.

The beauty of a work as a whole, rather than just the individuals it represents, may also affect how we emotionally and evaluatively respond to its contents, without that beauty giving us reasons drawn from facts in the fictional world to respond as we do. The beauty of an elegy does not tell us why we should feel a distanced and contained sadness for its subject—one of the standard effects of the genre—so much as prime or cause us to feel that way.[25] Similarly, the scale of a monument can evoke reverence toward its subject, without offering any description of the subject that would warrant that feeling. The architecture of Gothic cathedrals, comparably, does not only explicitly communicate theological commitments in its cross-configured plan, but is designed through its soaring elevations to induce the corresponding emotions of awe and disassociation from our earthly selves.

We are also often prompted to identify the material qualities of the media of visual works of art (roughness, austerity, fragility, pliancy) as figurative properties of whatever content the work embodies, evoking emotions that

---

[24] Dostoevsky (1866/1993, 4, 6).

[25] See Gilmore (2005). The beauty of a representation, through disposing us to feel a harmonious acceptance or even pleasure in what it shows, may interfere with other emotions that the represented subject should evoke on other grounds. See Chapter 9 for a related point with reference to the work of Sebastião Selgado.

don't reflect the properties of that content considered independently of the use of the medium. We see this in how a painter may dispose us to think of some content as ethereal or fleeting through depicting it with transparent washes, or get us to experience someone as being violent or powerful—as in de Kooning's *Women* series—through brushstrokes aggressively applied.

In Michelangelo's Roman *Pietà*, Mary's face is carved from a clear, unveined area of the marble, whose pristine quality is meant to elicit from viewers an imagining of Mary herself as unblemished in a spiritual sense. And Mary is represented as a young woman, not because we are to imagine that, in fact, she is so young (she appears younger than Jesus), but because such an appearance prompts us to see her as pure and ageless, unaffected by earthly decline.

Finally, as any graphic designer knows, the letterforms in which a proposition is inscribed shape its content's reception. Gothic type conveys sobriety and probity; some sans-serif types such as Helvetica convey clarity and generic contemporaneity; and the nominally sans-serif letterforms of Optima suggest both a modernist sentiment in their sleek lines and the permanence of grave markers in their proportions and serif-like swelling at their termini. These expressive dimensions figure in the typeface's use for the inscribed names of Maya Lin's Vietnam Veterans Memorial—a work of ancient function in a 20th-century minimalist style.[26]

One account of the relation between such features of a vehicle of representation and those of what it depicts describes the vehicle's design properties (beauty, texture, color, form, and so on) as *inflecting* the properties of what it depicts. Addressed in the context of pictorial representation, inflection is instantiated when, in virtue of a depiction's design properties, our experience of a depicted object seen in a pictorial representation is necessarily different from what it would be if the object were before us.[27] There is some debate over whether inflection is ubiquitous, or even a prototypical feature, in pictorial depiction. My interest here is only in how the appeal to inflection captures the way in which—no longer limiting this to pictorial works— the properties of a represented object may be fully characterized only with

---

[26] Hermann Zapf, Optima's designer, based the letterforms on those used for Italian Renaissance funereal stones. Some studies suggest that one's fluency in processing a text has an effect on the interpretation of its content. Hyunjin Song and Norbert Schwarz (2008), for example, reported that people who read identical exercise routines and cooking recipes printed in, respectively, difficult-to-read and easy-to-read type-forms, judged the routines and recipes as more difficult in the difficult type and easier in the easier type.

[27] See Lopes (2005); Hopkins (2010).

reference to properties of the vehicle, the style, technique, media, form, and so on employed in representing it.

In literary works, the orthographical vehicle by which the content of a story is represented typically plays no role in our (imaginative) experience of that content, save in cases in which a book's design conveys meaning, such as the large dot that ends a chapter in *Ulysses*, the period representing the atom traced throughout history by Primo Levi's *The Periodic Table*, or the blank pages in *Tristram Shandy*. However, we can still see the presence of inflection in the way in which formal or design features of a narrative (addressed from the external standpoint as an artifact) shape the nature of the fictional content toward which we are elicited to take an imaginative stance.[28]

Consider the effects on content of the wide variety of devices that belong to the formal and stylistic techniques of literary representation: the naming of characters (Becky Sharp, Willy Loman, Pecksniff, Naipaul's repeated emphasis on the honorific in his novel's titular character Mr. Biswas); the repetition of words ("nothing" and its cognates in *King Lear*); and the register (clinical, heroic, vernacular) of a description. All these serve to activate an evaluation of the represented events or individuals that doesn't stem from properties of the event or individual considered as if existing independent of the representation. The incidents in Kafka's *Metamorphosis* and *The Trial* are bizarre, but the matter-of-fact, quasi-bureaucratic language used to describe them evokes in readers only a sober, if curious, reckoning.[29] Such formal devices can evoke certain emotional responses to things represented in the fictions without such responses being warranted for analogous things in real life. That someone has the misfortune to be named Gradgrind in real life would give us no reason to assume he is rigid and dour.

It is difficult to identify any unitary explanation for how all such devices (the physical appearance of characters, choice of medium, formal properties, and so on) shape our evaluative attitudes toward the states of affairs they are employed in depicting. However, at least some appear to depend

---

[28] As noted in §2.3, Peter Lamarque (2014) argues that our access to the contents of fictions, when they are treated as works of literature, is typically *opaque*. That is, our reading of a given narrative qua literature is typically shaped by an interest in the way dimensions of its form function in the service of conveying its contents: how "textual nuances, implicit evaluations, narrator reliability, symbolic resonance, humour, irony, tone, allusions or figurative meanings in the textual content" give precise shape to the thoughts the content elicits (149).

[29] Adorno (1983) suggests that this rendering of wildly imaginative events in a normalizing language functions to lay bare the ways social repression is naturalized.

on well-studied automatic and subdoxastic tendencies.[30] One such tendency that has broad effects is the operation of an *affect heuristic*: a tendency to take the good or bad feelings experienced roughly contemporaneous with some state of affairs as an indication of the value of that state of affairs, despite the feelings having stemmed from a wholly independent source.[31] The heuristic operates in relation to particular emotions, when, e.g., I implicitly and irrelevantly take my antipathy toward the ugliness of a character as indicating his malevolence. However, the tendency is especially prevalent in contexts in which audiences are caused to experience certain kinds of *moods*—temporally extended (i.e., non-episodic) affective states that, unlike emotions, have no salient object of which they stand as evaluations.[32] Not being directed at any particular object prevents moods from having the force or vividness of ordinary emotions, yet allows them to have broad effects in shaping responses to any particular objects to which a work directs the audience's attention. For example, when a given mood is elicited in its audiences, it can lower the threshold for the particular mood-consistent emotions and associations that the work is designed to provoke.[33]

Moods also help sustain over time the attentional and informational processes that emotions depend upon.[34] When in a given mood, one continually "discovers" grounds for and confirmation of the mood outside of oneself.[35]

---

[30] Noël Carroll (1999) writes, "Through the manipulation of sound and image, filmmakers often address audiences at a subcognitive, or cognitively impenetrable, level of response. Loud noises—either recorded effects or musical sounds—can elicit instinctual responses from spectators as can the appearance of sudden movement. The movie screen is a rich phenomenal field in terms of variables like size, altitude, and speed, which have the capacity to excite automatic reactions from viewers, while the display of certain phobic and sexual material may also call forth responses barely mediated by thought" (22).

[31] Affect-based conclusions tend to be more likely when people lack the time, resources, or inclination to arrive at reflective judgments. The affect-heuristic model predicts, for example, that one who has a negative attitude toward nuclear power will, if under time-pressure, arrive at a comparatively more negative judgment of its risks vs. its rewards than if one had time to reflect. Slovic et al. (2002).

[32] Griffiths (1997) argues for the predominant view that moods have no intentional objects.

[33] Ekman (1994); Gray et al. (2001). For the role of mood in altering our attention to focus on mood-congruent elements in a film, see Smith (2003). On mood-congruent associations and memories, see Davidson (2004); Forgas and Vargas (2000).

[34] On moods and mood-like states resulting from affective priming see Clore and Colcombe (2003). On art and moods, see Carroll (2003a). More generally, on affective states experienced as giving information about objects in one's situation, see Clore, Gasper, and Garvin (2001).

[35] In an experiment designed by Jordens and Van Overwalle (2005), people who were directed to write an essay advocating for something that they disagreed with tended not to shift their attitudes in favor of the position. However, when they were unexpectedly given a significant payment during the study, their attitudes tended to shift toward agreeing with a heretofore rejected view. The authors hypothesize that "this manipulation puts them into a good mood. When contemplating how they feel about the essay topic . . . their good mood leads them to express much milder opposition. In effect, they 'misread' their affective state as information about the essay topic, and rate the latter accordingly" (Carruthers 2011, 137).

Indeed, that such moods can be elicited by processes whose workings and effects are outside of conscious awareness allows them to have effects on our evaluations, judgments, and decision-making that would not be as readily sustained if their sources were held up to cognitive scrutiny.[36] Sound, lighting, and editing techniques of film, for example, can elicit moods that, inter alia, direct the attention of viewers to the film's mood-congruent visual features, invoke mood-congruent expectations, and promote particular evaluations of characters.[37] If a viewer is unaware that the source of these effects is the work's mood, she is much more likely to attribute them to evaluative facts about the represented state of affairs in the film. Of course, a viewer must be aware in one sense of techniques, e.g., of editing—quick cuts, breaks in continuity, etc.—to experience the film at all. But this does not mean that she is aware that those techniques cause her to experience a given mood, or that the mood shapes her cognitions and evaluations of what she sees. Indeed, one marker of the experience of imaginative absorption or "transportation" is the relative diminution of one's awareness of a work's formal features qua formal features compared to one's awareness of the work's content.[38]

Another important process co-opted by artistic representations to cause emotions can be found in the kind of affective contagion described in §3.2: an automatic, largely unconscious tendency to conform one's facial expression, posture, vocalization, and behaviors to those of other people, and, as result, to share to some degree their affective experience.[39] Such mimicry has been shown to be reliably caused by a wide range of emotional responses or expressions such as laughter, embarrassment, and disgust.[40] Although operative in bodily deportment, the phenomenon is especially salient and well-studied in relation to facial expression. Ulf Dimberg and his colleagues showed that when subjects were shown images of happy faces, they tended to exhibit increased muscular activity in regions of the cheek muscle involved in smiling, but when they observed angry faces that activity increased in muscles below the brow involved in expressing anger.[41]

---

[36] For a discussion of studies showing people who take their independently caused moods as indicating relevant information about the merits of a given object, see Carruthers (2011, 136–37).

[37] Bolivar, Cohen, and Fentress (1994); Boltz (2001); Tan, Spackman, and Bezdek (2007).

[38] Green and Donahue (2009).

[39] Hatfield, Cacioppo, and Rapson (1992, 153–54).

[40] See Bavelas et al. (1988).

[41] Dimberg et al. (2000). Relatedly, similar cortical areas are activated when subjects imitate faces expressing emotions and when they merely observe those faces. Such facial mimicry also brings about the sorts of changes in autonomic nervous system activity, affecting heart rate, perspiration or skin conductivity, etc., that are associated with particular emotions. See Cacioppo et al. (2000).

As noted in Chapter 3, if such motor mimicry resulted merely in a spectator adopting the physiognomic expression of a target in a given emotional state, it would not be relevant to explanations of the actual experience of the emotions among audiences. However, there is significant evidence that, as Plato intuited, performing such motor mimicry can cause one to consciously experience the associated emotions, even when one is unaware of their source.[42] In studies of this "facial feedback" hypothesis, researchers found that merely forming the facial configuration associated with an emotion made one more likely to experience the emotion.[43] It isn't clear if the causal explanation is that people come to recognize that they've formed an emotion-consistent facial expression and that then causes them to look for grounds supporting the feeling, or if the facial expression itself causes the feeling. Studies (referred to in §3.2) in which Botox injections were used to diminish the sensory awareness participants had of their facial expressions support the latter hypothesis.[44] Here, even when individuals are unaware that they have been caused to adopt a facial configuration matching the expression associated with a given emotion, they tend to report experiencing that emotion.

The generation of such subdoxastic mimicry is particularly effective in eliciting emotions from audiences for visual art. For one's visual experience of, say, Francis Bacon's screaming pope, or Clint Eastwood's contemptuous snarl as he challenges a punk to "make my day," can be significantly similar, with respect to what is required for emotional contagion, as the experience of perceiving a person in the flesh.[45] However, the phenomenon may not be confined to cases in which one engages in an actual perception of a face, represented or real. For, as noted in §2.1, there is much evidence— behavioral, functional, and neurophysiological—of shared mind and brain processes in visual imagining and perceiving. Perhaps merely visually imagining a face, as when reading a story, can do the same job in emotional contagion, as perceiving one.[46]

Our susceptibility to emotional contagion may have adaptive origins in enabling conspecifics to behave in rapid and automatic ways as a consequence of seeing an emotional expression in another's faces, without requiring

---

[42] Adelmann and Zajonc (1989); Levenson, Ekman, and Friesen (1990).

[43] Zajonc et al. (1989); Hatfield, Cacioppo, and Rapson (1994).

[44] Hennenlotter et al. (2008).

[45] For affective contagion in the experience of film, see Coplan (2006, 2004).

[46] Plantinga (1999).

a conceptualization of what the other is feeling, or postulation about the emotion's source.[47] Feeling fear in response to seeing that emotion in another can make one ready to flee in advance of one's thoughts being formed about the other's feeling. However, such contagion can now be exploited by works of art to cause audiences to feel a certain way without giving them reasons to feel that way.

Indeed, the low-level, unconscious process of emotional contagion makes it possible for a work to evoke affective responses, and their concomitant evaluative perspectives, that conflict with more reflective, conscious, and higher-order affects. We may find ourselves coming to share in the anger of the morally deviant protagonist even as we consciously dissent from his evaluative point of view. As Goldie notes, "what is typical of contagion is that the agent is not aware of the contagion: the agent takes his experience as original and not as caught from another."[48] This means that a work of fiction may be designed such that, when audiences are "infected," they identify the putative justification of their emotion as some fact in the fiction, even though the emotion is arationally caused.[49]

Analogous kinds of motor contagion or mirroring may occur as well. Jörn Munzert and his colleagues found that, in general, when one imagines performing an action, there is activation, although attenuated, in the same cortical areas as when one really performs the action.[50] Indeed, an fMRI study indicated that when subjects merely silently read words related to actions involving the hand, leg, and head, the respective regions of the sensorimotor cortex, corresponding to the control of the different muscles in each of those actions, were activated.[51] Similarly, observing an action in a video

[47] Preston and de Waal (2002) propose that affective contagion developed in primates as a fast, subdoxastic process before the slower, higher-order, cortical-based processes of emotional expression and communication.

[48] Goldie (2000, 191).

[49] Clore, Gasper, and Garvin (2001) note that affective feelings, such as moods, generated by one source can cause people to make implicit attributions of value to another independent object (e.g., when bad weather affects how people answer unrelated questions about their life satisfaction): "Such attributions provide an object which gives affective feelings their information value, and in some cases their misinformation value" (126). They note that when a cause other than the object of the evaluative judgment was made salient, the effect of people's mood on their evaluation abated. On such mood attribution effects see also Kehner, Locke, and Aurain (1993); Siemer and Reisenzein (1998).

[50] Munzert, Lorey, and Zentgraf (2009). Merely observing an action readies the muscles one uses in performing the action. On musical and athletic performance see Pascual-Leone (2001).

[51] Hauk, Johnsrude, and Pulvermüller (2004). Brain regions activated when reading action words overlap with those activated when performing the actions, e.g., reading "run" or "kick" activates brain regions associated with moving one's foot. Pulvermüller (2005).

recording resulted in neural activity patterns similar to those activated when performing the action.[52] Again, that one experiences a motor readiness associated with some action shown in a fiction is not the same as being caused to experience the emotion that the represented action expresses. However, as noted earlier, one way to prime someone to experience an emotion is to cause her to adopt its characteristic bodily configuration.

Finally, as I will discuss in Chapter 8, a common dimension of verbal and cinematic narratives involves recruiting audiences to adopt a character's or narrator's point of view on some state of affairs, and thereby causing them to emotionally appraise those facts as that fictional individual would. Of course, insofar as that identification with a fictional individual proceeds from an inferential process by which we come to endorse her outlook for the same reasons we would endorse it in real life, such identification is no challenge to continuity. However, when at least part of our identification is caused through arational means, our evaluations may not have the grounding in reasons that would apply outside the fiction.[53]

Just as positive affiliation with a fictional character might not be justified by what we know of him, but still serve an artistic end, so our scorn for a character might be elicited by arational causes, yet be justified within the confines of the experience of a fiction. For example, there is a tendency, much studied in moral psychology, to unwittingly identify our largely automatic and low-level bodily responses to states of affairs as indications of their specifically moral worth.[54] This process, insofar as it is responsive to the right kind of features in those states of affairs, can be rationally defensible as an apt evaluation of the state of affairs in question. Physical revulsion in learning, say, of child abuse, is a justified experience and expression of moral disgust. However, studies of mere physical disgust suggest it is easily and spuriously elided with that moral disgust. Thus, someone's physically noxious odor or appearance may prompt one to make inappropriate moral, rather than just "hygienic," evaluations of him. This would be unjustified in the actual world, but it finds ready application in artistic representation, wherein a work may bring us to see a character as morally deviant through priming us

[52] Decety and Grèzes (2006); Buccino et al. (2001). Studies of motor imagery that compared the amount of time it takes to perform some action with that required to (fully) imagine performing it, find that the duration of the imagined movement roughly accorded with that of the real movement. Decety, Jeannerod, and Prablanc (1989).

[53] See Gernsbacher, Goldsmith, and Robertson (1992). More on this in Chapter 8.

[54] Prinz (2007); Haidt (2001).

with physical disgust elicitors and other aversive stimuli.[55] The moral disgust we feel for Fagin in *Oliver Twist* stems only in part from his sinister behavior. For that feeling is also supported by the text's references to his filthiness (his "greasy" clothes) and slimy bearing ("creeping . . . like some loathsome reptile"). These descriptions exploit our tendency to conflate feelings of mere physical discomfort with justified moral opprobrium.[56]

Let me stress that the devices by which an emotion is elicited in audiences may work *both* in causing one to feel a certain way about a fictional object and in giving one a reason (from the fiction) to feel that way. That is, there should be no assumption that because some feature of a fiction elicits a response unconsciously, that feature fails to provide a justifying reason for that response. For much of what we take to be appropriate, justified responses depends on only implicit awareness of their grounds. When the murkiness of a stage set primes us to feel fear, that can plausibly be described as the activation of an automatic, yet rationally justified, representation of the scene's evaluative qualities (darkness hides threats). And we may feel an emotion in response to a character's facial expression because we tacitly rely on it as a reliable indication of how to evaluate some state of affairs that the character perceives, but we do not. If so, the emotion is grounded in a reason that speaks to the facts (in the fiction) of the situation.[57]

However, it would be an unjustified optimism about unreflective emotional responses to assume that they all instantiate a reliable capacity to detect our individual or species-relative evaluative relation to things. As anyone not immune to advertising can attest, we may be explicitly aware that a fictional event or state of affairs doesn't warrant a given emotion (the facts within the depiction don't offer us sufficient reasons for the emotion), and still we *feel* it.[58]

---

[55] See Schnall et al. (2008) for studies showing test subjects were more severe in their moral judgments of various scenarios when exposed to morally irrelevant factors such as an unclean test environment.

[56] Schnall et al. (2008).

[57] It is also often the case that the presence of such emotion-eliciting devices can serve as reasons for our emotions, just because they can be employed as a signal by the author (or work) of what sort of events will soon occur, or what as-yet-unacknowledged feature of a character will be exposed. Indeed, a sense of foreboding might be created from just such non-specific indications of what is to come. These grounds for an audience's emotions are not internal to the fiction (not within the scope of the operator "it is fictional that . . ."), but are rather devices external to the fictional world that shape our attitude toward what is internal. I'm grateful to Gregory Currie (personal communication) for pointing out this distinctive source of emotion-justifying reasons vis-à-vis fictions.

[58] For an account of complimentary, simultaneous, or dual processing of information, see Greene et al. (2004). Kahneman (2003) discusses the degree to which processes identified with a lower automatic system are effectively monitored by those identified with a higher cognitive one.

Works of art often exploit the possibility of different deliverances of our justified cognitive awareness and our non-evidence-based subdoxastic appraisals. We are discomfited by the approach of an apparently harmless child because of the accompanying (non-diegetic) eerie music; we are surprised, along with the characters in a fiction, to find that the person with the pleasant visage turns out to be the serial killer. It runs counter to our implicit assumptions about evil to discover that Milton's Satan is attractive and charismatic—he is described in topoi associated with the heroic figures of Achilles and Aeneas—and he has none of the appearance of a foul fiend. Yet Satan becomes diminished as an object of our fascination as Milton's epic comes to enlighten us of his real nature. In the other direction, the initial visual repulsiveness of John Merrick, the title character in *The Elephant Man* (1980), is quieted as we come to empathize with him and recognize his dignity. Yet this change in our attitude is enhanced by changes in the film's presentation of Merrick's stance, complexion, and dress in the direction of normative standards of human appearance.[59]

Our familiar way of saying that it is make-believe that some fictional object has an emotionally relevant quality—that it is menacing, admirable, vile, disgusting, and so on in the story—tends to obscure the distinctions among the different means by which objects with such qualities are created. The devices previously described can play a role in generating what is fictionally true or part of the content of a work. But their *distinctive* contribution to that content is made, not through a description or representation of an object or event as bearing certain evaluative qualities, but through causing us to experience that content so as to impute such evaluative properties to it.

Imputing such properties is not merely projecting them onto the objects of a fiction, for objects of a fiction are in part constituted by properties that we are sometimes merely caused (without genuinely justifying fiction-given reasons) to attribute to them.[60] Causing us to have an emotion about a fictional character is one of the ways in which a work of art makes it the case that the character has the emotion's criterial properties. That is, in virtue of causing us to feel disgust toward Fagin, the work in part constitutes Fagin as morally disreputable. And once we conceive of a character as being in such a

---

[59] On this dynamic in the film, see Nehamas (2007, 59).

[60] See Thomasson (1999, 88–92) for a generative theory of intentionality according to which our attitudes toward non-existent objects play a role in their constitution. See also Zalta (1988). A work's way of presenting some content may, of course, not be successful in causing us to impute features to the fictional world. Cases of imaginative resistance (see Chapter 8) illustrate how we can have trouble following a work's prescription to imagine its contents as bearing certain evaluative properties.

way, we may find salient other features of his behavior or attitudes that would confirm that judgment. Of course, Fagin is disreputable for other reasons as well, those that are given in the fiction's description of his behavior.

In this way, the responses enjoined by such devices of a fiction are of a piece with those demonstrated in studies of human judgment and decision-making where people rationalize a response by appealing to factors that have no genuine role in producing the response.[61] We are induced to feel, e.g., an unjustified aversion to a character via informationally irrelevant processes, such as his ugliness or physical disgust-elicitors, but *rationalize* that response by judging him to be evil, untrustworthy, etc., i.e., as possessing qualities meriting our independently caused attitudes. However, I want to point to two differences between when these kinds of responses are occasioned by the contents of fictions and when occasioned by experiences of the real world.

One is that if we are aware of exhibiting such ungrounded responses in real life, we tend to try to work against them. Indeed, we often engage in such regulation and correction unconsciously. And even if we are sometimes (usually?) ineffective in countering these biases in ourselves, we still see them as defects calling for correction in *others*.[62] By contrast, it is often part of the project of our engagements with fictions, games, and other exercises of the imagination that we allow such biases to operate. Insofar, that is, as we desire to realize the values that those imaginative engagements offer, we may sometimes choose not to resist the (otherwise) unjustified attitudes they elicit from us.

The other is that fictions are often *designed* to exploit those biases, and have become effective in doing so through progressive research and development in the techniques of emotional and evaluative elicitation. Ordinarily, real-life experiences are much more haphazard and only contingently provide the bases for such biased responses. Fictions, by contrast, often depend on them for their success.

The contribution of audiences' emotions to the constitution of fictional objects is analogous to the projection that Hume finds in our aesthetic and moral responses to real things. For Hume, our "taste," the source of moral and aesthetic judgment, "has a productive faculty, and gilding or staining all natural objects with the colours, borrowed from internal sentiment,

---

[61] Nisbett and Wilson (1977). See also Johansson et al. (2005).

[62] The social dimension of such normative expectations helps save us from consistently falling prey to biases systematically related to what are otherwise rational reliances on heuristics in individual judgment.

raises in a manner a new creation."[63] When such sentiments are elicited by a work of fiction in accordance with how it is designed, they instantiate recognitions of the evaluative qualities constitutive of the fictional objects. In his *Modern Painters*, John Ruskin employs the concept of a *pathetic fallacy* in condemning the falsity and sentimentality he associated with late 18th-century poetry's attribution of emotional qualities to brute natural phenomena: descriptions of a landscape as indifferent, trees forbidding, clouds sullen, and so on.[64] The phenomenon he identifies, in which our emotional state or mood causes us to find reasons external to us that justify that feeling, may indeed result in false judgments about real states of affairs. However, my claim is that it captures one of the reliable modes through which we make true judgments about states of affairs in fictions.[65]

Richard Moran attributes to Kendall Walton's theory of make-believe the principle that if we have an emotional response to a fictional depiction of an object, that response depends on the degree to which the object resembles its real-life counterpart. Moran objects that what makes the difference between, say, a dry literal report of something and a literary description of it that provokes an emotion may not be more realism or verisimilitude but precisely artistic devices that would interfere with such realism. "In the theater," he notes, "we might think of the various nonmimetic effects of things such as music (including song), lighting, figurative language, pacing and compression of time, and other effects that . . . do not necessarily represent anything themselves, and indeed may be quite mimetically out of place in the scene presented." His point is that our emotions are not exclusively caused by things made "fictionally true" in a work, but by dimensions of presentation that may not contribute any fictional truths to a story on their own.[66] I agree with Moran in what I've said about those arational devices through which our emotions for a fiction are caused. However, Walton's picture

---

[63] Hume (1777/1975) notes that "the mind has a great propensity to spread itself on external objects" (Second Enquiry, appendix 1, para. 21). Through that process of projection we sometimes take a feature of our experience of the world as if it were an independent property of the world. See Walton (1999); Carroll (2014).

[64] Ruskin (1860). Wordsworth, one of his targets, says that we "spread the sentiment of Being over the earth."

[65] The phenomenon of projection I appeal to here can be seen in an influential experiment by Schacter and Singer (1962) in which participants were injected with adrenaline, while being told that the experiment concerned the effects of vitamin supplements on vision. When the subjects were exposed to different emotional cues in their environment, they identified the same feeling of arousal caused by the adrenaline with, respectively, different emotional states (fear vs. positively valenced excitement).

[66] Moran (1994).

could accommodate his objection by noting that, when those nonmimetic dimensions have had their effects on our emotions, it leads to our attributing additional fictional truths to the story—namely, those truths that would rationalize or make sense of the emotion that we are caused (say, through music or lighting) to form.[67]

Perhaps if a work is *too* effective in causing us to feel a given emotion—in "pulling our heartstrings"—we may charge it with being a debased form of art, or kitsch.[68] Indeed, the mechanical metaphor in that phrase, like "tear-jerkers," captures our disparagement of too-sure artistic effects. However, that point addresses how the aesthetic and artistic merit of a work of art is connected to the means by which it elicits our emotions, not the conditions of aptness of those emotions.[69] A preference for high art rather than melodramas need not be a desire for non-manipulative art but for an art whose machinery is better concealed.[70] Of course, one may reject the aesthetic appeal to sentiment altogether. Bertolt Brecht saw emotional elicitation in the theater as always susceptible to corruption.[71] And Muriel Spark, in characteristically acidic mode, diagnosed the too-sentimental pity that stories elicit for fictional victims as largely self-regarding. They let the reader

> go to bed feeling less guilty. . . . He has undergone the experience of pity for the underdog. Salt tears have gone bowling down his cheeks. . . . He is absolved, he sleeps well. He rises refreshed, more determined than ever to be the overdog.[72]

Of course, if we do generally respond to fictions in a way that gives free rein to our biases and subdoxastic tendencies, this does not mean that, in all cases, we ought to. I distinguished earlier between the reasons that speak to the moral, aesthetic, or instrumental aspects of an imagining and those that serve as warrants for the *representational* correctness of that imagining. But I acknowledge that non-representational considerations may be built into a theory of the proper ends as a whole that we should have in engaging with

---

[67] See Clore and Colcombe (2003).

[68] As in Greenberg (1971).

[69] Aristotle, for example, acknowledges that fear and pity can be caused by the spectacle or by the plot structure itself, but diminishes the former, which requires "less art," in favor of the latter, which "is better and argues a better poet" (1987, Book XIV).

[70] As Amanda says to Elyot in Noel Coward's *Private Lives*: "Extraordinary how potent cheap music is."

[71] Brecht (1964).

[72] Spark (2014, 79).

fictions. Perhaps we should not allow ourselves to have our irrational tendencies exploited by a fiction when, for example, it is designed to trigger highly fallible in-group biases and implicit associations in shaping judgments about a character with stereotypical racial or ethnic characteristics. Also, as Dylan Thomas registers in his "A Refusal to Mourn the Death, by Fire, of a Child in London," emotions caused by foolproof elicitors rather than reflective evaluations can fail to respect their object:

> I shall not murder
> The mankind of her going with a grave truth
> Nor blaspheme down the stations of the breath
> With any further
> Elegy of innocence and youth.[73]

Thus, there are sometimes strong *aesthetic* reasons why certain modes of producing an emotion would not make the emotion a fitting response to a work. One may be unimpressed by cheap or hackneyed dramatic effects, while still acknowledging that they succeeded in drawing out the work's sought-after response. There may also be *moral* reasons why an emotion is unmerited, as when the bigoted attitude expressed in a joke is instrumental to that joke's success in provoking laughter. And an aesthetic reason may also count as a moral reason for criticizing a work. As suggested in this chapter's epigraph taken from Pauline Kael's review of the *Sound of Music*, a work may be charged with employing artistically crude but effective devices to manipulate audiences in ways that undermine their autonomy: "Whom could this operetta offend? Only those of us who, despite the fact that we may respond, loathe being manipulated in this way and are aware of how cheap and ready-made are the responses we are made to feel."[74]

Those aesthetic and moral senses of merit are distinct from the narrow representational sense, and instantiate only some of the many pro tanto ways in which we may justify or condemn a response.[75] But failure of aptness in

---

[73] Thomas (2010).

[74] Kael (1965/2011) writes, "this is a tribute to freshness that is so mechanically engineered and so shrewdly calculated that the background music rises, the already soft focus blurs and melts, and, upon the instant, you can hear all those noses blowing in the theatre" (697).

[75] Goldie (2003) argues that a distinction between what emotions a story calls for and what emotions are ethically correct occurs in fictions, but not in relation to factual narratives, because the "coloring and shaping of a story" induces us to adopt its narrator's perspective (59–61). My argument, to the contrary, is that this potential distinction applies both in fictional and in nonfictional narratives. If our purposes in engaging with such narratives is predominantly for their truth (not

one or more of those registers does not touch on whether an emotion is apt as an evaluative representation: whether it presents its object's evaluative features correctly, and it is felt in virtue of that presentation.

Furthermore, we should make a distinction between whether our response to a work is appropriate, and whether it is appropriate that we allow ourselves to experience the work, knowing that it will call for such a response (see Chapter 9 for discussion). Photographs by Andres Serrano of corpses in a morgue, composed and lit in the style of baroque depictions of saints, are apparently designed in part to provoke a prurient fascination in their subjects, and indeed successfully garner that response. Audiences may judge that even if those works give one a reason in the representational sense to feel the emotions that they prescribe, one also has other kinds of reasons not to expose oneself to the conditions in which such emotions will be elicited. Sadness over Bambi's mother dying correctly presents it as a significant loss, but I may have reasons of self-respect to avoid being put in the position where that emotion can be drawn from me. We may thus have reasons pertaining to the work to respond as the work prescribes, but reasons independent of those, pertaining to the state of mind we would have in experiencing the work, to avoid that experience altogether.

5.4. Emotions and Functions

Discontinuity reflects, I suggest, the fact that the kinds of reasons that we countenance as justifying or challenging our emotions depend on the functions of the practices (or stances defining those practices) in which our emotions are elicited.

As we have seen, a reality-directed emotion typically has the function of accurately appraising the objective individual- or species-relative value of its object.[76] The only reasons that count in favor of the aptness of such emotions

entertainment), we approach them more transparently, "seeing through" the coloring and shaping of the story to form our evaluations of the facts that the story represents; if our purposes are directed to their entertainment value, we may want to adopt a nonfictional narrator's perspective—however unethical—as much as we may adopt a fictional narrator's perspective.

[76] No doubt, there are some circumstances in which our reality-directed emotions properly take on an ultimately non-representational function, as in the practices of conditioning or "covert sensitization." One trying to quit smoking or gambling might think of some aversive stimulus (say, rats or vomit) every time she considers the disfavored activity. When successful, these associations lead to a decreased desire for the object or activity by merely *causing* a negative emotion toward it. However,

in the narrow representational sense are those that speak to their objects' possession of whatever values the emotions impute to them.

Analogously, in some cases one's imaginative activity has an epistemic or practical role like that of beliefs and perceptions, where the function is to aid in, e.g., planning for the future, or discovering some truth about the actual world, our evaluative commitments, or what is metaphysically possible. Those aims are better realized if one's emotions are (1) based on reasons that speak to qualities of their object, and (2) not the arational result of some independent cause.

Many fiction- and imagination-directed emotions, however, are generated in practices that are constitutively oriented toward ends—such as pleasure, entertainment, and absorption—that don't require that the emotions always be rationalized by the facts of the objects to which they respond. One may feel warmly disposed toward a person depicted in a painting only because the beauty of the work is designed to cause one to feel that way. Even if that feeling is not justified by any facts depicted or rationally inferred about that content, it may be still be justified if one of the internal purposes of engaging with that work of art is to respond with the emotions the work is designed to solicit.

Another way of stating the above point is that, in response to the content of some fictions and imaginings—but not in response to the content of our beliefs and perceptions—the fact that we are merely *caused* to feel a given way may be a reason to feel that way. For the elicitation of a given emotion may be a means by which a fictional work of art or prescribed imagining gets its audience to attribute certain evaluative qualities to a fictional or imagined object. Thus, there are some kinds of reasons that justify an emotion felt toward a state of affairs represented in a fiction or imagining that would not justify that emotion when felt toward an analogous state of affairs in the real world.

Of course, the functions of any given fiction may be multiple, and, when multiple, not always mutually consistent. The realization of cognitive ends might be sacrificed for aesthetic ones or aesthetic ends for political ones. Correlatively, our ends in engaging with a fiction may be multiple, and these different ends can license respectively different reasons for or against our responses. If I watch *The Crucible* by Arthur Miller as an allegory of

---

here there is a distinction between having reasons (of a theoretical kind) to feel a given way and reasons (of a practical or instrumental kind) to cause oneself to feel that way. The latter kinds of reasons do not collapse into the former, although they might lead to their discovery.

McCarthyism in order to understand better our current political order, I want my emotional responses to be consistent with what they would be if the play's representation of political persecution were in relevant respects true; if I attend solely for the sake of absorption in a story, I don't have the same concern over whether my emotions are elicited for reasons that would also serve as justifications in the real world. What justifies my feelings may be different when the engagements within which those feelings are brought about have different purposes.

In the next chapter, I broaden the defense of discontinuity presented here to encompass not only affective responses, but responses of a more solely cognitive order as well, such as when we make judgments and inferences about what state of affairs holds in a fiction; what is likely to follow from that state; what are its causal antecedents, and so on. In other words, I ask to what extent make-believing is like believing.

6

Epistemology of Fiction and Rational Imagining

If Rawdon Crawley had been then and there present . . . the pair
might have gone down on their knees before the old spinster, avowed
all, and have been forgiven in a twinkling. But that good chance was
denied to the young couple, doubtless in order that this story might
be written.

—Thackeray, *Vanity Fair*, Chapter 16

6.1. Discovering What Is True in a Fiction

A primary dimension of our engagement with fictional works of art—
paradigmatically exemplified by literary, dramatic, and cinematic
narratives—is figuring out what is true in such representations, what the
facts are in the fictional world. These facts (or states of affairs) include not
only those that must be recognized for any genuine understanding of a story
to be possible—such that it was his own father whom Oedipus killed—but
also those that may be missed in even a largely competent reading, such as
that Emma Bovary's desires and dissatisfactions are fed by reading romance
novels.

How we uncover such fictional truth parallels in many ways how
we decide what is true in the real world. When forming beliefs, as well
as revising, transitioning among, and relinquishing them, we rely on
standard sources of evidence such as testimony, perception, memory, the
results of inductive and deductive inferences, and our affective responses.
These sources, when all goes well, provide the right sorts of reasons for
our beliefs: reasons that justify or serve as warrants for what we believe.
Analogous operations both supply and justify what we imagine to be true
in a fiction.

Apt Imaginings. Jonathan Gilmore, Oxford University Press (2020). © Oxford University Press.
DOI: 10.1093/oso/9780190096342.001.0001

For example, sometimes we rely on the testimony of a narrator who is largely transparent to the story. In such cases, we treat what is said as true by stipulation. Reading, "It was a dark and stormy night," we don't typically need to look for other confirming evidence in order to imagine that the description captures how things in the fiction are. In other cases where narrators or others in the text whom we rely on for information seem to be fully realized fictional characters, we may discount what they convey to us according to the degree of reliability we attribute to them. We don't accept, e.g., all the information supplied by Henry James's Maisie, who sees things with only partial comprehension through a child's eyes. Such discounting is of course what we do as good epistemic agents in response to testimony in real life. We also often infer what is true in a story, when it is not explicitly stated, from what is directly asserted to be true: I conclude that Charles Bovary (not a fully qualified physician but only a lesser *officier de santé*) must have botched the surgery he performed on the young groom's clubfoot because the boy's leg soon after develops gangrene. As noted in §2.2, other things that we imagine to be true in a fictional representation are not described by a text, nor inferred from those descriptions, but are imported into the fiction from our beliefs about the real world. For example, we tend to assume in reading a realistic narrative that, unless otherwise specified, the people it represents have minds and bodies much like our own. As Kendall Walton suggests, we adopt something like David Lewis's Reality Principle as a rule of thumb in filling out the implicit contents of a story on the basis of what is explicitly stated to be true in it.

Furthermore, just as I may be mistaken in my beliefs about the real world, so my imagining what is true in a fiction can be faulty—as it would be if I thought, say, the brawny peasant on a donkey that Don Quixote encounters really is the princess that he hallucinates; that Goneril's and Regan's professions of filial devotion to King Lear are actually sincere; or that Ganymede in *As You Like It* really is a young man within the story, not Rosalind in disguise. Intuitively, it seems that defects such as these that can occur in imaginings parallel defects that can occur in beliefs. For example, both beliefs and imaginings may fail to correspond to their object, may be held with an unjustified degree of credence or commitment, and may be arrived at via procedures that are not truth-apt (or "truth-in-fiction apt"), such as wishful thinking.

Philosophers and psychologists have worked out a substantial picture of the kinds of normative constraints that are constitutive of epistemic rationality when applied to beliefs—what rational criteria govern a person's formation, maintenance, transitions among, and relinquishing of her beliefs. My question here is whether such norms governing our beliefs about what is true in the real world apply invariantly to our imaginings of what is true according to fictions. In other words, taking p to be a proposition expressing some fact, is it rational to imagine that p is true according to a given fictional representation of the world if and only if it would be rational to believe, for the same kinds of reasons, that p is true in the actual world?

Let me describe two opposed answers, corresponding to the two offered in earlier chapters on norms governing emotions. On the one side, there are those who see imagining in response to a fiction to be rational according to the same norms that govern the rationality of beliefs. The norms of believing some fact and imagining some fact are invariant across the corresponding real and fictional divide. We will call this a commitment to doxastic continuity ("continuity" hereafter). On the other side, proponents of doxastic discontinuity ("discontinuity" hereafter) see the standards of rationality for forming beliefs about the real world as jointly inconsistent with the standards that govern imaginings of what is true in fictional worlds.

On the side of continuity is the intuition that our epistemic behavior in relation to the contents of fictions is very much like that in relation to actual states of affairs. Indeed, it isn't clear how authors could expect us to understand their fictions correctly—to import into the fiction what truths from the real world need to be imported, to infer what is implicitly true in a story from what is explicitly stated—were they not able to rely on readers' rational processes for discovery of facts about the world being taken "offline" and used to understand what is the case in a fiction.

The discontinuity view, however, appeals to the strong intuition that imagining exhibits a freedom that seems to distinguish it from many other representational states of the mind. It seems, for instance, that I can successfully imagine at will that almost any facts hold, but this cannot be said, both conceptually and practically, of other mental attitudes, such as remembering, desiring, perceiving, or believing, which are greatly constrained by the circumstances I find myself in and other memories, desires, perceptions, and beliefs that I already have.[1]

---

[1] The White Queen asserts that "sometimes I have believed as many as six impossible things before breakfast"; knowingly doing this in imagination seems possible, not so in belief.

As noted in §2.1, much recent work in cognitive psychology, neuroscience, and philosophy of the imagination supports the idea that there are several forms of *descriptive* or empirical continuity across the stances of belief and imagination.[2] The psychological mechanisms that process a belief-representation that *p* appear to operate in ways parallel to, and employ much of the same cognitive resources as, those that process a pretense-representation or imaginative representation that *p*. However, my question here is about the norms associated with those propositional attitudes: whether the criteria that govern the justification of our truth-apt attitudes also govern the justification of the imaginative attitudes by which we represent the contents of fictions.

In what follows I introduce and assess some considerations in favor of these two theses of continuity and discontinuity, both of which have a prima facie plausibility. Ultimately, I defend a version of the discontinuity thesis: for consumers of fictions, there are epistemic reasons to attribute facts to a fictional world that would not count as epistemic reasons to identify analogous facts in the real world. More generally, the norms in light of which our imaginings can be epistemically warranted are, as a whole, *inconsistent* with those in light of which our beliefs are epistemically warranted.

A few caveats are in order:

(1) There is no doubt that the concept of rationality when applied to either beliefs or imaginings requires careful qualification. There is no consensus over what theoretical rationality consists of, hence no easy way to ask whether all potentially relevant norms operate across believing and fiction-directed imagining.[3] In what follows I appeal to the putative invariance of only some of the most familiar and relatively uncontroversial criteria of theoretical rationality, not to exotic norms that only a perfectly rational person, say an android decision-theorist possessed of unlimited working memory, might be guided by. I will also not enter into the debate as to whether such normativity applies in the first instance to beliefs and only derivatively to believers, or to the converse (as in some theories of virtue epistemology). I assume that anything I say about the rational grounds for a belief can be translated into

---

[2] Representative studies are Byrne (2007); Harris (2000); Nichols and Stich (2000); Schroeder and Matheson (2006).

[3] In this discussion, I treat theoretical and epistemic rationality as largely identical capacities. In other philosophical contexts, however, the two may be distinguished, particularly in how the former but not the latter requires that one be sensitive to certain kinds of instrumental reasons pertaining to the achievement of one's cognitive goals. See Kelly (2003).

an attribute of someone's epistemic disposition to rely only on such rational grounds.

(2) Nothing I say here is meant to address the metaphysics of fictional worlds, or more mundanely, what makes something true in a fictional world (part of a story, make-believe, and so on). My only relevant commitment is to the idea that there is a criterion of representational correctness in what we imagine when we submit our imaginative activity to the objective constraints of a work of fiction, allowing that most fictions underdetermine what we may imagine of them consistent with correct comprehension. Let me also stress again that the locution "fictional world" should be understood as elliptical for "a fiction's representation of the world." As Currie notes, there are not, strictly speaking, fictional worlds. There is only one world that fictions, like any proposition, can falsely or truthfully represent.[4] Some of what is true in a fiction is also true of the world (that the Empire State Building is in New York), and some of what is true in a fiction is not true of the world (that King Kong climbs the Empire State Building). So the question of continuity is whether the norms governing our beliefs about the world apply invariantly to our imaginings about what is true in a fictional story's extended representation of the world. Are beliefs and fiction-directed imaginings rational, modulo their different objects, in the same respects?

(3) Finally, I do not address norms that govern the correctness or aptness of beliefs or imaginings, all things considered, but only those that govern their intentional, or more specifically, *representational* correctness. I allow that there may be practical, prudential, aesthetic, moral, and other norms in virtue of which one has a reason to put oneself in a position in which one will come to believe or imagine something. For sometimes, an epistemic reason to believe a given proposition might be trumped by an instrumental reason not to believe it, e.g., it would cause one to do something one would regret. There might be good epistemic reasons to believe that one's stock portfolio has declined but competing instrumental reasons to avoid that truth if it causes one to sell at the market's nadir. One might find it too distressing to imagine that a fictional protagonist is tortured, and choose to tolerate missing part of the story by thinking of its events as unfolding

---

[4] Currie (2014).

differently. But even if practical, moral, aesthetic, and other kinds of reasons can trump an epistemic reason, they do not silence it. The epistemic reason for the imagining remains applicable. My concern is only with the invariance or otherwise of epistemic norms governing how our beliefs and imaginings present their contents. Do the same standards of epistemic rationality apply to beliefs and fiction-guided imaginings? Not: Do the same standards of rationality in toto apply to the two domains?[5]

6.2. Continuity of Epistemic Norms

A continuity proponent might suggest that our abiding by the same rational standards for belief formation and transition is what creators of works of fiction rely on to let us know what is true in a fiction.[6] If a crew of astronauts crash-lands on a primitive planet ruled by apes but then comes upon the charred fragments of the Statue of Liberty, audiences can be expected to infer that the strange planet is actually Earth (!) in a post-apocalyptic future. If we are directed to imagine that a fictional world is governed by physical laws like our own, we are entitled to assume that a character in the fiction seeing an acquaintance reflected in a mirror must, in turn, be capable of being seen in the mirror by that acquaintance.[7] If our epistemic norms were not continuous, such identifications of the facts in a fiction would not have the systematicity and predictability that allow authors to communicate the contents of their stories.

It certainly seems part of the phenomenology of our engagement with fictions that we perform many of the same epistemic operations in imagining what is true in a fiction as we do in coming to believe what is true outside of it. We infer via deduction and induction from what is explicitly described as being the case to other facts of the fiction that are not so described—as when

---

[5] In §9.5 I address the relevance of non-epistemic norms to our adoption of certain fiction-prescribed morally defective attitudes.

[6] Defenders of the descriptive continuity of believing and imagining or pretending stress what Nichols (2006a) calls "inferential orderliness": that individuals working out what is true in a given pretense often make inferences that mirror those that they would employ if the pretense were in fact real.

[7] Currie and Ravenscroft (2002) write: "It is this capacity of imaginings to mirror the inferential patterns of belief that makes fictional storytelling possible. . . . If imaginings were not inferentially commensurate with beliefs, we could not draw on our beliefs to fill out what the story tells us" (13–14).

we debate what really happened at the end of Christopher Nolan's *Inception* (was it still a dream?). Drawing on the evidence of our affective and emotional reactions, we assign values to things represented in fictions just as we impute values to things in real life. We try to monitor the consistency among our imaginings in response to a fiction just as we monitor such consistency among our beliefs, sometimes giving up what we initially held to be true in a story as it unfolds. We think it is no more reasonable to decide what is true in a fiction according to how we desire events to transpire than we do in representing what is true in the real world. That I don't want Anna Karenina to take her life is no epistemic reason to imagine that in Tolstoy's narrative she somehow survives.

There are, of course, stories that seek to satisfy such dissatisfactions with what audiences are elicited to imagine, as in fan fiction that continues and sometimes revises a story without the sanction of the original creator. And there are interesting cases such as when the pseudonymous Alonso Fernández de Avellaneda determined that Don Quixote was in fact more pious than Cervantes posited in his creation of the character, and consequently wrote a long story featuring the fictional character sometime after Cervantes composed the first part of his novel, but before (a decade later) he finished the second. However, these imaginings are not epistemically justified by reasons internal to the original fictions, although they may be justified on aesthetic, moral, or other terms. Indeed, writers sometimes try to redeem characters from other writers' novels, say, because they see those characters or actual people like them as deserving of different attributes or experiences than those with which they were originally (fictionally) endowed. Thus, Jean Rhys's (1966) *Wide Sargasso Sea* offers an alternative imagining of the life and mind of the "madwoman in the attic" of Charlotte Bronte's *Jane Eyre* before her doomed marriage to Rochester.

In any case, audiences for fictions routinely discuss fictional characters and events *as if* they were real, debating the fine points of what a protagonist's motivations are on the basis of her behavior, or what their lives are like subsequent to the events narrated in the story. George Eliot's omniscient narrator acknowledges this in a report on her characters' histories at the end of *Middlemarch*: we can't "quit young lives after being long in company with them, and not desire to know what befell them in their after-years."[8] Whether

---

[8] Eliot (1998, 779). Authors (such as E. M. Forster and Tolstoy) speak this way of characters as well. A study by Taylor, Hodges, and Kohányi (2003) found that most of the 50 writers surveyed said they experienced their characters sometimes escaping their control, an "illusion of independent

or not the fiction is indeterminate with respect to such questions, the process of answering them seems to be governed by inferential norms that apply to the discovery of the nature of actual states of affairs.

It is also a standard rejoinder motivated by interpretative charity to the charge that a fiction is marred by a hole in its plot to show that it is possible within the constraints of the story that such an inconsistency can be explained away. Here we use the same reasoning we employ among our beliefs. If Charles Foster Kane died alone, the door to his bedroom closed, how did the press know that the last thing he said was "Rosebud"? Connoisseurs of the film ascertain that his butler must have heard him.

Finally, in forming beliefs about the actual world we rely on various modes of counterfactual imagining akin to our imagining what is true in a fiction. These include thought experiments, predicting the future, simulating another person's point of view, and appealing to scientific models featuring, e.g., frictionless planes, hermetically isolated populations, markets of fully informed buyers and sellers, and so on. The epistemic value and function of these imaginings is sometimes controversial, whether as a source of useful moral intuitions, scientific and social explanations, or truths about metaphysical possibility. However, a proponent of continuity would contend that the very possibility of counterfactual imagining serving as a source of knowledge about the real world depends on imagination and belief formation respecting the same inferential constraints.

Of course, some might embrace that latter point, not as an intuitive support for continuity, but as a *reductio* against the reliability of such products of the imagination, especially those intuitions drawn from highly artificial fictional scenarios such as runaway trolleys and dopplegängers emerging from teletransporters. If the norms governing our thinking vis-à-vis fictional truths are not continuous with those governing our representations of real-world truths, then such thought experiments may not be good sources of intuitions about morals and metaphysics in the context of the real world.[9]

Still, it may appear to be a major objection to the continuity view that there is an essential dimension of the process by which we discover what is true in a

---

agency." In an interview, Nabokov mocks the idea that fictional creations have a life independent of their author's dictates as a "trite little whimsy," and punningly adds, "My characters are galley slaves" (Gold 1967).

[9] That we form intuitions from thought experiments according to the same principles by which we discover truth in fiction is defended in Ichikawa and Jarvis (2009).

fiction that has no obvious analogue in the process by which we form beliefs about the real world. That is where, as introduced in §2.3, we take an *external* approach to the fiction as an ordinary artifact in our world and appeal to its style, tradition, function, genre, author, technique, and so on in imagining its contents: what is true from the *internal* perspective.[10]

In adopting such an external stance on a work of fiction we refer (like the narrator of *Vanity Fair* in this chapter's epigraph) to properties it has as a vehicle of representation but not (directly) to its represented content. By contrast, in adopting an internal stance, we refer to that content as if it were real or were a story being recounted by a real narrator. External features of a narrative do not lie within the scope of the operator "it is fictional that" or "it is part of the content that"; however, they cause us to adopt cognitive and affective attitudes toward what is. For example, some of P. G. Wodehouse's novels feature rural gentry raising an older child in the absence of a parent, who has died before the period of the story begins. We assume that the characters don't dwell much on that loss (even though it would be natural to import that assumption from real life) because we know it would be foreign to Wodehouse's comic aims. Similarly, we are usually correct in inferring that the party who appears guilty of the murder in the first few pages of a traditional mystery story is not genuinely the villain, for paradigmatic mystery novels don't give up the game that early. More specific knowledge than the genre of a work might serve the same function. A viewer of the film *Clueless* about a group of American high-school kids can make reliable predictions about various turns in the plot if he's familiar with its acknowledged model, Jane Austen's *Emma*.

However, such appeals to what is true *of*, but not *in*, a work of fiction do not count against the continuity thesis. For, in principle, if we had access to such an external source of understanding our world—say, through providence, fate, or karma—we would indeed be able to use it to infer what is true in our world. If Augustine's "City of Man" is in fact but a profane prelude to the "City of God," this is not one among many facts constituting the temporal world, but a truth about it described from the outside. No such more-than-human knowledge is available to us. But, if it were, it would serve as an appropriate source of beliefs about what is true in our world as much as external features of a story serve as a source of what to imagine as true about its world. The possibility of such an external discovery about one's life furnishes, of course, an

---

[10] For discussions of internal and external stances on a fiction, see Lamarque (1996); Currie (2010).

opportunity for artistic invention, as in *The Truman Show*, about a character whose days are unwittingly choreographed for the sake of a television series, and *The Comforters*, a novella with theistic intimations by Muriel Spark, in which Caroline discovers that she is only a character in a fiction (she periodically hears a keyboard typing) and resolves to frustrate her Author's plans.

6.3. Discontinuity of Epistemic Norms

Let us turn to the discontinuity view, which also seems prima facie plausible. This is the view, recall, that the rational norms that govern the formation of imaginings with respect to what is true in a fiction can be inconsistent with the rational norms that govern the formation of our beliefs. Sometimes, as in Shelley's Romantic primer, *Defence of Poetry*, this is construed as the denial that reason has any role in the activities of the imagination.[11] In other formulations, such as that which I adopt here, imagination vis-à-vis fictions is reason-governed, but perhaps—this is the question—not subject to the same norms of reasoning as believing. I want to first address, and suggest we reject, the most familiar point appealed to in favor of the thesis of discontinuity, one that pertains to the unconstrained contents of fictions. In its place, I introduce a defense of discontinuity that I think better survives philosophical scrutiny.

The most familiar point made in favor of discontinuity is that it is a highly salient feature of our engagement with fictions that they call for us to imagine things as true that are not, and sometimes could not be, true of our world. Descriptions in some fictions prompt us to infer the existence of radical physical and metaphysical departures from ordinary life. If we can form representations via the imagination of fictional states of affairs that are so different from the actual world, that process would appear to abide by epistemic norms distinct from those that govern beliefs.

But that observation based on the contents of fictions does not challenge continuity. For a proponent of continuity can plausibly propose that what is embedded in the content of those fictions is some principle in light of which it is rational of us to infer the (fictional) truth of its fantastical dimensions. If we accept that it is true in the state of affairs represented in Kafka's *Metamorphosis* that human beings *can* wake up as insects, then we don't in

---

[11] Shelley (1821/1909).

any straightforward way depart from ordinary rational judgment if we imagine on the basis of the narrator's description that Gregor Samsa has indeed greeted the morning as a bug. This is just as when Alice concludes from matters being so "queer" in general in Wonderland—shrunken, she swims in a pool of her own tears—that it's reasonable to speculate that the mouse she encounters can speak French.

We might ask whether it would be rational to imagine that such fantastical states of affairs hold in a fiction if there were not a principle holding within the fiction that licenses such imagining.[12]

However, it is difficult to conceive of how we might encounter such a fictional representation of such fantastic things that doesn't contain an implicit physical or metaphysical principle permitting such departures from ordinary reality. For if, on independent grounds, we could be confident that there is no such principle in a given fiction (we are assured that the author has only realist aims), the most reasonable interpretation would be that we are reading a story recounted by a highly misinformed or delusional narrator. We would be pressed to infer, that is, that our source for the facts in the fiction is like Poe's narrator of *The Tell-Tale Heart*, one who only imagines all that he describes to be true. In such a case, there are no genuinely fantastical states of affairs in the fiction, just someone who believes in them.

I suggest that a better argument for discontinuity can be found, not in the sundry contents of fictions, but in some of the myriad techniques by which they elicit our imagining of those contents. My proposal is that certain kinds of experiences generated by a fiction can serve as (rational) grounds for the imagination of facts holding in the fiction when those experiences are reliable indicators of those facts. More formally, when an experience E in reading a fiction is a reliable indicator that p in the fiction, E is a (pro tanto) reason for imagining that p. This structure of justification holds as well in relation to beliefs: an experience E can serve as a reason for a belief that p if E is a reliable indicator that p.[13] However, despite that parallel, a fiction can provide an experience that justifies imagining something to be true in the fiction while an analogous experience of the actual world would not justify an analogous belief.

---

[12] On principles of generation, see Walton (1990, 138–40).

[13] I appeal here to a "reliabilist" notion of epistemic justification that does not preclude other grounds of justification. For a defense of an epistemic reliabilism as an exclusive account of justification, see Goldman (1992).

Let me begin with an illustration drawn from the last chapter. It is true that in *Oliver Twist* Fagin is physically grotesque, as we learn from the narrator's attention to his greasy clothes and matted hair. Yet we imagine him as morally corrupt as well via the text's exploitation of our well-studied irrational tendency to conflate feelings of mere physical disgust with justified moral opprobrium. No doubt, other facts internal to the fiction also explain and serve as reasons for that imagining just as they would in an analogous case of belief, such as that he exploits children. But those facts do not exhaust the pro tanto reasons warranting that moral judgment.[14] For in engaging with such a work, we implicitly accept a norm under which such physical disgust is a reliable indicator of such moral facts about its object. Of course, no such reliable relation, hence no norm sanctioning an epistemic reliance on it, holds in the actual world. A feeling of disgust prompted by someone's filth in the real world would not offer a reason for judging him immoral. This demonstrates how some of the facts that we imagine are warranted in virtue of other facts that we imagine, where an analogous justificatory relation between the one set of facts and the other would not hold outside of our engagement with the fiction.

In what follows I characterize a few such cases in which works of art exploit automatic or subdoxastic tendencies in causing us to imagine certain propositions to be true.

I make two claims. First, such phenomena serve as evidence of a descriptive discontinuity in what can serve as the basis of, alternatively, imaginings and beliefs. Second, more controversially, these cases reflect normative discontinuity as well. They show how the causes of what we imagine to be true in a fiction can instantiate epistemic reasons for those imaginings even when they would not be good reasons for analogous beliefs about the actual world.

One kind of example, as noted in Chapter 5, is found in genres of art where physical appearances of characters—their beauty or ugliness, stereotypical racial or ethnic features, deportment, size, and so on, lead us to imagine (correctly in relation to the story) that they have certain virtues or vices of character and certain kinds of capacities. Ugliness, for example, is often employed to provoke a judgment of nefariousness or evil intentions even though, of course, that would not be a proper inference between such a perception and belief.[15]

---

[14] See Schnall et al. (2008).

[15] On the halo effect, see Dion, Berscheid, and Walster (1972); Nisbett and Wilson (1977); Norton (1997).

Also noted in that chapter, we are often solicited to construe the literal qualities of the media of some types of visual works of art as literal properties of whatever content the works depict, evoking a judgment about properties of a represented scenario that is not grounded in its properties considered independently of the medium of representation. A film may cause us to think of the lives it depicts as contented through presenting them in warm tones and soft focus or a state of affairs as menacing through the use of cold blues and grays.[16] Finally, the names of places and characters, e.g., that of Roger Chillingworth, the cerebral husband of Hester Prynne in *The Scarlet Letter*, induce us to attribute properties to their holders that the mere possession of a name in real life would not indicate.[17] As I'll describe more fully in §6.4, we may in some cases recognize those material and formal devices as indicating the communicative intentions of an author as to what facts should be imagined to hold in her fiction. In that respect, the respective grounds of our imaginings and beliefs are consistent. However, let me describe some ways in which sometimes the reasons for our imaginings do not count as reasons for analogous beliefs.

We often exhibit highly irrational forms of in-group/out-group bias in favoring even arbitrarily individuated communities in which we are primed to recognize our membership. That bias is easily exploited in inducing us to judge as objectively valuable the ends of the characters in a fiction with whom we are made intimate—say through having us simulate their perspective— even if independent of the fiction we wouldn't believe that those are good ends to have.[18] We hope that the fictional investors' baroque financial- market strategy succeeds, even though we know that it means a grievous loss to others whom the fiction leaves unidentified (as individuals) and thus out- side our concern.[19] Indeed, the devices employed to prime our identification

---

[16] Compare the metaphorical transfer proposed in recent experiments that address the processing of tactile information: in one, volunteers asked to assess the quality of candidates for an alleged job tended to rate those applicants whose resumes were attached to heavier clipboards as being, them- selves, more serious (i.e., "weighty"). Ackerman, Nocera, and Bargh (2010).

[17] The tendency to attribute features to a thing based on associations triggered by its name is, of course, exploited regularly outside of fictions, as the brand names of pharmaceuticals—*Ambien, Lunesta, Halcion, Viagra, Celebrex, Abilify, Lyrica, Rogaine* (whose original name *Regain* was blocked by the FDA for overpromising)—attest. Note that some studies suggest that placebo effects are intro- duced merely in substituting a brand-name medication for an equivalent generic version. See Sapone et al. (2009).

[18] For a demonstration of an arbitrary categorization of individuals generating in-group bias, see Otten and Moskowitz (2000).

[19] E.g., in Adam McKay's 2015 film, *The Big Short*, a partly fictionalized film portrayal of mortgage defaults and the collapse of housing values in 2008.

with a character can lead us to appraise the facts in a story as that fictional individual appraises them even if a description of such facts outside of a fiction would be unlikely to garner that evaluation.[20] We recognize Tony Soprano's need to eliminate the police informers in his organization, countenancing his violent means as unfortunately required to realize his ends, instead of objecting to the ends themselves.

Our tendency to see actual events as having a narrative-like structure that goes beyond mere causal connectedness can be relied on by authors to supply the kind of closure and unity among fictional events that traditional plots require. It could only be figuratively true of a person's life, or of a romance, that it had an organically structured and internally related beginning, climax, and denouement, but it can be literally true in a fictional world that such is the case. As both prosecutors and con artists know, embedding facts within an aesthetically satisfying narrative is more convincing than merely stating the facts and explanation outright. A successful narrative can gloss over major explanatory and causal gaps in what we are to imagine as true, without thereby having any less claim on us in evoking that imagining. The narrator of Proust's novel tells us, from a first-person perspective, of his life and emergence as a writer. But certain sequences, particularly those where he recounts the affair between Swann and Odette, could not have been witnessed by the young Marcel despite being described, and by us imagined, as if he were there. The seamlessness of the narrative gives us reasons to imagine certain states of affairs as obtaining in the fiction even though other facts in the fiction should make those states of affairs impossible.[21]

In his remarks about the nature of moral demands, Nietzsche portrayed our psychological need to attribute a meaning to suffering as leading to unjustified beliefs about its redemptive significance: e.g., that it is a test of character, a divine punishment, or curse.[22] But works of fiction regularly rely on that tendency to endow objects and events with a significance that is then treated as objectively and independently possessed by them. In, for example, *It's a Wonderful Life*, the character played by Jimmy Stewart undergoes various travails which, satisfyingly, come to appear to have existed for the sake of his eventual enlightenment. Graham Greene's Catholic novels such as *The End of the Affair* similarly invite an appeal to the workings of faith to explain

---

[20] See Gernsbacher, Goldsmith, and Robertson (1992).

[21] Aristotle (1987) notes in the *Poetics* that, in the construction of a plot, "what is impossible but can be believed should be preferred to what is possible but unconvincing" (chap. 24).

[22] One of the themes of his (2006).

the transformations their characters undergo, as if suffering has a final as well as efficient cause.

We also readily accede to a faulty form of understanding—the *fundamental attribution error* or *correspondence bias*—of people's motivations in seeing their actions as explained by stable character traits and deep psychological dispositions or motivations, rather than much more powerful situational factors.[23] This tendency distorts our understanding of real people's behavior, but it is often successfully relied on by traditional fictional narratives (perhaps it is essential to certain genres) in systematically eliciting from us insight into why characters in the fiction behave as they do.

Those are just some of the general ways that fictions draw on our automatic and subdoxastic tendencies, including our common biases and heuristics, to elicit our imaginings. A more specific catalog of such devices might show how particular kinds of biases can be indexed to the successful functioning of, respectively, particular categories or genres of fictions. For example, there is the bias of the "hot hand" in which we unjustifiably tend to believe that gamblers or ballplayers can enjoy streaks, that they can be "on a roll," or "in the zone," where these aren't merely short runs in a random process.[24] This may be the result of a confirmation bias, but whatever the psychological explanation, it seems tailor-made for every film about an underdog team trying to make it to the championships.

Studies of what has been called the *rhyme-as-reason effect* suggest that statements that rhyme are taken to be more truthful or insightful than those that don't, even when the meaning is held constant.[25] People judge "woes unite foes" as more accurate than "woes unite enemies" although the meaning is (roughly) the same.[26] This may be an instance of a more general phenomenon in which a statement's truth is unwittingly evaluated on aesthetic terms, which can include the fluency with which a statement is processed.[27] In any case, it is a cognitive bias friendly to popular music where, in the midst of absorption, we exhibit cognitive, affective, and behavioral signs that suggest we imaginatively accept the singer's claim of eternal devotion, promise of wild

---

[23] On the explanatory limits to relying on a notion of character see Doris (2002); Wilson (2004); Krahé (2010); Upton (2009); Appiah (2008).

[24] Tversky and Kahneman (1971).

[25] Compare Nietzsche's (2001) remark: "even the wisest of us occasionally becomes a fool for rhythm, if only insofar as he *feels* a thought to be *truer* when it has a metric form and presents itself with a divine hop, skip, and jump" (85–86).

[26] McGlone and Tofighbakhsh (2000).

[27] McGlone and Tofighbakhsh (1999).

aspiration, or justification for violence and mayhem, even though we would not believe those avowals if they were assertions about real things.

In many of these cases we implicitly impute to a fictional world the facts that would rationalize our irrational responses. This rationalizing, if adopted in relation to our beliefs, would be of only a spurious sort. For in the cases I've described we do not discover genuine (fictional) evidence of what we imagine to be true, but, rather, are caused to impute that evidence to a fiction and treat it as existing there independent of our imagining. In this respect, our way of preserving our rationality—treating, e.g., our physical disgust for a character as a correct recognition of vices that would genuinely warrant moral disgust—exemplifies the widely studied phenomenon of *cognitive dissonance*: people are systematically motivated to reduce the dissonance among their cognitions, even when doing so isn't justified by their sources. Employing spurious rationalization aimed at reducing cognitive dissonance is not a truth-conducive manner of forming beliefs. However, when provoked by a work of fiction, such rationalizing can be a truth-in-fiction conducive manner of imagining.

Of course, artists may exploit not only our tendencies to think in these ways to make certain things true in their fictions but also to create unexpected or ironic discoveries, such as that a character has qualities that run counter to what our automatic responses would impute to him.

The epistemic errors and departures from rationality exemplified in the activation of these tendencies are importantly, for my purposes, systematic. If we were not systematically biased or irrational in certain ways in forming our beliefs, creators of works of art could not predictably exploit such tendencies and rely on them to direct our imagining of what is true in a work. Our imagining from such tendencies would not be truth-in-fiction tracking. An author wouldn't know that—or wouldn't reflect in her writing an implicit awareness that—she could elicit the desired response, unless her readers would standardly have such biases. Furthermore, while many of the cases I describe illustrate how a work can prime us to attribute certain truths to the fiction, such priming is not just an arational form of causation to which the application of epistemic norms would be irrelevant, i.e., a category mistake. Rather, such priming employed by fictions can be systematically directed at particular ends.[28] That is, unlike experiments in which a participant may be differentially primed to adopt one of a plurality of different perspectives on

---

[28] Appel (2011).

some essentially ambiguous state of affairs, the priming performed by a fiction is usually systemically directed at the discovery of what is true in it, what sorts of things it is *correct* to imagine.[29]

6.4. Discontinuity and the External Perspective

One way for a defender of continuity to respond to the phenomena I have described would be to say that, while they illustrate how the epistemic norms that govern our beliefs don't always govern our fiction-prescribed imaginings, this only shows that such imaginings are often epistemically unjustified or irrational. Authors exploit some of our irrational dispositions to cause us to imagine certain things to be true in a fiction that we would not, on the basis of like causes in real life, be justified in believing. There is no discontinuity in epistemic norms if the illustrations above confirm only that we are by and large epistemically rational in what we believe but epistemically irrational in some of what we imagine.

The problem with this way of describing such cases is that we need to preserve a distinction within our responses to fictions and imaginings between instances in which our responses are epistemically rational and others in which they are, indeed, irrational. In some cases, that is, fictions are designed to exploit our subdoxastic tendencies to reliably cause us to recognize what is true in a story. In other cases, those tendencies lead us to misunderstand a story, to attribute facts to it that the text is not designed to elicit us to imagine, as when irrational prejudices cause one to wrongly assume that a given character is, say, an unsuitable marriage partner for someone of a different race or ethnicity, despite there being no indication in the story that this should be imagined to be so. If it were the case that all otherwise ungrounded imaginings we form due to the activation of such tendencies describe above are epistemically irrational, we would not be able to distinguish between the kinds of responses that, *in virtue of* their irrationality in truth-apt contexts (1) lead to a correct recognition of what is true in a fiction, and (2) lead to a failure of comprehension.

Another approach for a defender of continuity might be to say that the preceding examples do not show that we exhibit otherwise epistemically irrational tendencies in our fiction-prompted imagining. Rather, they

---

[29] Bargh and Chartrand (2000).

demonstrate that we are epistemically rational by ordinary standards in inferring what is true in a fiction from recognizing how the fiction is designed to affect us. One might suggest, for example, that in these illustrations, we rely on external factors of the work to imagine what is fictionally true in the same epistemically warranted way in which we form ordinary beliefs: I come to infer that something is true in a fiction from my recognition that the author or artist has designed it in such a way as to make my discovery of that truth possible.

However, the problem with that defense of continuity is that not all such elicitations to imagine function that way. For there are two routes through which our imaginings of what is true in a fiction can be prompted. One route, posing no threat to continuity, is exemplified by the way characters are named so as to give us reason to believe something about their qualities. There, our imagining that the character has that quality indeed follows from an ordinary rational process of relying on the communication of an author or testimony of a reliable narrator. The nouveau riche Veneerings do live a life of superficial gloss; Daffy Duck really is a daffy duck; and Thwackum, the tutor in Fielding's *Tom Jones*, does have a penchant for the cane.[30] In the other route, however, the names of characters do not give us reason to believe something about their qualities, but, instead, are designed to cause us to attribute those qualities to those characters through, e.g., activating stereotypes or implicit associations. There the fiction presents a character or state of affairs as having one property and our response to that property causes us to correctly imagine the presence of another property, even though the two properties bear no genuine real-world explanatory connection.

So there is a distinction here between (1) those truths that we attribute to a fiction because we recognize the communicative intention of the author—or the convention of the genre (this is compatible with continuity) and (2) those truths that we attribute to a fiction as a result of having some experience of the fiction about which we may be unaware of a communicative intent.

Finally, a defender of continuity might say: if it's true in the fiction that, e.g., Fagin is morally corrupt, the beautiful person is intelligent and honest, the mobster's ends are merited, and so on, then that justifies imagining such things as true. *Whatever* the means might happen to be that such fictional truths are conveyed to us, they are fictional truths and therefore we

---

[30] As if the thought expressed in Plato's *Cratylus*, that names and nature are internally related were true.

are justified in imagining them as such. But that does not employ an adequate concept of justification. A belief that p is not justified in virtue of "p" being true if the formation or acceptance of the belief did not arrive in the right way. It must not be, e.g., an accident, a knock on the head, or a deviant causal chain that explains why one believes that p. Having dreamed that my car won't start is no reason to believe that it won't start, even if, in fact, the battery is dead. Speaking of a fiction from the internal perspective, one does not have direct access to any non-stipulated facts; the only *internal* evidence one has for imagining what is true within a fiction is what else one imagines to be true in the fiction, including that the narrator is reliable.

For the rational norms governing beliefs do not speak directly to their contents in isolation, but rather to the reasons in favor of their formation or retirement, and to their relations—such as their consistency—while they are held. Accordingly, just as we have certain commitments to what kinds of processes by which a belief comes about can render it justified, so we have commitments to what kinds of processes are appropriate means for an imagining to come about, in virtue of which it is justified.

6.5. Reasons and Functions

Although in making the case for discontinuity I've referred to the various tendencies exploited by fictions as irrational dispositions when they are activated in veridical contexts, it is a mistake to assume that, when seen from the broadest perspective, they always instantiate defects or evidence of improper functioning in our reasoning. There may have been evolutionary trade-offs in which the emergence of these sometimes faulty modes of cognition and behavior allowed the development of other more consistently beneficial forms. Or they may, say, reflect evolutionary history not being able to pass over a fitness valley required to attain a more optimal state. And, serving as heuristics, they may reflect, e.g., efficiencies in the formation and transmission of beliefs, and asymmetries in the cost of making an error in judgment and the benefit of getting it right. "Better safe than sorry" is a low-cost/high-benefit policy when deciding whether what has the shape and movement of a snake should be treated as if it is, indeed, a snake.

My interest is in the fact that our recognizing the suboptimal aspect of these tendencies leads us to *try* to correct for them in theoretical reasoning with our beliefs. Of course, as the literature on biases and heuristics show, we often fail. But we do not recognize an epistemic norm calling for us to engage in such correction in response to fictions—when, that is, such ways of thinking are exploited by the fiction in order to reveal what in the story holds true. Indeed, one of the standard critiques of thought experiments is that, while aspiring to elicit reasoning governed by appropriate inferential norms, their conclusions are often illicitly dependent on literary conventions (character continuity, temporal contiguity that implies causal connectedness, events interpreted as confirming a theme such as fatalism or the uniqueness of humanity, and so on).[31] Insofar as thought experiments can be cleansed of these illegitimate influences, they would function better; but it would be odd to propose that literary fiction would better realize its aims if cured of analogously "distorting" influences.

As in the last chapter's explanation of discontinuity over affective norms, I suggest that discontinuity in our epistemic norms for believing and imagining demonstrates that the reasons we count as justifications for our cognitive representations depend on the functions of the practices in which those representations are formed.

Beliefs are typically, if not essentially, directed at accurately representing things as they are.[32] Accordingly, the only reasons that count in favor of a belief in its representational dimension are evidential reasons, those that speak to its truth and to the reliable means by which that truth is obtained.

Analogously, in some cases one's imaginative activity has an epistemic or practical role analogous to that of belief and perception, where the function is to aid in discovering some truth about the actual world, as when we need to plan for the future. That purpose is better realized if one's imaginings are based on reasons that speak to the objective qualities of, and relations among, what the imaginings represent.

Many fiction-directed imaginings, however, are generated in activities with ends—the wide variety of interests we have in artistic experience—in virtue of which they can be epistemically warranted on grounds that would not count as justifications for analogous beliefs. One may decide that a character in a film is trustworthy because she has a, so to speak, honest face. Even if that judgment is not justified by an inference from any facts imagined to hold in the fiction, it may still be justified if it is part of the design of the

---

[31] See Sorensen (1992, 263–65).

[32] Exceptions may be found in the sort of motivated believing and reasoning involved in, e.g., thinking of oneself as a better athlete than one is in order to perform better than one would if one adopted a wholly accurate appraisal of one's ability. See Starek and Keating (1991).

work that it induces audiences to see that character as having that property. To capture this distinction in an area at one remove from fictions, consider the casino detective who by day scrutinizes card players in order to expose any illicit sleight of hand, but by night joins the audience of the performing magician who employs the same tricks as the cheating gamblers. His professional aims during the workday require him to resist the card shark's exploitation of perceptual biases, say, the lag in our perception of motion wherein our sensory experience of an object is sustained for a fraction of a second after it has been removed.[33] However, his aim during the evening is to enjoy the magic show, and this means that no such bias in his perception is to be guarded against or corrected for. What grounds our representations of things in contexts of make-believe need not be consistent with what grounds those representations in contexts of belief.

[33] See Stone (2012).

7

Tragedy and Desire

Edgar:O thou side-piercing sight!
King Lear:Nature's above art in that respect.

—King Lear, 4.3

In earlier chapters I looked at two kinds of relations—*affective* and *epistemic*—between our attitudes about fictions and those about the real world. Here, I address a third kind of relation—a *conative* one. I ask whether our desires for what happens within a fiction are, or should be, consistent with our desires for what happens outside of it.

7.1. Desires and the Paradox of Tragedy

In earlier chapters I asked, with reference to their representational dimensions, how our responses to fictions compare to those to what we take to be real. How do emotions present their objects across the real-fictional divide? Can imaginings of what is true according to a fiction be justified in the same ways as beliefs about the actual world?

Although desires instantiate another significant kind of prescribed response to the contents of fictions and imaginings, the question of whether they exhibit normative continuity requires a distinctive form of analysis compared to those offered for emotions and beliefs. This is because desires differ from those other attitudes in their direction of fit. The satisfaction conditions of both emotions, as evaluative representations, and other representational states such as beliefs, are given by how the world is. We can assess those states by reference to their correspondence to the facts. By contrast, a

Apt Imaginings. Jonathan Gilmore, Oxford University Press (2020). © Oxford University Press.
DOI: 10.1093/oso/9780190096342.001.0001

desire's satisfaction conditions are given not by how things are, but by some state of affairs the desire aims to bring about.[1]

One might propose that desires can be addressed with respect to at least one representational dimension, that specified in the theory of desires as essentially presenting their objects as good. In that view, a desire that p is an impression or registration in some way that it would be good if p.[2] If that were true, we could ask of a particular desire a question analogous to that we posed for emotions and imaginings: Does it *correctly* present its object (here, as good), and is it experienced in virtue of that presentation? However, that approach is unpromising. For, as critics have noted, many things we desire seem from our own point of view to be neither good for us nor good simpliciter.[3] Of course, desires can follow from and imply the acceptance of representational states such as beliefs and perceptions. But addressing desires on the basis of just those representational dimensions does not address desires qua desires. Hence, the need for an approach that recognizes their distinctive direction of fit.

The question of whether the norms governing our desires are invariant across fictions and the real world could be asked in connection with any sort of imaginative representation. However, I focus here on the kinds of fictions, sad or painful ones, in which our desires for what is internal and external to the work seem, most saliently, to come apart. For example, when watching a tragic drama, we appear to want the protagonist not to suffer and yet want the play to be performed such that she does. Such works of imaginative literature seem to instantiate cases in which what we desire of the real world does not square with what we contemporaneously desire of conceptually related states of affairs within the fiction. Yet, whether the apparent disparity in those responses expresses a discontinuity in the norms governing our real-world and fiction-directed desires depends on how the desires are interpreted. We need a clearer sense of what content is to be attributed to each kind of desire, and an answer to whether those directed at fictions are sufficiently of the same kind as those directed at actual states of affairs for the question of discontinuity to even arise. In what follows I try to clarify the nature of these desires, identify their content, and assess the philosophical relevance of any mutual inconsistency they may exhibit. I conclude by arguing that tragedy's

---

[1] I only register here that desires have a direction of fit opposite that of beliefs; the proper interpretation of that difference is contested. See Anscombe (1957); Schueler (1991).

[2] See Stampe (1987).

[3] See Stocker (1979); and Velleman (1992).

capacity to elicit genuinely inconsistent desires is a condition of its artistic success.

Let us start with David Hume's identification of a puzzle arising in connection with works of art that cause us to suffer:

> It seems an unaccountable pleasure, which the spectators of a well-written tragedy receive from sorrow, terror, anxiety, and other passions, that are in themselves disagreeable and uneasy. The more they are touched and affected, the more are they delighted with the spectacle; and as soon as the uneasy passions cease to operate, the piece is at an end.[4]

It is not puzzling that works such as tragedies provoke both pleasure and pain, for many non-perplexing experiences do as well. Nor is there any oddity in feeling pain as a necessary condition of feeling pleasure, for many ordinary circumstances have that structure. Rather, Hume's enigma is that our pleasure seems to be internally related to our distress. Feeling such pain is not a contingent cost but an essential element of the pleasure in question, without which it would not be as desirable. One could delight in blood-red sunsets even if they were not caused, as it happens, by aerosol pollution, but one would not derive certain pleasures from tragic dramas if they did not provoke their characteristic kinds of grief.[5] As Hume notes, audiences are "pleased in proportion as they are afflicted."[6] Yet how best to describe this puzzle, beyond the noncommittal sketch already given, remains contentious.

On the one hand, we often pursue and take pleasure or satisfaction in works of art in ways that are ostensibly explained by their elicitation of painful, disvalued, or disagreeable feelings: fear of a movie's monster, disgust for the simulated viscera in a painting, shock and trauma in a video game, cringing embarrassment for a television comedy's heedless characters, alienation through punk rock, grief in listening to a threnody, disorientation entering into an installation, and boredom and acedia, as might arise in watching Andy Warhol's eight-hour continuous footage of the Empire State Building, filmed from a static point of view.

---

[4] Hume (1987, 216).

[5] See the April Fool's Day, 2006, broadcast by National Public Radio on the "Positive Opera Company" that installs happy endings in the otherwise depressing productions of *Madame Butterfly, Don Giovanni,* and *La Bohème.* "We're in troubled times," explains Hamilton Banks, the project's director.

[6] Hume (1987, 217).

On the other hand, our engagement with such works does not conform to the prima facie plausible assumption that we tend not, and ought not, to pursue experiences for the sake of distress, pain, annoyance, or other aversive feelings, and that when we must undergo such experiences we do not, and should not, value them for their disagreeable dimensions.

This conundrum is usually identified as "the paradox of tragedy," although, as the preceding examples show, it is instantiated in many different kinds of experiences beyond the theater. Attempts to dissolve the paradox typically introduce reasons for why, despite what appear to be our usual dispositions to avoid pain and distress, we may be rationally motivated to pursue experiences of art that elicit disagreeable feelings. Among other values, tragedy offers certain kinds of pleasures which may distract us from, compensate for,[7] be converted into a palatable form of,[8] or arise as a meta-response to,[9] the pain it causes: an affective stimulation that we desire, whether its valence is positive or negative;[10] an opportunity to clarify our emotions;[11] an intrinsically valuable enlightenment about the nature of suffering;[12] a safely distanced experience of suffering; and an opportunity to contemplate our own vulnerability to loss.[13] Referring to the last point, Samuel Johnson writes that "the reflection that strikes the heart is not, that the evils before us are real evils, but that they are evils to which we ourselves may be exposed."[14]

Some of these reasons better serve to identify the conditions under which we desire to experience tragedies, than to justify that desire. If, for example, an artistic medium allows us to experience suffering in a safely moderated form, this tells us of the circumstances under which such an experience can be desirable, but not why. And none of those explanations is prima facie exclusive of any of the others.

---

[7] See Carroll (2003b). Note Aristotle's (1987) posit of a compensatory pleasure we take in acquiring knowledge through looking at renderings of things whose actual sight we would find painful, "such as the forms of the basest animals and of corpses" (chap. 4). Even if this is true of the first occasion, it isn't clear that such an exchange is available upon subsequent viewings of the same image, in relation to which the putative knowledge has already been acquired.

[8] Hume's solution in "On Tragedy."

[9] See Feagin (1983).

[10] Hume's interpretation of l'Abbé Dubos. Compare this to measures employed by psychologists of people's dispositional desires for emotionally provocative experiences, e.g., Maio and Esses (2001).

[11] As proposed in interpretations of Aristotle's notion of catharsis. See Nehamas (2015).

[12] See Schier (1983). In some accounts, this enlightenment is identified as conducive to moral value of some sort. See Ridley (2005); Budd (1995).

[13] Lucretius (2001) identifies the general dynamic: "'tis sweet / To mark what evils we ourselves be spared; / 'Tis sweet, again, to view the mighty strife / Of armies battled yonder o'er the plains, / Ourselves no sharers in the peril" (Book II, 5–9).

[14] Johnson (1765/1968, i.77–78).

When the problem is construed in general terms, many kinds of engagements beyond those of art fall within its scope. Hume refers to religious sermons and oratory as provoking, like fictional dramas, a pleasure in distress.[15] We often find satisfaction in nonfiction works, e.g., in historical narratives, even as they generate pity or anger. Many people are titillated by lurid and disturbing journalism that has little cognitive or practical value. Others find the violence in bullfighting or boxing repellent but enthralling. A long-distance runner might find satisfaction in exercising to the point of exhaustion. And merely for a thrill, one might eat too-hot chili peppers, risk one's physical well-being, or imagine inordinately nauseating or frightful circumstances. Leontius, in Plato's *Republic*, morbidly ogles the bodies of people executed outside the city walls even as he recognizes its deviance: "he pushed his eyes wide open and rushed towards the corpses, saying, 'Look for yourselves, you evil wretches, take your fill of the beautiful sight!'"[16] Augustine speaks in the *Confessions* of a similar "cupiditas oculorum"; and Dante, alluding to Augustine, offers an analogously self-accusatory and exculpatory explanation of his slow pace through Hell: "The many people and their ghastly wounds / did so intoxicate my eyes / that I was moved to linger there and weep."[17]

The puzzle arising from our engagement with tragic works of art assumes that they call for a response that contrasts with that which we tend to exhibit in a class of normal cases. However, the wider the range is of relevantly similar experiences such as those surveyed earlier, the more dubious is the premise that initially gives rise to the puzzle: viz., our finding value in some experiences in virtue of the negative feelings they evoke is so unlike our other sorts of attitudes and behavior that it requires some distinctive explanation. If we have that response in many contexts outside of our engagement with tragedy, then its paradoxical air is difficult to sustain. We might still want to know what we desire in tragedy, or why it gives us pleasure, but there would be no special *paradox* of tragedy calling for a solution.[18] Indeed, we may

---

[15] Hume (1739–40/1978, I.iii.9).

[16] Plato (1975, Book IV, 439e–44b).

[17] Augustine (2006, Book 6); Dante (1980, canto 29, 1–4). When Augustine tries to explain his attraction to tragic drama ("Wretched, I loved at that time to be made sorry, and sought out matter to be sorry at") he rejects the more general explanation that we take pleasure in showing mercy or compassion for others. Such mercy would imply a desire that the sorrows of characters be eliminated, yet, as he notes, spectators desire that they be continued (taking pleasure in one's own sadness, one "sheds tears of joy"). He calls that pleasure in grief a "wretched madness" (Book 3, chap. II).

[18] I draw here from the analogous objection to the putative paradox of fiction-directed emotions developed in Richard Moran (1994).

contrast those sorts of socially normative pursuits in which one takes satisfaction in one's distress with other sorts that *do* call for a special explanation, such as pathological practices of masochism and self-harm.

Yet there is still something puzzling about *what state we are in* as audiences for tragedy and similarly aversive works of art, whether or not it is also puzzling that we seek to put ourselves in that state. This is a condition in which we both (1) contemplate a work from an external perspective, as an artifact designed through its plot, medium, language, and so on to achieve certain artistic ends; and (2) imagine the objects, events, and facts of the story internally, as if they were real, or described by a real narrator. We are pleased by, value, or desire what occurs in the work from an external perspective, yet we feel sadness or some other sort of aversive attitude toward what occurs in the work described from an internal perspective.

Thus Peter Lamarque writes, "When Othello kills Desdemona, viewers are appalled by the senselessness and injustice of it, internally and imaginatively. Yet externally, reflecting on the remorseless logic of the drama, they accept that there can be no other outcome."[19] In some sense we don't want Desdemona to die, yet we want *Othello*, or the particular performance of the play, to be such that this event occurs in it.

How should we characterize these two attitudes constitutive of our engagement with a tragedy?

Although many sorts of affective, evaluative, and conative responses enter into an engagement with tragedy and other arts that cause antipathy, I will address just one kind of apparently conflicting attitudes: the desires instantiated in the state described earlier.[20]

By focusing on competing desires, we can better clarify what sort of tension inheres in our enjoyment of tragedy and other distressing forms of art without entering into debates over whether or not emotions can be contrary to desires, or contrary to one another.[21] Of course, it may be disputed that our two desires are mutually inconsistent, but at least we can recognize the prima

---

[19] Lamarque (1996, 163).

[20] That we may characterize the tension paradigmatic of tragedy in terms of not just emotions, but also desires, has been noted by commentators such as Neill (1993).

[21] Of course, many explanatory connections can be drawn between emotions and desires. Emotions are sometimes cited as causes or rationalizations of desires. Desires are sometimes cited as causes or rationalizations of emotions. Some kinds of emotions can be characterized as partly constituted by desires: envy and disappointment, e.g., respectively reflect the presence and frustration of what one wants. However, not all emotions on all occasions lend themselves to such a characterization: anxiety, e.g., does not always involve a desire for its cause (e.g., a job interview) to be eliminated. For theories that identify desires with emotions, see Green (1992); Gordon (1990).

facie tension in desiring that a performance of *King Lear* includes Cordelia's death and not wanting Cordelia to die.

Let's begin by identifying three different proposals for identifying the objects of the apparently competing desires?[22] They may be

(1) alternative fictional states of affairs, e.g., Cordelia dying and not dying;
(2) alternative versions of the work of fiction, e.g., *King Lear* and *King Lear Revised*; or,
(3) respectively, the work of fiction and the state of affairs it represents.

In some cases (1) is a good characterization of the objects of the competing desires evoked by a fiction. In Book 6 of the *Iliad* Hector rebuffs Andromache's pleas that he not depart for the battle in which, he acknowledges, he will die. We desire for him to remain with her and their child, and we desire for him to leave, as he insists he must. These desires cannot be mutually satisfied within the constraints of what the work prescribes for us to imagine. But such a tension does not generate a philosophical problem, for such an incompatibility between different desires for an imagined state of affairs has a ready parallel in the unfortunate but hardly puzzling incompatibility between desires that we can experience for things in real life.

If (2) describes our desires, then we both want the work not to be changed, and wish that it were in some significant way different. No doubt, this is a plausible account in some cases. We want *Titus Andronicus* to be an extravaganza of bloodletting and dismemberment—its artistic power partly resides in its gory marvels—yet, at the same time, we would like the work not to be so unrelentingly violent. Perhaps what it aspires to could be achieved in other ways. Our desires about the work are in conflict, as it cannot satisfy them both. Desiring a work to be other than it is can seem incoherent if one takes every feature of a fictional work to be essential to it. However, we can intelligibly express such a desire in a pro tanto manner: I want *Titus* to exhibit such violence insofar as it demonstrates the self-destructive fury of revenge, yet I do not want the work to exhibit such violence insofar as it is furnishes a revolting spectacle.[23]

---

[22] My focus on desires here and throughout is heavily indebted to Currie (2010b).

[23] Or in a 17th-century context, we may say we prefer a particular version of the play, e.g., Nahum Tate's 1681 revision of *King Lear* in which, joyously, Cordelia lives and marries Edgar and Lear regains his throne.

However, it is a problem with (2) that it presents us not just as *sometimes* ambivalent about our desires concerning the contents of tragedies but *necessarily* ambivalent. It would entail that the proper experience of a tragedy requires that one be torn between a desire that it be performed as it is, and a desire that it be performed without its distressing elements.[24] Yet while we may occasionally criticize a work for some feature that, if eliminated, would make the work better, our doing so is not an essential feature of the proper response solicited by successful tragic drama.[25]

This leaves us with (3): we desire that the *work* be such that it represents some state of affairs, S, as obtaining, yet we desire that S not obtain. This doesn't specify what state of affairs we wish were otherwise, but an intuitive answer is that it is the object of our aversive emotions or negative evaluative appraisal. In what follows, I refer to this conjunction of conflicting desires as our *external and internal desires* for a tragedy or similarly antipathetic art. The modifiers indicate the location of the object of our desires, not the desires themselves.

Not every kind of distressing form of art can be naturally described in terms of the desires it evokes. Our engagement with many works can be better captured in terms of our emotions. Caravaggio's early *Sacrifice of Isaac* shows the instant at which Abraham, grasping his son's neck and drawing his knife, is restrained by an angel who seizes his wrist.[26] As I imagine seeing a beseeching Isaac and the angel staying his father's hand, I feel both horror and relief. These emotions do imply certain correlative desires—that Isaac be freed and Abraham stopped—yet those desires seem secondary, and their content, if meant to fit the contested theme of the story in Genesis, less easily identified.

Some philosophers argue that we cannot have desires for events or states of affairs that have already taken place, or are otherwise impossible to bring about.[27] They propose that we speak instead of *wishes* for such things, or to

---

[24] Currie (2010b) notes, "It is not possible, on this account, to experience [*Othello*] as a tragedy *and* to want wholeheartedly for it to be a work in which Desdemona dies; one must want it to be a work in which she dies, and want it not to be one" (636).

[25] A compelling dissention from the standard view that Cordelia's death is a dramatic necessity in the play is advanced by the Shakespearean critic A. C. Bradley, who dismisses the sentimentalism of the happy ending provided by popular alternative versions, such as Nahum Tate's, yet holds that Cordelia's and Lear's destruction is unmotivated by the plot, more like a "bolt from a sky" than an inevitable consequence of the drama. His desire that Cordelia be saved is motivated not by "philanthropic feelings," but by a "dramatic sense." I'm grateful to Sandeep Sreekumar for alerting me to this passage.

[26] Circa 1603, Uffizi, Florence.

[27] See Anscombe (1957).

what we *would desire* in some counterfactual state of affairs. Others disagree, finding it plausible that one can have such desires as that one had taken a left turn earlier on the drive, or that one were several years younger.[28] This may be a solely a verbal dispute. In any case, one can avoid referring to desires concerning how the plot of a work unfolds by speaking instead of yet-to-be experienced tokens or instantiations of those works. We want, e.g., the performance we will attend, the version we will read, etc., to be such that some state of affairs, S, obtains in it.

The puzzle raised by our conflicting internal and external desires concerning a tragic or otherwise distressing work of art is that, when conjoined, they seem to present our engagement with such works as *essentially* fraught with conflict. Satisfying one desire entails a failure to satisfy the other. Here even an exemplary work of tragic drama appears always to promise more than it can deliver. Yet to respond by scaling back one of our desires, e.g., to convince ourselves not to care whether Cordelia dies in *King Lear*, would be to fail to fully appreciate and comprehend the tragedy—one whose design *merits* both desires.[29]

Thus, it seems that we are oddly conflicted or inconsistent in the feelings we have about such works. It appears that we desire something that we also don't desire. Or that in experiencing such tragedies we seek to satisfy incompatible desires. If this characterization of our engagement with aversive art forms entails that we are irrational, then we should consider ways in which the characterization might be mistaken. For it is at least prima facie implausible that works of art as ubiquitous as these ask us to occupy an irrational state as a condition of their proper appreciation.

Indeed, we need to preserve the idea that an irrational response is possible, without being often or always present, in order to distinguish between forms of comprehension and appreciation that rest on rational grounds and those that fail to do so, via, for example, succumbing to wishful thinking that a given fact holds in a fiction when the work clearly prescribes imagining otherwise.

---

[28] In many models of the explanation of behavior desires are referred to as encompassing a wide range of "pro attitudes" including wants, wishes, wills, instincts, strivings, urges, yearnings, appetites, and drives. Distinctions among these states may be significant in different explanatory contexts, but the common use of the generic "desire" in their place casts doubt on there being a clear conceptual distinction between wishes and desires sufficient to deny that we have desires about states of affairs that cannot be changed.

[29] Alex Neill (1993) notes that to attribute such a scaling back of desire to audiences would oddly imply that "what we regard as valuable about certain works of fiction involves wishing that they were other than they are" (10).

In what follows I address two attempts to demonstrate that there is no con-flict, and thus no threat of irrationality. I argue that each is unsatisfactory. In their place, I argue that there is, indeed, a genuine conflict. However, I show that that conflict does not entrain the charge of irrationality. Finally, I show how, in positive terms, our having such conflicting desires in the experience of tragic works of art is not only fully rational but also reflects a criterion of tragedy's success qua tragedy.

7.2. The Two Desires Do Not Conflict

In one proposal, no conflict—and thus no conflict suggestive of irrationality—holds between our desires because they are directed at different objects. Our external and internal desires are *aspectival*: one pertains to the work as an ar-tifact in the real world and the other to the contents of what the work asks us to imagine. Any apparent inconsistency here is due only to how we represent and refer to the object of our desires. What we feel is a desire that *p* with re-spect to its dimension A and a desire that *not-p* with respect to its dimension B. The upshot is that I do not desire both that *p* and that *not-p*.

An apparent inconsistency between two desires about the same object can, it is true, be dissolved sometimes when they are shown to be directed at dif-ferent properties of the object. One may desire to drink a glass of whiskey in virtue of its taste but desire not to drink it in virtue of its inebriating effect. These desires are not necessarily inconsistent as the conditions of satisfac-tion for the two desires are not internally related. A desire for the whiskey's taste and a desire not to be inebriated by it can both be satisfied under some conditions (e.g., one could develop a high tolerance for alcohol). But this is not the case with the relevant desires formed in experiencing a tragic fic-tion. My desire that a performance of *King Lear* be such that in it Cordelia dies, and my desire that she not die, cannot be jointly satisfied under any conditions. They are necessarily inconsistent desires.

A related approach is to treat the objects of our desires as distinct, mutually exclusive, foci of our attention.[30] To the extent that appreciation of a tragedy demands that we alternately shift our attention from the artifact-work (its design, staging, meter, and so on) to what we are prompted to imagine by the work, our desires may not come into sufficient closeness for us to register

---

[30] See the attention-based theory of desire in Scanlon (1998).

their conflict. Such distinct foci of attention may also result from several inferential steps being required to recognize that the two desires are in conflict. To charge a person with irrationality for trying to satisfy two essentially conflicting desires would only be plausible—if it is plausible—if the conflict between the desires is one that a reasonable person would be able to recognize. Certainly, many of our current desires are in conflict without our realizing it and it would set an inordinately high bar for our rationality to require that all those conflicts be eliminated. However, in the characterization offered here of our desires, the conflict does not go unnoticed. Indeed, at the end of the play, as Lear holds Cordelia's lifeless body, we want his confabulation that she still breathes to turn out to be true, yet we recognize that the poignancy of the scene depends on that wish being to no avail.

Finally, one may propose that there is no conflict between our desires if they are supported by reasons of a pro tanto sort. Employing the earlier example, we may say that one has reason to desire to drink the glass of whiskey insofar as one likes its taste, yet one has reason to desire not to drink it insofar as one wants to remain sober. Appealing to pro tanto reasons brings out the distinct, non-conflicting sets of considerations that, from an agent's perspective, respectively justify his or her distinct desires. One might thus propose that one has reason to desire that Cordelia survive because she is blameless and sincere, and reason not to desire that outcome because her death is an essential feature of a deeply moving work. However, this characterization fails to capture the nature of our desire for Cordelia to survive. We may be caused to form that desire through being shown that she has such admirable qualities. Those qualities serve as reasons why we come to desire for her to live. But, once formed, our desire for her to live is not for her qua a bearer of those qualities. Rather our desire is (we imagine) for her welfare as a particular being whom we care about. In this sense, our imagined attachment to characters in fictions can be formally akin to the attachment we have to real individuals through friendship or love—a kind of concern not appropriately characterized by pro tanto reasons of the preceding sort.[31] One might come to love another for certain qualities the other possesses, but once that love is formed, its survival need not be correlated with the survival of those (or any particular) qualities.

---

[31] On our attachment to characters in tragic works see Wilson (2013).

7.3. There Is Only One Genuine Desire

Some theorists argue that what we have identified as a conflict of desires over a work of tragedy is only apparent, for one of those putative desires is only an imaginative counterpart of a real desire: an *i-desire* that shares some, but not all, of a real desire's functional roles.[32] Their proposal is that such i-desires are related to genuine desires in a way analogous to how imaginings are related to beliefs. Desires and beliefs have as their content some proposition about the real world; i-desires and imaginings have as their contents propositions that are true in a fiction, pretense, or other form of make-believe.

Employing the concept of an i-desire in identifying our attitudes toward a tragedy, we may say that we have a genuine, real-world, desire that *King Lear* be such that it represents the king's decline in status and descent into madness, yet we only in imagination desire that he not undergo such losses.

Some of the reasons why desires for fictional states of affairs seem to be internal to a pretense match those reasons in §3.3 for why emotions felt for fictions seem to lie within the scope of our imagining. For example, one might deny that I genuinely desire that a tragic character not be harmed because I don't display the behavioral or motivational accompaniments of genuine desires. I might turn away from a performance, or close a book that I'm reading, but these reflect desires to end my experience of the fiction, not to act on my desire for some state of affairs in it.

As noted in that earlier discussion, it isn't obvious that we exhibit *none* of the markers of being motivated to act on desires when we know their contents are fictional. Watching some harrowing event represented on stage, we do not climb onto the proscenium to intervene. However, we may exhibit other tendencies to act, by grimacing, recoiling in our seat, or, less automatically, trying to discover a place within the represented scenario—on stage or in other media—where an affected protagonist could seek refuge. Or we may recall facts in the story, or consider facts that the story permits us to import into it, that would help the character: the presence of a weapon, vulnerability in an attacker, some strategy to turn the tables on an antagonist.

Nonetheless, the defender of i-desires might note that such behaviors can plausibly be classified as merely part of the activity of understanding the content of the fiction, trying to discover what is true in it. It may also be that such

---

[32] Although it is not clear that the concept is always employed in the same way, such imaginative counterparts of desires are variously identified as *i-desires* (Doggett and Egan [2012]); *desire-like imaginings* (Currie and Ravenscroft [2002]); and desires held *offline* (Goldman [2006b]).

behaviors reflect a continuum between experiences of fictions, such as theatrical and literary works, which are organized around propositional imagining, and the experience of fictions such as video games, virtual reality, and interactive stories where behavioral pretense is invited. If we do continue to notice, e.g., the ways in which in a fiction a character *could* escape her peril, even though we know we are meant to imagine that she *cannot,* our cognitive behavior might better be described not as aiming to affect those fictional events (that is to *act* on our putative desires), but as identifying real-world defects in the construction of the plot.

A stronger rejoinder to the "no motivation" objection to the genuineness of our desires for what is solely make-believe is that desires tend to motivate only in connection with relevant beliefs, and no such beliefs, e.g., that one *can* intervene, are present in one's engagement with fictions.[33] Many kinds of desires, such as those about the past, seem genuine but not acted on because the relevant beliefs about how to realize those desires are lacking. The absence of motivation to act on one's fiction-directed desires can be explained in the same way. One refrains from acting on one's desires internal to the fiction because one believes no intervention is possible, not because the desires are not genuine.

Some theorists have argued that if our desires for what is internal to a tragedy were genuine, this would impose on audiences an unacceptably odd kind of disappointment. We would be disappointed over either the shape of the work or what happens in it. For these proponents of i-desires, describing our experience of tragedies as constitutively disappointing is counterintuitive. If, however, one of those putative desires is only an i-desire, then its not being satisfied in the fiction generates no real disappointment, only a feeling of, e.g., sadness that would serve as an appropriate appraisal of the fiction's contents.

It is not clear here where the burden of proof lies. It is prima facie plausible that one can regret, bemoan, or express disappointment over some event that occurred in a work of fiction. Edmund Wilson objected to what he took to be Emma's failure in Austen's novel to be cured of her "infatuation with women" and lamented that in the fictional world she would likely find a new protégée to replace Harriet. Indeed, that readers of a fiction sometimes don't cease to feel sadness for the death of a novel's protagonist even after they put the story aside suggests that one's desire for some imagined state of affairs can

---

[33] See Carruthers (2006).

be disappointed. If one experienced no feeling evincing disappointment in reading that Anna Karenina takes her own life, this would suggest that one had *neither* a desire nor an i-desire for her well-being. Of course, the proponent of i-desires might suggest that what the reader feels after finishing the work is only an imaginative counterpart of genuine disappointment. Then, however, the putative objection—that we should resist assuming our internal desires are genuine if doing so entails an experience of disappointment—is much weaker.

What might explain the apparent counterintuitiveness of attributing disappointment to audiences of some fictional work is a mistaken inference that such attribution would imply a reduction in the work's artistic value.[34] That need not be so, for the disappointment at issue here is over a state of affairs that one imagines to have obtained, not over the real-world degree to which the work realizes its artistic ends. Indeed, such disappointment may reflect the work's power in generating such desires for what is only fictional.

7.4. There Is a Conflict between Two Desires but Not an Irrational One

The approaches represented in §7.2 and §7.3 both assume that the internal and external desires that audiences form in relation to a tragedy threaten to present an irrational conflict when conjoined. They try to block that attribution of irrationality by demonstrating that the conflict is only apparent. A different tactic I want to propose here is that we acknowledge that there is a conflict in an audience's all-things-considered desires, but deny the assumption that having such conflicting desires is irrational. To desire, in reading *Anna Karenina*, that the novel portray Anna's death is in a serious tension with the desire that Anna not die. Yet we can rebut the charge that there is some apparent defect in this conjunction of attitudes by noting that it is difficult to identify any norm that would render having such a set of desires systematically irrational.[35]

---

[34] Doggett and Egan (2012) remark that the deaths of Romeo and Juliet "are an occasion for a distinctive sort of saddened affect, but they are not an occasion for any kind of aesthetic disappointment—not even aesthetic disappointment that's more than compensated for by aesthetic benefits" (282).

[35] For an analogous and incisive argument against i-desires, see Spaulding (2015). See also Kind (2011).

Let us first consider those desires in light of norms of theoretical rationality—constraints governing a person's formation, maintenance, transitions among, and relinquishing of her beliefs. Note: it might seem that norms of practical rationality are most relevant here. However, to the extent that such practical norms apply to one's desires, it is qua desire's role in explaining one's intentions or actions. In the case of our desires for tragedy, no such intentions or actions are present that could serve as data for the assessment of the desires. So here I will primarily consider norms of theoretical rationality. In the next section, however, I will show one way in which our desires for tragic works can be assessed by a norm of a practical, specifically instrumental, kind.

According to one plausible rational constraint on our beliefs, we ought not to fully adopt or endorse two inconsistent beliefs when we recognize that they cannot both be true. A less stringent rational constraint is that, faced with a salient inconsistency between two of my beliefs, I need not give up either or both, but ought to assign a lesser degree of credibility to each, or give them a less-than-full endorsement in any role they play in my inferences.

Is there any comparable consistency requirement for desires? We may have inconsistent desires because they are based on inconsistent beliefs. This points only to a potential defect in theoretical rationality, not in the rationality of the desires.[36] Alternatively, we may have inconsistent desires where their conflict is due to their conditions of satisfaction: they cannot both be satisfied in this world (a contingent inconsistency), or cannot both be satisfied in any world (a necessary inconsistency). But if having either kind of set of inconsistent desires can count against one's rationality, it would not be for the reasons that holding a pair of contrary beliefs can be irrational. To knowingly hold two inconsistent beliefs, each with full credence, is to represent the world as existing in two incompatible forms, and thus to betray some defect in how one acquired, or reasons with, those beliefs. By contrast, knowingly having inconsistent desires need not express a defect in how they are acquired or held. For their inconsistency may be solely due to fact that the world does not cooperate in allowing their joint satisfaction.

---

[36] Thus, some accounts of the rationality of desires do not address them qua desires but for the beliefs or epistemic processes upon which the formation and holding of the desires depends. See, e.g., Brandt's (1979) account of "rational desires" as requiring the possession of available information, no failures of logic, and vivid imaginings of their states of satisfaction. See also Blackburn's (1988) proposal that there is a "logic of attitudes" in which it is irrational to want both *a* and *not-a*.

Another rational constraint on our beliefs pertains to their coherence. If I believe p and believe that p entails q, I rationally should believe q (or at least not affirm its negation, given that there are many facts that we are indifferent to that are entailed by our beliefs). An analogous principle might seem to hold for desires.[37] However, on many occasions one can desire p and believe that if p then q without desiring q. I desire to play loud music late at night, even though I'm sure that this will wake my neighbors. Yet I don't want to wake my neighbors.

According to a different candidate for a norm of coherence among desires, if I know that p is necessary to realize my desire that q, I ought to have at least a defeasible desire that p. If, e.g., I know that attending cooking school is necessary for me to realize my desire to become a chef, I ought to have at least a defeasible desire to attend cooking school. However, this principle admits of many exceptions. Consider a case featuring competing desires that is somewhat analogous to our engagement with tragedy. I have a standing desire for my game of tennis that it be highly competitive and close-scoring, for it's less fun when one player dominates the other. Yet even when, on occasion, preserving a close score depends on my opponent winning the point, I may rationally never have the desire, not even a defeasible one, that he succeed. I want the game to be even and competitive, yet in playing I fully want every point to go my way.

Finally, in rationally forming our beliefs, we rely on standard evidentiary sources such as testimony, perception, memory, inductive and deductive inference, and our affective responses. When all goes well, these sources provide the right sorts of reasons for our beliefs: specifically, reasons that justify what we believe. Thus, it is irrational to form a belief on the basis of a reason that doesn't speak in favor of its truth, e.g., that it would be good if the belief were true. Some philosophers argue that, analogously, we may criticize a desire for the reasons that, from the agent's point of view, are taken to warrant it.[38] It counts against the rationality of someone's desire to bet on horses if it's based on the belief that this is a reliable method of saving for retirement. This is a criticism of a desire as both theoretically irrational, in depending on a faulty belief, and practically irrational, in not contributing to the satisfaction

---

[37] Doggett and Egan (2012) write that "having the desire about the fictional character (at least) rationally requires that one have the corresponding desire about the content of the fiction, since as you well know, the only way for the fictional character to have the property that we desire him to have is for the content of the fiction to make it so" (284–85).

[38] See Dancy (2000): "we can in general understand desire as a response to a perceived reason" (38).

of the person's more primary desires. However, neither of these forms of criticism applies to the competing desires operative in responses to tragic drama. Typically, in responding to a work of sufficient artistic merit, each desire (externally about the play, internally about a character's fate) is justified by the reasons one would have for forming them; and neither desire tends to conflict with one's primary interests. Of course, only one of these desires is satisfied, raising the question of whether it is rational to regularly form a desire that one knows will be frustrated. In the next section I take up the rationality of the higher-order desire to have this experience—prototypical of tragedy—of forming and only partially fulfilling our lower-order desires.

7.5. The Conflict Is Rational in Light of a Third Desire

We see from the preceding discussion that in none of the familiar terms with which we speak of theoretic irrationality do the desires required for the appreciation of fiction appear systematically irrational. However, while one's worry over a putative irrationality in our conflicting desires may have abated, one might still wonder if such desires have any rational standing at all. For one may conclude from the preceding discussion that our desire for a given state of affairs in a fiction is merely *arational*, not susceptible to rational justification or criticism. In this way, desires about the contents of a fiction would be comparable to other mental states that have representational content, such as dreams, but which are not appropriate objects of rational appraisal. As we saw in earlier chapters, we may assess one's cognitive response to a work in asking whether what one imagines conforms to what the work prescribes one to imagine. And we may assess an affective response to a work over whether it is true in the work that the emotion's object has the qualities that justify the emotion. But how might we show that our conative responses to a tragedy are appropriate subjects of rational evaluation?

We may begin by noting that we can criticize a desire felt for some feature of a fiction if it betrays a cognitive misunderstanding of what is true in the fiction. I may want Iago to succeed in his sinister schemes, say, because I identify with his envy of Cassio and his resentment over not being promoted by Othello. Yet the drama does not present the success of Iago's plans as meriting such a desire. My desire thus presents those plans in the fiction as having evaluative qualities that are contrary to what they exhibit in the fiction. Of course, in a work in which there is greater ambiguity in what audiences are meant to desire, or an artistic failure in motivating such desires, such criticism may be unfounded. The important point is that our desires for some fictional state of affairs may be appropriately evaluated for their fit with the evaluative qualities that the work presents the state of affairs as exemplifying. They may be assessed, that is, for their fit with what desires the work is designed to evoke. Of course, even when our desire for some state of affairs in a tragedy is shown to be rational in this light, it still appears in conflict with the external desire we have about the work of fiction, which we presume raises no special question of rationality. Even though each desire can be individually justified, their *conjunction* remains without a rational justification.

I propose that having such conflicting desires is rational in an *instrumental* sense of a peculiar kind.[39] A rational *second-order* desire of ours is satisfied through having the two *first-order* desires. That second-order desire is for the realization of one or more of the goods—such as pleasure—featured in the solutions to the paradox of tragedy surveyed in §7.1. The reasons that justify one's motivation to pursue those goods also serve to justify one's having the internal and external conflicting desires constitutive of the experience that realizes those goods. In other words, the rationality of the end of satisfying the higher-order desire renders rational the joint possession of the conflicting lower-order desires. Let me try to justify this claim.

Sometimes when a person has one desire that has as its object the acquisition of another desire, the person's reasons for the former are also reasons for the latter. Suppose I desire to improve my health but believe that I can do this only if I form the desire to exercise. There, improving my health can be my reason both for desiring to exercise and for desiring to acquire that desire. However, in other cases, there is no such "transitivity" of justification. A scientist studying caffeine addiction might choose to develop a desire to drink several cups of coffee each day. There, her reason each morning for desiring the coffee (its stimulating effect) would not be identical to her reason for desiring to have that desire (to learn about the addiction).[40]

Our experience of tragic and other distressing works of art can instantiate a structure of desires of the second kind. The answer to what justifies our lower-order desires is distinct from the answer to what justifies our higher-order desire to form those lower-order desires. We have a desire to form both

[39] I am indebted here to Joyce's (2000) instrumental account of the rationality of fiction-directed emotions generally. On instrumental rationality, see Fehige (2001).

[40] For this point, see Frankfurt (1971).

(1) the painfully frustrated desire that Lear recover his standing, and (2) the happily satisfied desire that *King Lear* be performed such that, in the fiction, Lear loses his kingdom and identity. Each desire is explained and justified by a different reason: we want Lear not to lose his kingdom because he is the victim of treachery and we pity him in his decline. But, at the same time, we want the performance to include these events because Lear's struggle to hold on to his kingdom and his identity is a source of the work's great pathos. And we desire to *form and sustain* those two desires because, by virtue of experiencing the frustration of the first and the satisfaction of the second, we garner one or more of the benefits proposed in those resolutions to the paradox of tragedy canvassed earlier. So there are three desires constitutive of our engagement with tragedy:

(1) a desire that a work be such that something, S, occurs in it;
(2) a desire that S not occur; and,
(3) a desire that one have both (1) and (2).

My claim is that we are instrumentally rational in forming and having the conflicting desires (1) and (2) because having both those desires is necessary for the satisfaction of desire (3).

One might object that having a desire is not an action and thus not the sort of thing that can be justified by the instrumental role it plays in achieving some rationally desired end. Digestion and respiration are normally necessary for one to act on a given intention, yet even if acting thus is perfectly rational, this does not make digestion and respiration rational. However, the proper object of rational assessment is our *acting so as to form our lower-order desires*. We do that in choosing to experience a tragic or otherwise painful work of art, assuming we can roughly predict the desires or kinds of desires that it will provoke in us. We decide, for example, to attend a sad drama instead of a light comedy; read an elegy rather than a satire; or see a film by a director known for works of unrelenting bleakness.

In each case, we act on our desire to form desires central to the experiences of these works. We don't, that is, want the things such works cause us to desire independent of experiencing the works. The potential value of satisfying the desires arises only in the context of one's being "committed" to the story.[41] Indeed, sometimes, after forming these desires, one no longer wants

---

[41] The satisfaction of our desires in tragedy instantiates what George Ainslie (2013) calls an

to have them. Contemplating the inevitable frustration of one's wish for a happy ending, one closes the book or stops the film, intending to eliminate the conditions under which the desires' existence is sustained.

Many of the desires that we form as audiences for a work of art are not sufficiently predictable so as to be assessed in terms of instrumental rationality. Yet the fact that complexes of desires, broadly described, are respectively indexed to different genres and other categories of art, as well as to particular artists, performers, media, and venues, suggests that in some cases these desires are, indeed, knowingly acquired or formed when we choose to attend, read, see, etc., the work that elicits them. In other words, it is the function of these works to provide certain relatively predictable experiences, and our desires to engage with them qua tragic or painful work of art are desires to realize those functions.

My proposal is not committed to the claim that any given mental state can be rendered rational in virtue of instrumentally serving the satisfaction of some bona fide rational desire.[42] The costs of forming, having, and satisfying the lower-order instrumental desires may outweigh the benefit of satisfying the higher-order final desire. Indeed, we should notice that our higher-order desire for the experience of tragedy does not always justify the formation of the two lower-order ones. In a particular case, the rationalization can fail. A work can be so disconcerting that our desire to experience it for the sake of, e.g., a compensating pleasure is not warranted. This is rarely the case in relation to great works of painful art, in that their greatness consists in part in offering us reason to undergo the pain that a proper comprehension of them elicits. However, we must allow that sometimes the satisfaction of the higher-order desire to experience such a work isn't worth the disquiet that its activation of lower-order desires results in.[43]

---

endogeneous reward. This is a satisfaction of a desire, like the desire to win at solitaire or the desire of an addict to satiate his craving, that is valuable only within the context in which the desire is elicited.

[42] More generally, we should heed Donald Davidson's (1982) concern over the explanation of irrationality: "The underlying paradox of irrationality . . . is this: if we explain it too well, we turn it into a concealed form of rationality; while if we assign incoherence too glibly, we merely compromise our ability to diagnose irrationality by withdrawing the background of rationality needed to justify any diagnosis at all" (184).

[43] In his *Preface* to Shakespeare's plays (1765/1978), Samuel Johnson notes, "I was many years ago so shocked by Cordelia's death, that I know not whether I ever endured to read again the last scenes of the play till I undertook to revise them as an editor."

In distinguishing the structure of these three types of desires, we can identify an important condition of a tragedy's success qua tragedy.[44] It is that the
work generates precisely the *conjunction* of the conflicting first-order desires.
If we have an external desire that a tragedy be performed such that its heroine
dies and yet no internal desire that she not die, this would signify a failure
of the work to elicit our concern for that fictional individual. By contrast, if
we have the desire that she not die but no preference over whether the work
is such that her death occurs in it, this would mean that we care about what
merits our desires for what we imagine to exist, but not for the work's artistic
ends in eliciting those desires. In such circumstances, we sometimes judge a
work as sentimental, manipulative, or meretricious in virtue of successfully
evoking and frustrating our desires for a fictional character's welfare without
offering us sufficient artistic returns to justify our having formed that (ultimately frustrated) desire in the first place.

Our engagement with tragic works in *general* is rationally justified by the
values that solutions to the paradox of tragedy attribute to that experience.
However, this does not eliminate the risk one takes on in an engagement with
any particular painful work of art: for there one may develop a desire that one
need never have formed, but that, once formed, becomes a desire that one
wishes one didn't have.

---

[44] I refer here to a condition not of that genre only—conventions of which have included, e.g., that
its subject be noble and its style elevated—but of other works as well that we seek knowing of the
aversive responses they elicit.

8

Discrepant Affects

> Poetry is a rationalized dream . . . there are truths below the surface
> in the subject of sympathy, and how we become that which we under-
> standingly behold and hear.
>
> —Coleridge, *Notebooks*, II, 2086

> Bull, ya ain't an oil painting but you're a fascinating monster.
>
> —Mae West, *Klondike Annie*

In earlier chapters I addressed the question of whether our engagements with
states of affairs represented in fictions and other works of the imagination track,
in normative terms, our attitudes toward analogous states of affairs in the actual
world. I asked that question of our emotions, belief-like representations, and
desires. Here I address evaluative (especially moral) attitudes toward fictions
that are distinguished by being in conflict with the attitudes one would tend to
endorse if their objects were real. Against accounts that seek to explain away
such deviant responses to fictions, I argue that they are genuine.

8.1. Deviant Imaginings

Most audiences of fictions have had the experience of rooting for someone
in a make-believe story whom they would find contemptible in real life;
desiring something in a fiction that they would feel disdain for if they thought
the scenario of the fiction were real; and morally evaluating or emotionally
appraising behavior in a fiction contrary to how they would judge analogous
actions in the actual world. Shaun Nichols calls these kinds of cases "discrepant affects."[1]

---

[1] Nichols (2006b, 464).

Apt Imaginings. Jonathan Gilmore, Oxford University Press (2020). © Oxford University Press.
DOI: 10.1093/oso/9780190096342.001.0001

Some familiar illustrations: audiences worry with Tony Soprano over threats to his Mafia dominion; we feel relief when the cannibal Hannibal Lector eludes arrest after a characteristic meal, and when Patricia Highsmith's sociopath Tom Ripley strangles his way out of imminent exposure; players of *Grand Theft Auto* enjoy driving over pedestrians; pornographic depictions can evoke desires that would not be felt for the real thing; Godzilla thrills us as he (she?) flattens buildings like empty milk cartons; Warhol's repeated imagery in his *Disaster Series* of car crashes, race riots, and electric chairs elicits not disquiet, but dispassion; it's funny when an anvil lands on Wile E. Coyote's head or when Kenny, a cartoon child on *South Park*, is predictably killed in one episode after another; it feels good to see Beatrix Kiddo enact her bloody revenge in *Kill Bill*; and characters such as Gide's immoralist, Raskolnikov, Shakespeare's Richard III, and the conniving politician Frank Underwood / Francis Urquhart (aptly known by the initials "F.U.") of *House of Cards* serve as our confidants, objects of identification, and guides. In Nichols's illustration, we are not horrified, but amused, when the B-52 pilot Major Kong in *Dr. Strangelove* rides a nuclear missile, as if it was a bucking bronco, on its catastrophic course to earth.

Most of the illustrations in studies of this topic feature fictional characters who elicit from audiences morally deviant attitudes of approval or endorsement.[2] However, those cases may be better understood as illustrating a more general phenomenon involving real-world-inconsistent evaluative attitudes toward potentially any kind of fictional content, including characters, events, and states of affairs. In relation to *Dr. Strangelove*, for example, our amusement in the event which portends mass death and destruction is not easily explained as an alignment with a given character who has a positive attitude to what occurs—we don't share the deranged relish of the gung-ho Major Kong.[3] Furthermore, although works of fictional art supply the most vivid cases, ordinary imagining can be a source as well. As my ostentatious dinner host swans into the dining room with a teetering tray of desserts, I might chuckle inwardly at the thought of his tripping on the rug, yet not find it funny if that really occurred.

---

[2] Carroll (2004) dubs this the phenomenon of "sympathy for the devil." For his explanation of the effect, see the discussion later in this chapter.

[3] An alternative approach, although not explicitly argued for by those who focus on our alignment with particular characters, is to disaggregate kinds of discrepant affect and subject different kinds to different explanations.

Limits to such divergences between our evaluative attitudes toward states of affairs in fictions and in the real world have been probed in recent discussions of *imaginative resistance*.[4] There it has been observed that while we are usually able to imagine a wide range of counterfactual situations, such as the bizarre scenarios of science fiction, certain kinds of fictional representations are comparatively difficult to entertain: among them, those in which we are to imagine that what we believe to be morally deviant is morally good. By contrast, in cases of discrepant affect, there is no such difficulty: we appear to readily respond to a fictional scenario in a way contrary—with respect to our evaluative dispositions—to how we would if it were real.

In what follows I try to distinguish genuine cases of discrepant affect from those that only seem to belong to that category, and I survey some tentative explanations of the phenomenon. I'll refer somewhat indiscriminately to emotions, moral judgments, desires, as well as less easily individuated feelings of alignment, endorsement, "rooting for," and approval, as all exemplifying kinds of *evaluative attitudes* whose token evaluative representations count as cases of discrepant affect. My focus is thus broader than Nichols's on discrepant emotional responses. I proceed here assuming that any token discrepant affect is likely to have multiple, interdependent dimensions: inter alia, a desire that a character succeed in his deviant moral ends, an affiliation or "taking sides" with such a morally bad actor, a pleasure in a state of affairs which is not, from our usual point of view, genuinely merited, an approval of some action or outcome that we would typically not value, an indifference to something that one ordinarily would condemn. The point is that these evaluative dimensions are usually not amenable to being characterized as solely reflecting moral judgments. Nor are discrepant affects as I refer to them here usually identifiable with just an emotion, whose fit to its object could be addressed in the representational sense discussed earlier in §4.1. Rather, such responses are better characterized as expressions of *valuing*, "a complex syndrome of interrelated dispositions and attitudes, including, at least, certain characteristic types of belief, dispositions to treat certain kinds of considerations as reasons for action, and susceptibility to a wide range of emotions," in Samuel Scheffler's formulation.[5] Adapting that account to apply to our responses to fictions, I'll assume that non-instrumentally valuing some object O involves (1) a belief or imagining that O is good, worthy,

---

[4] Gendler (2000); Moran (1994); Walton (2006).
[5] Scheffler (2010).

or valuable according to contextually salient standards of value; (2) a susceptibility to experience certain context-dependent desires or emotions consistent with those beliefs or imaginings; and (3) a disposition to experience those desires or emotions as merited.

Furthermore, the discrepant affects that I will discuss are, importantly, only those that are prescribed by the works that elicit them. They instantiate, that is, *apt* responses to the fictions—ones that track how the fictions present their contents.

Finally, here and in most other discussions, discrepant affects are identified as evincing a disparity between the alignment we experience with immoral individuals in a fiction and the antipathy we would feel were we to encounter them in real life. However, I want to point out that this particular assignment of approval and contempt may be only contingent. A misanthrope may discover a teary-eyed affection for his fellow beings portrayed in fiction, while continuing to scorn lumpen humanity in his daily affairs.[6]

8.2. Why Discrepant Affects Are a Philosophical Problem

Why should a misalignment between the value we accord a fictional object and an analogous object in real life seem puzzling? Couldn't we quickly dissolve the puzzle by recognizing, as I note in Chapter 5, that we do not respond to a fiction's representation of x as we do to x (in the real world) just because our response in the fictional context is to *x as represented* by the fiction. Our access to a fictional object (state of affairs, event, person, and so on) is, in Peter Lamarque's expression, *opaque*. Such opaque readings reflect how the events, characters, and states of affairs of a narrative are constituted by the manner in which they are represented, i.e., how they are essentially connected to the descriptions used to characterize and refer to them.[7] Perhaps we adopt a deviant evaluative attitude toward some fictional x because x as represented by

---

[6] I thank Gregg Horowitz for this observation.

[7] As used here, the opacity of narrative can be understood in relation to the imputation of opacity to many ordinary non-literary contexts of predication, wherein terms that refer to the same thing cannot be substituted for each other, *salva veritate*. Such opaque contexts often arise when the contents of propositional attitudes such as belief and desire are reported: e.g., "Tom believes that Bob Dylan is an important musician" does not entail "Tom believes that Robert Allen Zimmerman is an important musician" even though Dylan and Zimmerman are the same man. However, as Lamarque (2014) explains, the preservation at issue in literary fiction concerns not the truth of a proposition but the contents of a narrative (6).

the fiction is such as to elicit that attitude (one that wouldn't be elicited by x itself). That seems right, but furnishes only a partial explanation. The difficulty is in explaining what about the fictional object as represented enables it to provoke a moral response that is contrary to what we would express in ordinary circumstances.

For in the standard case, a fictional object elicits an evaluative response from audiences because it is represented so as to conform to what would evoke that response in real life. Creators of fictions systematically garner certain responses by exploiting our tendency to predictably judge fictional people, states of affairs, behaviors, and so on, in ways that conform to how we (would) evaluate such things in the real world. Kendall Walton alludes to this general practice in saying, "I judge characters by the moral standards I myself use in real life."[8] Discrepant affects are puzzling because they seem to be glaring exceptions to that default mirroring relation between our attitudes toward fictions and real things.

In this chapter, I canvas three kinds of explanations of discrepant affects. In §8.3, I discuss and argue against a set of explanations that are based on grounds *internal* to fictions. These accounts try to identify properties or states of affairs within a fiction that justify what (only) *seem* to be atypical responses. In this approach, there turn out to be no genuine discrepant affects, despite appearances. For what elicits and justifies our seemingly non-normative responses to a fictional scenario, these accounts say, are just those factors that would elicit and justify such responses if the scenario were actual. In §8.4, I appeal to the features involved in simulating the point of view of a fictional character to argue that discrepant affects are genuine, and result from a breakdown in the quarantine that keeps our imagined evaluations distinct from our genuine ones. In §8.5, I consider an objection to that approach, which appeals to a set of explanations on grounds *external* to fictions. The objection holds that we don't really have non-normative responses to their contents, we only pretend to do so.

One caveat: I acknowledge the artificiality of the way the problem of discrepant affects is posed in this chapter. Our evaluative perspective on both real people and fictional characters (events, states of affairs) is often constituted by a complex, shifting, and internally inconsistent set of attitudes. Thus, to speak here of there being only one kind of prevailing attitude toward a

---

[8] Walton (1994, 37).

fiction is to sacrifice some real-world complexity for simplicity of philosophical exposition.

8.3. Explanations on Internal Grounds

Let us start with Nichols's own explanation of the asymmetry. Employing *Dr. Strangelove* as an illustration, he proposes that

> the set of inferences and activations we have about [an] imaginary scenario is shaped by our desires about what happens in that imaginary scenario. When it comes to the real world, we have powerful and consuming desires for the survival of human life.... When it comes to black-comedy, we typically do not have such powerful desires.... Hence, we are not compelled to draw out disturbing inferences like *billions of innocent people will die horrifically painful deaths*.[9] This explains differences in our affective responses by appeal to differences in their contributory desires. As noted in §2.3, we typically represent in the imagination only a highly selective subset of the propositions that are true in a given fictional story. Our interests and desires, prompted and directed by the text, determine what that selection is.[10] Thus Nichols can plausibly propose that the desires that are operative in our experience of a comedy such as *Dr. Strangelove* don't lead us to infer certain truths that would interfere with our amusement—such as that the bomb will cause mass death and destruction. That proposition doesn't enter into our affective mechanisms at all.[11]

The problem with adopting Nichols's proposal as a comprehensive solution is twofold. First, we need an explanation of the relevant emotions and other evaluative responses, not just the desires. It is dubious that all evaluative responses, or even just those implicated in discrepant affects, enjoin desires. Evaluations are sometimes cited as causes and rationalizations of desires. And desires are sometimes cited as causes and rationalizations of emotions

---

[9] Nichols (2006b, 472).

[10] For research on how one's desires or goals in following a fictional narrative selectively affect the activation of one's beliefs, associations, and memories, see, e.g., Noordman and Vonk (1992); Zwaan, Magliano, and Graesser (1995); van den Broek et al. (2001).

[11] "[T]he explanation for the asymmetries is *not* that the affective mechanism itself responds differently to imagining that *p* and believing that *p*. Rather, the asymmetries arise because the affective mechanism is sent quite different *input* depending on whether one imagines that *p* or believes that *p*" (Nichols, 2006b, 472).

and other evaluations, as, e.g., envy and disappointment respectively reflect the presence and frustration of particular kinds of wants. However, not all evaluations lend themselves to such a characterization. Feeling admiration for an object need not commit one to having any particular desire concerning it. This is not to deny that Nichols's explanation helps to understand a restricted domain of discrepant emotions that *do* follow from the possession of relevant desires. There, the explanation succeeds. Second, even if all cases of discrepant affect could be explained by differences in desires, we would still be left with the quandary of *why* we have such differences in desires. Such asymmetries in our desires are just as puzzling as asymmetries in our emotions and other evaluative attitudes. We might ask, for example, why we do not have desires for the preservation of human life in the imaginary scenario? Isn't that just the sort of desire that would normally be triggered by the threat of catastrophe that the movie portrays?

Whereas Nichols's account points to how fictions can preferentially provoke certain desires, a related explanation stresses the ways fictions can frame their contents so as to direct our attention, interests, and inferences.[12]

For example, facts in a scenario that are criterial for one kind of emotion can be highlighted, while those criterial for emotions that would interfere with a sought-after response can be diminished.[13] Even though we would be revolted learning of them occurring to a real person, we may be amused by the torments of a character in an action film, where certain dimensions of the fictional circumstances are made salient and others downplayed, such as the brain injuries typically caused by knock-out punches, car crashes, and the like. One such framing technique is to present the bad character for whom our sympathy is directed as the *least bad* of those around him. Perhaps we identify with a recognizably immoral character, not for his intrinsic merit, but because others in the fictional context are much worse.[14] Alternatively, that anti-hero may be presented as possessing what in pursuit of benign ends would count as virtues (say, courage and cunning); and the work's directing our attention to those qualities, over the wrong ends to which they are employed, elicits feelings of affiliation.

The problem with relying on such framing techniques as an explanation of discrepant affects is that the techniques are hardly peculiar to the generation of evaluative responses by imaginings. Framing devices such as

[12] This is discussed in Chapter 5.

[13] Carroll (1997).

[14] As noted in Carroll (2004). See also Murray Smith (1999). Smith notes: "The internal moral system of the texts makes a character attractive relative to other characters."

contextual clues, evaluative anchoring, and manipulations of saliency, affect our judgments of real states of affairs. This is vividly apparent in politicians' rhetoric, tabloid journalism, and advertising imagery, but, as the discussion of framing in Chapter 5 notes, such effects occur in ordinary decisions and evaluations as well. If such widely observed devices of framing explain discrepant affects, then such counter-normative kinds of responses to fictions would not seem anomalous, calling for an explanation. But they do seem anomalous; that is a source of their artistic interest.

That is, part of the pleasure we take in identifying with evil characters, or adopting normatively deviant points of view, is our awareness both that (1) we express in our judgments, emotions, and perhaps behavioral tendencies, certain evaluative attitudes toward the contents of a fiction, and that (2) those attitudes are wrong, unmerited, blameworthy, etc. I know one ought not to root for people like Bonnie and Clyde who, in real life, conducted a murderous crime spree, but when they are played as charming outlaws by the attractive actors Warren Beatty and Faye Dunaway in Arthur Penn's 1967 film, I do. Such self-aware "guilty pleasures" (pleasures here that depend on some conscious recognition of their norm-discordance) are not consistent with the ordinary cases of being swayed by framing effects to evaluate a given content in the frame-consistent way. In those ordinary cases, one experiences one's frame-influenced response to some content as if it were norm-consistent. No doubt framing effects typically contribute to the elicitation of the point of view prescribed by a work.[15] My concern is that an appeal to them isn't sufficient to explain the elicitation of normatively deviant points of view.

Perhaps discrepant affects result from *compensatory* pleasures. Our being on the side of the villain is, so to speak, the cost we bear for certain benefits, e.g., the frisson of feeling sympathy for the devil. This is a cost that we don't typically want to incur in relation to real-world moral monsters (even if we acknowledge that sometimes it can be advantageous to temporarily align our feelings with them). The approach here is related to Nichols's recourse to attention-focusing desires as an explanation of discrepant affects. However, Nichols focuses on the desires *internal* to a fiction: desires about this or that state of affairs that the fiction has us

---

[15] In a discussion that seeks to show common mechanisms serving rhetoric and artistic representation, Arthur Danto (1981) proposes that "it may just be one of the main offices of art less to represent the world than to represent it in such a way as to cause us to view it with a certain attitude" (167).

imagine as true. The compensatory pleasures approach by contrast focuses on desires *external* to the fiction, namely, the desire to experience whatever works of that genre typically offer when one responds with the evaluative attitudes that the work prescribes. I think this approach is partially right in that it reflects a significant difference between the kinds of justifications that support our attitudes toward a fictional scenario. If asked why I identify with a morally good character, I can appeal to such reasons as her kindness and courage. These are reasons pertaining to the object of my emotion. By contrast, if asked why I identify in counter-normative respects with a disreputable character such as Humbert Humbert, I can at best appeal to reasons as to why I want to have the experience of being on his side—it's entertaining, taboo, enlightening, and so on. These are reasons that pertain to having the experience of that mental state.[16] It would be no explanation to appeal to his intrinsic qualities: that he is "a shining example of moral leprosy," in the novel's frame-narrator's diagnosis.

However, even if such compensatory pleasures do explain why people permit themselves to enter into a state in which they find themselves on the side of people within fictions whom in reality they would despise, such pleasures do not tell us how to characterize that state itself. An analogous worry confronts explanations of discrepant affects that appeal to the particular functions in the realization of which they are evoked. Perhaps the initial attraction one feels for Satan in reading *Paradise Lost* is invited by the poem as spiritual therapy designed to expose one's fallen state.[17] However, even when we explain the existence of such an experience by appealing to the point of the work—in Milton's epic, to render us "surprised by sin"—we still need to ask how to describe the state of mind that experience enjoins.

A final answer is that discrepant affects are explained by differences in pro tanto evaluations. I'm attracted to the venal politician for his clever strategizing but not for his viciousness. The drug dealer Stringer Bell in *The Wire* invites our admiration for enrolling in business classes at the university in an effort to rise above being a street thug, but not insofar as he pursues that

---

[16] The distinction between object-given reasons—reasons that derive from features of the object of one's desire—and state-given reasons—reasons that derive from features the desire would have if one possessed it—is advanced in Parfit (2001). However, there is no consensus on how best to characterize the difference. See also Rabinowicz and Ronnow-Rasmussen (2004).

[17] See Fish (1998). Gaut (2007) describes a similar strategy in *Lolita*: readers are led to discover their moral fallibility in having fallen under the sway of Humbert.

finance-and-marketing degree to enlarge his narcotics operation. This is the predominant explanation proposed in the psychological literature on why we like evil characters.[18] Such pro tanto evaluations are likely enhanced by the serial nature of some of these examples, where a character's bad behavior in an early television episode becomes less salient in our thoughts about him than his praiseworthy behavior in the broadcast of a later one. Of course, these perspectival attitudes explain at least some part of our alignments with immoral characters, and to the extent that they are operative, there is no genuine discrepancy.

Still, it is not clear that the pro tanto approach correctly identifies the phenomenology of our approval or endorsement of anti-heroes. For, once established, our attitude to those characters isn't so perspectival. We care for at least some of these characters themselves, not just insofar as they have one trait or another. That is (as noted in §7.2 of fictional characters generally), our allegiance to an immoral character is at least sometimes akin to our relations to such things as friends, lovers, and sports teams. A pro tanto evaluation may be part of the process by which we come to care for such things, but once we care, that allegiance is not explained by the content of that evaluation. Jane may have come to love James in ways explained by his kindness and beauty but her love of him is not equivalent to, nor wholly dependent on, her love of those qualities. A person just as kind and beautiful wouldn't necessarily merit Jane's love as well.[19] So some fictional characters might be such that I like them only insofar as they exhibit certain traits, but others can gain my allegiance as fictionally represented particular individuals, not just as bundles of qualities.

Furthermore, as we saw in Chapters 5 and 6, our affective and cognitive evaluations of people are often affected by evaluatively irrelevant qualities of the person or context. Analogous findings exist in the moral domain: our moral judgment of a person can be contaminated by nonmoral reasons, such as our attitudes toward his appearance.[20] This suggests that while the contents of our pro tanto evaluations are conceptually distinct, they may not always be held distinct in practice.

[18] See, e.g., Oatley (1999).
[19] See Nehamas (2016).
[20] Wilson and Brekke (1994).

8.4. Simulation, Mirroring, Contagion

The preceding approaches aim to *rationalize* discrepant affects, that is, to demonstrate how they only appear to run counter to our typically invariant evaluative perspectives. But is there a way to preserve the phenomenon, that is, explain these discrepant fiction-directed affects without claiming that they are ultimately consistent with our real-world attitudes? In what follows I want to consider the prospects of explaining discrepant affects as stemming from a breakdown in normal activities of imaginative simulation, specifically a breach in the quarantine that keeps the content of imaginings distinct from that of real-world-directed mental states.

I will explore the proposal that simulating the deviant evaluative attitude of a fictional character, or the attitude a fiction as a whole presents toward its contents, causes one to genuinely adopt that attitude. In other words, the norm-discordant evaluative attitudes elicited by the fiction do not remain completely encapsulated within the imagined representation, but come to compete with, or temporarily supplant, our stable, real-world-oriented evaluative attitudes.[21] This phenomenon is vividly illustrated by James Harold in Ralph Fiennes's account of coming to identify with his portrayal of the cold-hearted Nazi Goeth in *Schindler's List*: "It's not a rational thing. . . . If you are playing a role, you are immersing yourself in thinking about that character— how he moves, how he thinks. In the end he becomes an extension of your own self. You like him."[22]

Simulation has been identified with many different kinds of operations, including both the self-aware cognitively mediated processes of imaginative identification, empathy, and perspective-taking, and the more automatic, non-deliberative, unconscious processes of mirroring and affective contagion. Each operation involves a distinctive causal mechanism, and theorists disagree over their comparative strengths in giving us an understanding of others' minds, and also whether the more automatic processes should be identified with simulation at all. I draw on each sort of process in what follows without making any commitment as to which ones should count as

---

[21] On the limits to imaginative quarantine in cognition, emotion, and behavior, see Gendler (2006).

[22] Harold (2000); Fiennes's interview with John Darnton (1994) is entitled "Self-Made Monster: An Actor's Creation." See also Harold (2007). Alluding to that potential permeability between what we believe and what we imagine, Gregory Currie (1995c) notes the dangers posed to ourselves and others if "imagining alien values carried with it the possibility that we may actually come to have those values" (258–59).

simulation proper. Here, at least, they are mutually reinforcing. Specifically, I will suggest that these processes can work in tandem in encouraging us to see certain fictional characters as like us and to see ourselves as like the fictional characters.

Recall from §3.2 that, in simulating a fictional character, I imagine having her beliefs and desires and occupying her situation. Then, adjusting for other relevant differences between us, I attribute to her the emotions or other states that I discover this process generates in me. I can discern what she feels from what I'm caused to feel when I imagine what it would be like, in relevant respects, to have her particular perspective on her situation. However, just as I don't confuse with my own the initial mental states that I adopt in imagining the fictional scenario, so I don't confuse with my own the emotions and other states generated in me as a consequence of that simulation. Still, by imagining of myself that I am in her circumstances, and discovering what feelings this imagining gives rise to, I can learn through non-inferential means something about her state of mind. More precisely, starting with what I take to be true in the fiction, true of the character, and so on, I can discover through simulation further facts about what the fiction represents as the character's state of mind.

A successful process of simulation is conducted entirely "offline," meaning that the simulator never loses track of which of her mental representations belong to her target and which originate with her. I may imagine having Richard III's malign ambition "to prove a villain / And hate the idle pleasures of these days," and from that predict and understand his behavior, but I don't take his motivations for my own. I may imagine what it is to see the world leached of human intimacy, as a novel by J. G. Ballard presents it, but I need not genuinely construe reality that way myself. The contents of my representation of a character's mental states are usually kept quarantined from the contents of my own. However, I want to describe some general contexts in which such quarantine is regularly breached, both in the simulation of real people and in our engagements with fictions. I will suggest that discrepant affects are explained by those breaches in the barriers that shield, specifically, our own evaluative attitudes from those of malevolent characters whose psyches we imagine inhabiting.[23]

---

[23] The following potential defects in the processes of simulation are often cited in discussions of the limits and unreliability of empathy. See Goldie (2011). Here I suggest that those liabilities serve as the conditions that make possible artistically valuable discrepant affects.

One kind of failure of imaginative quarantine occurs when we take thoughts that belong to ourselves and inappropriately attribute them to the target of our simulation.[24] The psychological literature refers to this contamination as *projection* or *egocentrism*.[25]

Some studies show that people have difficulty inhibiting the attribution of, specifically, their own beliefs to the targets of their simulation. In one experiment, people who were well informed about a corporation were asked to predict what people who were less informed would identify as the corporation's likely earnings.[26] The well-informed people knew the others were less informed, and yet they couldn't discount the proprietary knowledge that they held when they assessed the others' beliefs (the so-called curse of knowledge). A similar form of contamination occurs in *hindsight bias*, in which our knowledge of how some current state of affairs came to be causes us to overestimate the extent to which others had the capacity to predict it.[27] Finally, such contamination occurs in the common tendency to overestimate the extent to which our own mental states are discernable by others—a confusion that takes the immediacy of our access to our own thoughts as an indication of their transparency to people around us.[28]

Other forms of egocentrism occur in our attributions of evaluations to others. Exhibiting the *endowment effect*, people who own an object tend to overestimate the price people who don't have the object would pay for it, and people who don't own the object underestimate the minimum price people who have the object would accept. Each party mistakenly projects its own valuations onto the other.[29]

Specifically affective forms of contamination arise in contexts in which one is unable to discount one's own emotional response to some scenario in the process of trying to empathize with someone else's.[30] Adam Smith describes

---

[24] Alvin Goldman (2006b) notes the variety of ways in which simulation is threatened by one's own genuine states seeping into the representation of another's and contaminating the process. Individuals are more likely to project their mental states onto others whom they perceive to be similar than those whom they take to be dissimilar. Ames (2004). See also Goldstein and Cialdini (2007).

[25] Such contamination in an agent's representation of another's mind with the agent's proprietary knowledge is familiar from young children's difficulties in false-belief tests. See Birch and Bloom (2003).

[26] Camerer, Loewenstein, and Weber (1989).

[27] Fischhoff (1975).

[28] Gilovich, Savitsky, and Medvec (1998).

[29] Van Boven, Dunning, and Loewenstein (2000).

[30] When students were asked to perform a highly embarrassing task, wearing a large sandwich-board reading "Eat at Joe's," those who consented predicted that 62% of their peers would also agree to do it, whereas those who refused predicted that only 33% would agree. Participants let their own embarrassment affect their prediction of that of others. Ross, Greene, and House (1977).

this effect in explaining how, in feeling sympathy for the dead, we imagine what it would be like to be in their place, without sufficiently inhibiting our current conscious awareness of things: "the idea of those circumstances, which undoubtedly can give us no pain when we are dead, makes us miserable while we are alive."[31]

This contamination of our representation of another's emotion with our proprietary feelings is particularly salient in contexts in which the emotion is resistant to cognitive monitoring. A vegan might unreflectively attribute disgust to her meat-loving dining companion when the latter's casserole—advertised as vegetarian on the menu—is discovered to contain ground beef. Studies of affective forecasting demonstrate how often our current pleasures or pains elicited by imagining an event mislead us about the feelings actually experienced by our future selves when the event transpires.[32] For example, people systematically discount how deleterious they will judge some state of affairs according to how far in the future, or removed from one's current context, it is stipulated to take place. I think the credit-card debit I incur today is no threat to my finances, but my future self will disagree; lottery winners, contrary to what they anticipate, have been found to be not much happier a year or two after winning than they were before.[33]

Finally, consider the instances in which our beliefs and emotions about an actor contaminate what we imagine of his character. We saw in Chapter 2 how facts in a fictional scenario are often imported from facts about the real world. In some cases, we may imagine of a fictional character in a film that he is large and swarthy because the actor playing him is large and swarthy. In other cases, that an actor looks a certain way may not be a reason to imagine that character appears that way. However, often what we know of an actor, such as his bad behavior in real life, can contaminate our imagining of the characters he plays. We may misattribute our antipathy for the actor to the character whom we are supposed to admire. The reverse effect occurs as well, as audiences reportedly allow their imaginings of the qualities of a fictional character to affect the qualities they attribute to the person who represents him. Those playing the role of fictional doctors are treated as if they have medical expertise.[34]

---

[31] Smith (1759/2010, part1, sec. 1, ch. 1).
[32] Gilbert and Wilson (2007); Gilbert et al. (1998).
[33] Brickman, Coates, and Janoff-Bulman (1978).
[34] Tal-Or and Papirman (2007).

Violations of quarantine going in the other direction, where certain target states of our simulation become salient in our own behavioral, cognitive, and affective responses, have already been noted in connection with the source-monitoring errors discussed in §2.1. There we saw how claims made by a character in a fictional story can affect readers' beliefs in direct proportion to how trustworthy the story represents the fictional character as being.[35] In other demonstrations, readers formed beliefs endorsing assertions made in fictional texts even when those assertions were identified to the readers, prior to their exposure to the text, as false.[36] That influence persisted even when readers were reminded that the beliefs they formed in reading the text were based on a fictional story.[37]

The effects of imaginative processes on our real-world attitudes has also been regularly demonstrated in research on video-game players' inter- and post-game emotions, evaluations, and behaviors (although the degree and longevity of such effects are highly disputed).[38] The particular mechanism through which such games have such effects is obscure. A plausible explanation is that players experience a temporarily diminished capacity to separate their real-world attitudes from those the game prescribes for their adopted roles.

Of course, even if that explanation is true, it is perilous to generalize from the effects of video games on players to analogous effects on audiences of fictions of other sorts. Their interactive nature, the possibility of rebooting to achieve a different outcome, and a player's or avatar's capacity to be continually restored to life, may make video games unrepresentative among fictions in their effects on evaluative attitudes. Still, note how the widely assumed possibility of habituation and desensitization to the violence depicted in that and other forms of media could obtain, if they obtain, only if there were some

---

[35] Appel and Mara (2013).

[36] Eslick, Fazio, and Marsh (2011); Marsh and Fazio (2006).

[37] Green et al. (2006).

[38] A meta-analysis by Paik and Comstock (1994) of 217 studies between 1957 and 1990 found that exposure to media violence had a short-term, moderate-to-large effect on actual physical violence. A meta-analysis conducted by Anderson and Bushman (2001) of 42 studies involving approximately 5,000 individuals found a statistically significant, albeit small-to-moderate, relationship between watching violent media and aggressive behavior later in life; see also Anderson and Bushman (2002). A review by Browne and Hamilton-Giachritsis (2005) in *The Lancet* of studies on media violence held that, cumulatively, the research supports the position that exposure to media violence, especially among younger children, leads to aggressive tendencies, desensitization toward violence, and lack of sympathy for its victims. Although these studies demonstrate an influence on post-game hostile attitudes, the effects were seen to diminish rapidly. See Barlett et al. (2009). The extent to which the correlation demonstrated in these studies indicates a causal relation is, of course, a significant concern. See Ferguson et al. (2014).

elision between audiences' attitudes toward imagined violence and their attitudes toward its actual occurrence. After all, the worry is not that people will become inured to *fictional* depictions of violence, but that they will somehow become insensate, in virtue of those depictions, to the real thing.

In any case, there appear to be socially positive effects of simulation that are consistent with the undesirable results already mentioned. These are found in experiments designed to determine whether imagining being in the shoes of another—e.g., by writing a first-person narrative from a target's perspective—can attenuate biases that permeate intergroup encounters.[39] These studies find a reduction at least immediately after the simulation in the previously measured bigoted attitudes among participants, even in cases where those attitudes were only implicit. Compared to a control, participants who simulated the perspective of a person from an out-group subsequently exhibited more favorable implicit and explicit evaluations of the out-group; reduced their reliance on the typical processes by which people rationalize—against contrary evidence—maintaining stereotypes of others; and behaved in encounters with confederates in the experiment who belonged to the out-group in ways that expressed a more positive evaluation.[40] In those respects, simulation appears to have led participants to see members of the out-group as more like themselves, and this resulted in more positive associations and greater feelings of affiliation.[41]

Less cognitively mediated effects on our evaluative and affective attitudes can be found in various forms of automatic mimicry, including processes of mirroring and affective contagion, as described in §3.2.[42] Unlike standard processes of mind-reading, these connections to others emerge unintentionally, and, at least initially, without awareness of their occurrence. However, as noted in Chapter 5, there is substantial evidence that such mimicry can cause one to experience the correlative affective state of one's target, even if one is unaware of that state's grounds.[43] Mirroring may thereby support and sustain the higher-order and self-aware process of simulation through making certain attitudes caused by a target of simulation more accessible to

---

[39] Todd and Galinsky (2014).
[40] Todd and Galinsky (2014).
[41] Davis et al. (1996).
[42] Hatfield, Cacioppo, and Rapson (1992).
[43] E.g., when individuals unwittingly adopt a facial configuration that matches one generally associated with a given emotion, they are more likely to report or express experiencing that emotion. Adelmann and Zajonc (1989); Levenson, Ekman, and Friesen (1990).

a simulator.[44] As I try to discover how you feel through imagining being in your shoes, I am likely to be primed to attribute to you the emotion caused in me by my matching your posture, movement, facial expression, vocalization, and so on. Indeed, some research on explanatory connections between empathy and behavioral mimicry suggests that there is a direct relation between the strength of people's scores on tests measuring the capacity for taking the perspective of another and the degree of their tendency to engage in behavioral mimicry of others.[45]

Furthermore, the focus on another's behaviors or attitudes involved in such mimicry may encourage a diminution in one's awareness of one's self. Kaufman and Libby found such diminution to be a precondition of a kind of extreme empathy that they call *experience-taking*, which disposes one to undergo changes in one's judgments, attitudes, and behaviors toward an alignment with those of the target of one's empathy. This relation shapes our reading of fictional narratives, Kaufman and Libby note, in that the less one is made aware of one's own identity as one follows a narrative, the more likely one is to adopt the affective and evaluative attitudes of the story's protagonist.[46]

Some theories of behavioral and affective mirroring suggest that it reflects a fundamental human disposition to engage in pretense and imitation, often unawares. Subjects who interact with an experimenter who rubs his face will tend to rub their own faces, even when they are unconscious of having observed the behavior.[47] Children engage in imitation continually, and some research suggests that the main difference in this respect between us and them is that they lack the capacity for inhibition that we've developed.[48] Studies of people with brain lesions support this idea that our tendency to imitate others is a default mode of behavior—a disposition of any social species—and will occur unless inhibited by social context or cognitive control.[49] For example, patients who have lesions in the frontal brain areas that usually enable inhibitory behavior tend to automatically copy an experimenter's actions even when they are odd or contrary to social norms, such as putting on two pairs of eyeglasses.[50] Also, people are able to perform imitative tasks

---

[44] See Goldman's (2011) account of how both higher simulative and lower mirroring processes work in tandem in a person's attempt to understand and predict the behavior of another.

[45] Chartrand and Bargh (1999, Study 3).

[46] Kaufman and Libby (2012, 5–6); Goldstein and Cialdini (2007).

[47] Chartrand and Bargh (1999).

[48] See Carlson, Moses, and Breton (2002); Moses (2001).

[49] Dijksterhuis (2005); Barkley (2001); Kinsbourne (2005).

[50] Lhermitte, Pillon, and Serdaru (1986).

more quickly than non-imitative tasks, and their gestures are faster when they've been primed by similar gestures even if the priming gestures bear no relevant relation to the task.[51] Although the concept of mirroring refers to many kinds of mimicry (affective, cognitive, behavioral), a much-discussed but still preliminary neurological explanation of our imitative tendencies appeals to the operation, specifically, of mirror neurons in the human brain, the activation of which occurs along with both an individual's own performance of intentional actions and the observation of those actions when performed by others.[52]

Finally, studies of priming effects, based both on imagined representations and on real experience, suggest that being exposed to a concept or prototypical embodiment of some trait can influence one to exhibit that trait in one's behavior and attitudes (assuming, of course, that one independently has the capacity to do so).[53] For example, compared to controls exposed to neutral words, study subjects who were exposed to words associated with aggression subsequently judged other people to be more hostile,[54] were faster to identity a weapon among other objects,[55] behaved in a more aggressive manner themselves,[56] and appeared more motivated to find occasions to engage in aggressive actions.[57]

No doubt, those arational and automatic kinds of imitation are quite different from the cognitively mediated forms of identification one adopts in relation to fictional characters. However, that dissimilarity should not count against the low-level processes supporting the higher modes of imaginative identification. As we saw in the remarks made by Ralph Fiennes, adopting the speech and deportment of another can affect one's own attitudes in ways that also seem arational and outside of cognitive control.[58] Consider the common proposal in analyses of literary narration that an internal perspective on a protagonist's mind, supplied either through a first-person

---

[51] Prinz (2005); Hurley (2008).

[52] Decety and Chaminade (2005); Obhi and Hogeveen (2010). The role of mirror neurons in imitative identification with others is contested. For criticisms, see Heyes (2010). On problems in the interpretation of the original studies of similar mirror neuron systems in macaques, see Hickok (2009).

[53] See Goldstein and Cialdini (2007). For recent skepticism about the strength of such priming effects, particularly with respect to behavior, see Shanks (2013).

[54] Higgins, Rholes, and Jones (1977).

[55] Meyer and Schvaneveldt (1971).

[56] Carver et al. (1983).

[57] Todorov and Bargh (2002). The mechanisms here may be varied, including the prime making the aggressive trait more accessible in a person, activating behavioral scripts, and triggering associations with other ideas.

[58] See Currie (2010a, 100–106).

narration or third-person free indirect discourse, is especially conducive to establishing a reader's identification with the character. Part of that identification might be conscious and deliberate as we discover and assess the character's reasons for her attitudes and behavior. However, another part may instantiate a more automatic form of mimicry, as we adjust our own evaluative attitudes, objects of attention, and desires, to match the character's sensibility through which the contents of the fiction are presented. Wayne Booth notes in this respect how Jane Austen promotes our affiliation with Emma despite her conduct: "By showing most of the story through Emma's eyes, the author insures that we will travel with Emma rather than stand against her."[59] I assume here that seeing things through Emma's eyes does not mean only discovering her reasons for acting as she does. Recall, also, the affective misattribution effects in which a person takes a given mood or emotion as an indication of the value of some wholly independent object.[60] Perhaps the pleasure we take in the formal or aesthetic dimensions of the representation of an anti-hero causes us, without providing relevant reasons, to evaluate the character's attitudes and motivations more favorably.

Most cross-contaminations between imaginings and truth-apt representations are readily corrected in experience. If through deep absorption in a story I come to believe that I have Sherlock Holmes's powers of observation, my frustrating attempts to exercise that skill in the real world will typically set me right. However, the obdurate facts of the real world are much less likely to reveal to me that I've conflated imagining *valuing* or *desiring* some object with really valuing or desiring it. This, I suggest, is why it is plausible to describe cases of discrepant affect as consisting in a difference between our genuine evaluative attitudes during and sometimes subsequent to our absorption in a fiction, and those evaluative attitudes we tend to exhibit independent of that encounter. In imagining that we've arrived at some strange island in a film, we never come to believe that we've left the theater, but in imagining that some evil character's ends are as desirable as he construes them, we may come to genuinely desire those ends in the fiction ourselves. In a letter to Hans von Bulow, Wagner grandly extols works of art for having just this consequence, "communicating the strongest and

---

[59] Booth (2010, 245). See also Miall (2000, 43). Austen performs the contrasting maneuver with other characters who might be more sympathetic than Emma, by withholding from a reader their interior perspectives.

[60] For a discussion of studies showing people who "misread" their independently caused moods as indicating relevant information about the merits of a given object, see Carruthers (2011, 136–37).

most unusual feelings to a listener in a such a way that . . . he . . . involuntarily assimilates even what is most alien to his nature."[61] After a performance of Wagner in 1917, the conductor Otto Klemperer, perhaps succumbing, said to his sister, "when I like Wagner, I do not like myself."[62]

8.5. Explanations on External Grounds

A natural objection to my proposal might start with the observation, already noted, that while a confusion between imagining and belief will often be readily exposed in one's experience, this is not true of a confusion between imagining oneself holding some deviant evaluative attitude and really embracing it. If this is so, then what evidence demonstrates that discrepant evaluative attitudes are genuinely formed among one's real attitudes, not merely entertained in one's imagination? If, that is, my behavior doesn't reveal that I've taken on some alien evaluative perspective as my own, it isn't clear on what evidential basis a discrepant attitude can be attributed to me.[63]

In other words, for some fictional state of affairs S, how do we determine which of the following situations, (1) or (2), I am in?

(1) I imagine that {I have the fictional character's beliefs, desires, moral perspectives, and so on}. And, in virtue of that, I evaluatively respond to S consistent with those attitudes.

(2) I imagine that {I have the fictional character's beliefs, desires, moral perspectives, and so on, and, in virtue of that, I evaluatively respond to S consistent with those attitudes}.

In (1) my evaluative attitude is external to what I imagine; it is one I genuinely have about what I imagine. In (2) my attitude lies within the scope of the imagining; it is attributable only to the target of the simulation. I only imagine having that evaluative attitude, just as I only imagine having the beliefs

---

[61] From a letter to Hans von Bulow, quoted in Edwards (2008, 52).

[62] Heyworth (1996, 125).

[63] Thus, discussions of simulative and empathetic processes are sometimes too hasty in proposing that they result in genuine changes in one's evaluative attitudes, e.g., that readers of a narrative "let go of key components of their own identity—such as their beliefs, memories, personality traits, and in-group affiliations—and instead assume the identity of a protagonist, accepting the character's decisions, outcomes, and reactions as their own" Kaufman and Libby (2012, 2). See also Oatley (1999). Perhaps such readers only imagine of themselves that they have assumed those dimensions of the protagonist's perspective as their own.

and desires of the character that serve as inputs to my affective and evaluative mechanisms.[64] If there isn't some way of demonstrating that what are identified as discrepant affects have the structure of (1), then we have reason to be skeptical of there being any genuine cases of discrepancy. For it's clear that there's nothing puzzling about my pretending to desire, as I perform the role of Iago, the destruction of Othello, or merely imagining of myself that I take pleasure, as an evil sorcerer, in turning people into toads. In those cases, our attitudes are part of the pretense—we only imagine of ourselves that we have such feelings.

For discrepant affects to be more than merely apparent, we need to be confident that such evaluative attitudes sometimes exist outside the operator "it is imagined that," but are directed at what is within its scope. Only then can the evaluations that we seem to evince in response to the contents of a fiction be genuinely contrary to those that we are disposed to express and endorse in our responses to veridical representations of the world.

My proposal is tentative, for there is comparatively little behavioral evidence that distinguishes between when evaluative responses to a fiction are genuine and when they instantiate merely "playing along" with the fiction in adopting the evaluation it prescribes.[65] We've seen some evidence of behavioral consequences from the simulation of norm-discrepant attitudes in the research on violent video games and the studies of empathy extended to members of out-groups. However, shifts in our evaluative attitudes in engaging with a fictional character wouldn't typically call for commensurate shifts in behaviors in which those attitudes could be expressed. Little of one's behavior in, e.g., following Raskolnikov's murder of the pawnbroker could show whether one merely pretends to accept, or actually comes to sanction, his lack of remorse. Of course, what counts as evidence here can be debated. Perhaps we should recognize, e.g., sincere assertions of one's attitudes toward deviant characters and sincere attempts to rationalize their bad behaviors as among the behavioral outcomes of norm-discrepant attitudes.

---

[64] This discussion parallels that in Chapter 3 of the debate between realists and irrealists over whether emotions generated by fictions are "genuine," or at least of the same explanatory kind as everyday reality-directed emotions. Note that one's position on fiction-directed emotions may not determine one's view of fiction-directed evaluations, despite the close connection between the two kinds of attitudes.

[65] Contrast that with the empathetic identifications with others that are prescribed under experimental conditions, for which there is substantial empirical evidence of short- and medium-term behavioral and attitudinal effects. See Todd and Galinsky (2014); Paluck and Green (2009).

I suggest that we look at how audiences respond to the contents of a fiction once their identification with a morally deviant fictional character has been established. Subsequent to my identifying with a protagonist (on whatever grounds) I do not continually ask myself, as events in the fiction unfold, what emotions, desires, or evaluations are called for where those events touch on the fictional character. I just respond with the evaluative perspective that reflects the furtherance of the character's own interests or desires. The character's evaluative outlook forms the framework through which I assess the events that concern him. (An analogous account would apply where the object of our identification is the work's point of view on the states of affairs it represents.)[66]

For example, when Tony Soprano achieves his aims, I feel satisfaction; when Humbert Humbert finds his path clear after Lolita's mother is dispatched by a truck, I feel something like relief; when I learn of the police detective zeroing in on Hannibal Lector, I want him to find the means to escape; I'm frustrated when my poor skills prevent me from performing the morally objectionable video-game maneuvers for which points are awarded. These responses correspond to evaluations and emotions that the respective works are designed to provoke. However, unlike the way our initial alignment with the morally deviant character or perspective must be generated, these responses subsequent to that alignment don't need to be continually motivated by the fiction. They just follow from the general evaluative outlook that we take on in our identification with the character's or work's perspective.

If we were merely pretending to have adopted that evaluative perspective, we would need to consciously decide how, consistent with the perspective, one should feel about this or that event as it occurs. Yet that isn't part of the phenomenology of such engagements. Rather, we tend to respond to such events in a way parallel to how we respond to events in our own life, *from* our evaluative perspective, where we do not continually ask how, given our evaluative dispositions, we should feel.[67] One doesn't *choose* to imagine that the protagonist's sociopathic behavior in the novel merits one's endorsement; rather, one discovers in one's imaginative experience that one has judged the behavior so. I allow that the phenomenology of this engagement is only a defeasible reason in favor of our evaluative states being genuine; as we saw

---

[66] See Currie (2010a, 106–7).

[67] Of course, difficult moral decisions might require such self-conscious consideration of what one's evaluative disposition requires.

in §3.3, irrealists argue that the apparent genuineness of the emotions we feel for fictions is compatible with their being internal to a pretense. We may be mistaken, that is, in attributing a genuine evaluative attitude to ourselves when, in fact, we've only imagined having that attitude.

A second objection to this approach might be that the workings of simulation are sufficient to explain our discrepant evaluative attitudes; and thus the appeal to a failure of quarantine is unnecessary. One might begin by observing (according to the realist about fiction-directed emotions) that we can feel fear through imagining, of what we see on screen, that we are pursued by an axe-murderer; or sadness in imagining, of some description in a novel, that it represents a real child's loss of a parent. In such emotional elicitations, we do not need to posit any confusion between the contents of our imagination and truth-apt states such as belief and perception. Why, the objection asks, do we need to posit some breakdown in the barrier separating pretend from truth-apt evaluative attitudes in the case of discrepant affects? It seems that deviant evaluative responses can, like emotions, arise just from the imagination, specifically, just from *imagining* having the immoral character's beliefs and desires.

The problem with this objection stems from an asymmetry between ordinary emotions or evaluations and those that are discrepant. Our feeling an emotion for some fictional state of affairs is typically explained by reasons in the fiction that justify the emotion—reasons that speak to the emotion's criterial qualities (as in §3.1). Sadness over a fictional event arises because the event counts (fictionally) as a significant loss. And when such emotions are not elicited by a recognition of what merits such an emotion, as in the arationally generated instances discussed in Chapter 5, such reasons are projected into the fiction. If we are caused to feel fear solely because of the eerie soundtrack playing while we watch a film, we impute to the fictional state of affairs some fact that would justify the fear—e.g., some impending danger.

However, by contrast with both those kinds of cases, discrepant affects do not result from facts that are recognized in or projected into the fictional scenario that would justify the deviant attitude. In discovering that we feel an affiliation with Humbert Humbert, we don't impute to him the property, e.g., of (secretly) being a decent person who despite appearances does no harm. It is *never* true in the fiction that Nabokov's protagonist secretly merits our allegiance. Nonetheless, we give it to him. Indeed, if we recognized such a fact rationalizing our putatively deviant attitude as holding within the fiction, then the attitude wouldn't be deviant. It would be comparable to discovering through our affiliation with the Beast the goodness that Beauty should have recognized all along.[68]

Let me close with a final consideration in favor of seeing discrepant affects as explained by a quarantine breakdown: one's partial awareness of the discrepancy of one's responses often enters into the pleasure they offer (the "guilty pleasure" referred to in §8.3). Discrepant affects are often associated with feeling gratification over something about which one believes one should feel a degree of embarrassment or regret, e.g., on grounds of taste or morality.[69] Without such awareness of its discrepant nature, adopting a non-normative evaluative perspective could not, *as such*, be a source of enjoyment. One would take one's response as consistent with what one would have— and what would be merited—were the fictional events to actually occur. It is sometimes part of properly comprehending a work, and experiencing what makes it artistically valuable, that we respond to its fictional states of affairs in ways contrary to how we would, should, and would want to respond to them if we knew that they were actual. Indeed, in response to the worry that the genuineness of such attitudes is undermined insofar as they don't survive very long post-engagement with the work of fiction, one might observe that, deprived of the engagement-supported pleasure of holding such attitudes, it is unremarkable they would dissipate or be replaced with non-discrepant ones. [70]

I should clarify that I have not argued that *any* evaluative or emotional response to the contents of fictions must stem from a breakdown in quarantine. I've addressed the question in the form of "How can you like Tony Soprano, he's a sociopath?" not "How can you like Tony Soprano, he's a fictional character?" For typically, from the internal perspective, the grounds

---

[68] See Norton et al. (2003) for a study of how observing an individual with whom one aligns oneself, albeit one engaging in behaviors contrary to one's evaluative attitudes, can motivate one to unconsciously change one's own attitude in order to alleviate one's experience of dissonance and unease.

[69] This is especially common in the experience of certain kinds of offensive jokes, but I suggest that the dynamic holds for fictions in general.

[70] In a discussion of cases that instantiate discrepant affects, Murray Smith (1995) distinguishes between instances of what he calls "alignment" with a character, wherein we follow a character, seeing things from his point of view, and "allegiance," wherein we adopt, consciously or not, the evaluative stances of the character and endorse them. Smith rightly denies that alignment always leads to allegiance. In response, James Harold (2005) objects that Smith perhaps paints a too optimistic picture of the top-down control we have over our more automatically elicited feelings. That debate seeks to establish whether discrepant responses have implications for our moral dispositions. My bar is lower: I've tried only to explain how genuinely discrepant affects are possible. I leave open the question of whether these have any long-term effects on one's evaluative dispositions.

a fiction offers for the attitudes it prescribes toward its contents would also serve as grounds for those attitudes if the fiction were true.[71] Grief felt over the death of Cordelia is justified for the same reasons that grief felt over the death of an analogous person in real life would be. By contrast, the genuinely discrepant attitudes that we adopt toward fictional states of affairs are not justified according to norms of evaluation that apply to such attitudes in real life. Instead, breaches of quarantine lead us to adopt the norms to which the fiction or fictional characters subscribe. Milton's Satan wills "Evil be thou my Good." While absorbed in that narrative, it becomes our good as well.[72]

---

[71] In this I differ from theorists who appeal to a breakdown in simulation as a resolution of the paradox of fiction, i.e., how it is possible for us to have emotional responses to what we believe to be only imagined. Gordon (1995) for example, argues that imaginative quarantine only imperfectly keeps emotion-recognition from producing affective contagion. According to his simulationist theory, off-line representations of others' emotions can "switch" online.

[72] I am grateful to Susan Feagin for substantial comments on an earlier version of this chapter's argument.

9

Artistic Functions

What pleases these lovers of toys is not so much the utility, as the aptness of the machines which are fitted to promote it.

—Adam Smith (1759, Sec. IV)

In earlier chapters, I proposed that we can explain the existence of inconsistent affective norms across fictions and real life by appeal to differences in the functions of our engagements with those domains. Here I argue for that implicit functional dimension of artistic practices. I also show how a functional account of artistic evaluation provides an answer to the question of when, if ever, the moral and artistic value of a work of art are internally related.

Each of the four preceding chapters concluded with an explanation of why in our affective, cognitive, conative, and evaluative engagements with fictions, the norms governing our attitudes are not invariant across fictional (or imagined) and real contexts. My explanation was that the kinds of reasons that we countenance as justifying our emotions, imaginings, and desires depend on the *functions* of the practices in which those mental representations are elicited.

Thus, sometimes our imaginative activity has an epistemic function, where we deploy our imaginative capacities to discover what is true. One finds this in such practices as thought experiments, planning for the future, and assessing the past. In such cases, the ends of the activity impose a norm on our affective responses that they track what our responses would be if the content of the imagining were true. Here the purpose of the activity is less well realized if this and other relevant epistemic norms are not respected. Some criticism of the utility of thought experiments accordingly notes the ways in which the responses they invoke often unwittingly violate the appropriate truth-conducive norms by which they should be constrained.[1]

---

[1] For criticisms along these lines see, e.g., Dancy (1985); Thagard (2014).

Apt Imaginings. Jonathan Gilmore, Oxford University Press (2020). © Oxford University Press.
DOI: 10.1093/oso/9780190096342.001.0001

Other times, our imaginative activity has functions that are not associated with the pursuit of truth, but other ends. In the case of art and play, these ends include entertainment, absorption, vicarious experience, distraction, and so on. Here the norms that govern and guide one's responses are not exclusively truth-apt. It matters, in part, whether our affective responses fit their objects-as-presented within the fiction or imagining; that fit may require abiding by norms different from those governing the justification of affective responses to the real world.

But this explanation faces a categorical objection, alluded to in Chapter 1, that works of art, and by extension our engagements with them, don't have functions. That claim, appearing under various guises associated with the idea of artistic autonomy, treats any functions attributed to a work of art as irrelevant to our experience of it qua art. The worry this raises for my account is that if the function of a work of art is not essential to its identity—or our experience of it—as art, then appealing to such functions in an explanation of our responses will miss the mark. In what follows I offer an account of the nature of such functions that should dissolve that objection. I then discuss how that account allows us to address, in a limited fashion, when moral considerations are relevant to the evaluation of a work of art and the affective responses it may prescribe. Moral considerations were largely eschewed in my earlier account of the aptness of our attitudes toward fictions. I reintroduce them here.

Before going further, I want to note that this chapter departs from the others in its focus on the ontology and evaluation of works of art. Its relevance to the arguments offered so far is that it supplies a fleshed-out account of what it is for the function of a work to determine, in part, the relevant attitudes that are appropriate to it. However, my appeal to functions in this chapter is detachable from my arguments for discontinuity. That is, the truth of discontinuity does not depend on the adequacy of the functional explanation I've alluded to earlier and address more fully here.

I also hasten to add that appeal here to the functions of our mental attitudes should not be conflated with the theory of *analytic functionalism* in which different kinds of mental representations are type-identified, or individuated, via the patterns of interactions they exhibit with other components of one's mind and behavior. One can be a functionalist about the distinctions among mental states without accepting that there can be contrary functions (i.e., purposes) realized by fear when based on the content of a belief and fear when elicited by the same content of an imagining.

Finally, I recognize that it's artificial to speak of a univocal function of any imaginative activity; a richly developed practice that exploits our imaginative capacities will likely operate with several functions—perhaps sometimes with mutually incompatible realizations. We may imaginatively represent the future to, inter alia, make decisions about what course of action to take based on how visualizing alternative situations makes us feel; take pleasure in anticipation; or while away the time. Likewise, our engagements with fictions might aim to realize certain aesthetic forms of value, but they can also have epistemic ends—we choose to read this novel rather than that because of what it will tell us about human nature, the distant past, and so on. And, of course, one function may be realized by way of satisfying another. My point is only that the norms of aptness, fittingness, or rationality that govern our responses in our imaginative activities depend on the functions of those activities, however multifarious, culturally contextual, and potentially revisable those functions may be.

Let me now begin to specify what kind of function is at play in determining such norms.

One very general approach would be to say that such functions are determined just by the reasons people have for engaging with imaginative representations. One might read a nineteenth-century realist novel with the narrow aim of determining how some actual technology (e.g., a laundry mangle) was employed in the period in which the book was written. There, of all the propositions the novel elicits one to imagine, one would want to adopt as beliefs only those propositions that are true. By contrast, one might engage with a scientific text solely for entertainment, as a Creationist might perversely read *On the Origin of Species* as a masterful exercise of science fiction. Analogously, one might construct counterfactual stories to test our intuitions about our concepts and values, or do so solely for the sake of wonder, where one does not care that one's responses track those that one would have if the events of the story actually occurred. Thought experiments about brains in vats and malfunctioning transporters are the stuff both of philosophy seminars and of fantasy fictions. To stay with works of art, there is in principle no constraint on the ends for which a work can be harnessed, however ineffectively it might do the job. As Nelson Goodman noted (borrowing one of Duchamp's injunctions), a Rembrandt can be used as an ironing board.

However, I want to identify one kind of function that should be distinguished from all those that are defined by the uses to which people can put works of art. This is the function that is *constitutive* of the work: the function that a work is designed to fulfill as the particular work of art that it is. Thus, for example, it is a constitutive function of many detective stories to elicit feelings of suspense, curiosity, an attitude of problem-solving, and surprise. A detective story may be read, e.g., to learn the language in which it is written or discover the popular poisons of the era it depicts. But those functions would be independent of its constitutive function.

That the functions for which we employ works of art are not constrained by their constitutive functions is true of artifacts generally. "Sad-irons" serve as doorstops and book ends, presumably more effectively than they once performed their functions of pressing clothes. However, it is highly plausible that the value of works of art qua art is typically best realized if our ends in engaging with them are guided by the artistic functions with which they are designed. By "guided" I do not mean *determined*. Rather, I appeal to the uncontroversial assumption that works of art that merit our attention qua art typically offer greater artistic value when our engagement with them is shaped by their intrinsic features, including what they are designed to do. Works of art with little artistic value may be sometimes better experienced ironically, or used in the service of experiences that depart from what they were designed to bring about. And some practices of criticism encourage audiences to interpret works "against the grain," as Roland Barthes does with Balzac's *Sarrasine* in *S/Z*. However, those alternative practices make sense only against a background practice in which our ends in engaging with a work of art are typically realized in being guided by the work's ends. Responding to an elegy as an elegy, a horror film as a horror film, means engaging with such works, insofar as their features allow, to some substantial degree with an eye toward the functions they embody. Thus, in what follows I focus on the functions we have in engaging with a work where those functions (ends, aims, purposes) are essential to the works—they would not be those works without those functions.

9.1. Functional Theories of Art

Any attribution of functions to art must contend with the position held by many philosophers of art that, although artifacts typically have functions, works of art belong to a special class of artifacts that have no function. Certainly, one prominent strain in Romantic and modernist thinking is that art has no function qua art, that it is "autonomous," to be experienced as "purposeful without purpose," or "set free."[2] And recent Anglo-American philosophy has significant defenders of the view that art has no essential purpose or function.[3] Stated without qualification, that position is implausible given that at least some artifacts clearly (1) do have functions, and (2) are paradigmatically works of art (e.g., statues to commemorate persons or events; paintings designed to decorate rooms; music written for dances; satires designed to mock public figures; fables written to convey moral platitudes; stained glass designed to instruct the illiterate). According to a more refined proposal, works of art do not have such functions qua works of art. This claim can most plausibly be construed in an evaluative sense: the satisfaction of a function is relevant to the evaluation of an ordinary functional object, such as a tool, but not to the evaluation of a work of art. Let me address some reasons why theorists have held this view.

One motivation for denying the relevance of functions to the evaluation of art is that, if it were correct to say that we evaluate a work of art in light of the satisfaction of a function, this would counterintuitively suggest that it is only whatever good is instrumentally furnished by the satisfaction of the function that we care about, not the work of art.[4]

The value of an ordinary functional artifact may be typically exhausted by its value in satisfying its function. If two corkscrews remove a cork equally well (i.e., cleanly, easily, reliably, etc.), they are equally good as corkscrews. An ordinary artifact, to the extent that it is evaluated as an instance of a functionally defined kind, is typically judged for its success in satisfying the ends characteristic of that kind, not for the material or mechanism by which those ends are satisfied.

However, when we evaluate a work of art in light of its achievement of its ends, that evaluation is typically not based on merely the discharging of those ends, without regard to how that happens to occur. Our interest is rather in the ends *as realized* by the means: that is, how the material or structural medium of the work discharges a function. This is not always the case; our concern, for example, for whether a lullaby is good instance of its kind might address only whether it helps a child to sleep. However, usually our evaluation of a work of art addresses what the work achieves *and* the manner in

---

[2] See, for example, Hegel's remarks in the *Lecture on Aesthetics* devoted to art after its end.

[3] See, e.g., Beardsley (1981); Lamarque (2010).

[4] Malcolm Budd (1995) writes, "If music is of value as a means to an independently specifiable end . . . , then it must be possible that there should be other, and perhaps even better, means for achieving what music aims at; so that music could be dispensed with and replaced" (29).

which that achievement is realized. One takes pleasure in the reflection on the past prompted by an elegy, but that pleasure lies not only in the reflection but in how the particular poetic construction elicits it. Two films might produce feelings of fear or dread in audiences, and yet one be judged a greater work for causing that response in a more subtle manner. Our appreciation of a work is in part an appreciation of its ends in light of the means by, or in which, they are achieved, not just of its ends.

Some theorists would say this means-end evaluation of works of art demonstrates that what we really care about are the means by which a work of art is designed to achieve its ends, not that the ends are realized. Our identifying the function of a work might help expose what its artistically relevant properties are, but we evaluate those properties, not the end to which they contribute. For example, we may recognize an ancient sculpture of Apollo as a great work of art for its sculptural qualities, even if we place no value on its function, to have been discharged through those qualities, of honoring the god. But this sort of example shows only that if we do not find an end of a work of art valuable, we may still find its means valuable for reasons (say, aesthetic reasons) that are independent of their being the means to that end. One can marvel at the cinematic techniques of D. W. Griffith's influential *The Birth of a Nation* and still condemn the film's point to which those ends are marshaled of glorifying the KKK. Indeed, we can assign distinct evaluations to a work of art's successfully realized function; to the means by which that function is realized; and to the function-as-realized-by those means.

A proponent of the nonfunctional view could respond that while art may be properly evaluated with reference to the satisfaction of a function, there is a (more central) source of artistic value that does not correspond to a function. That value is typically identified as aesthetic value: the intrinsic value of one's experience of a work of art's aesthetic properties. The view that art ought to be evaluated on *exclusively* aesthetic grounds finds few contemporary defenders (except, indirectly, among those who equate aesthetic value with whatever value art has as art). However, we can see that *even if* it were true that the proper evaluation of works of art is only, or primarily, for the aesthetic value they furnish, such aesthetic criticism could not ignore all points, purposes, or functions of art. For it can be an aesthetic property of a musical work that it expresses a certain emotion; of a minimalist work that it provokes a certain kind of awareness of one's body or stance; of a joke that it makes one laugh. To evaluate these works for such aesthetic features is to attend to the points, purposes, or functions that they are created and presented to achieve.[5]

Some philosophers suggest that furnishing such aesthetic value is not just a function of art but an *essential* function of art. The idea here would be that the sculpture of Apollo, in virtue of being a work of art, has the essential function of furnishing aesthetic value, whatever other—say, religious—functions it might have. It might appear that such an account is a nonstarter in light of the obvious objection that there are many works of art that furnish no aesthetic value. However, that objection on the basis of counterexamples would not, in itself, be decisive. For an artifact may have a function yet be unable to satisfy that function. A flat tire is still a tire. So, just because something doesn't satisfy a function that is attributed to it does not entail that that function is wrongly attributed.

It should be noted that if works of art *always* satisfy a function simply in virtue of being works of art then reference to that function cannot explain why one work of art is a good—or better—instance of its kind. If, say, art as a kind has the putative function of enhancing community ties, as in some anthropological accounts, or grounding class distinctions, as in some sociologists' views, then successfully discharging those functions, because a property of all art, does not enter into determining the value of any particular instance of art qua art.[6]

In any case, the problem in treating an aesthetic function as an essential feature of all art concerns the causal and historical commitments such functional attributions must make. Insofar as the function of any given work of art is supplied by the intentions from which it was created, the proponent of an aesthetic function of art must hold that all works of art are created from intentions that refer to some aesthetic end. However, that would not be consistent with any plausible empirical account of the history of art. The point is not that many works of art have been created that do not aim, specifically, at beauty, for aiming at ugliness is, indeed, trying to achieve an aesthetic effect. Rather, many works of art are not created in light of aesthetic concerns at all. Many medieval works of art, conceptual works, and works of other sorts are centrally organized around cognitive, spiritual, and other non-aesthetic

---

[5] Stephen Davies (2006) argues further that the aesthetic evaluation of a functional object (or work of art with a function) that has non-incidental aesthetic properties *always* takes into account the contribution of such aesthetic properties to the satisfaction of its function.

[6] See, e.g., Bourdieu (1984) for the sociological claim; and Gell (1998) for the anthropological perspective.

ends. Appropriation art, for example, is in many cases designed to have the appearance, but not the aesthetic properties, of the artwork that it copies (the aesthetic properties of the original are only referred to, not possessed, by the work of appropriation).

My assumption in what follows is that there is no answer to what the function of art qua art is other than those found in the empirical study of what functions art has had or has. Those functions fall into a variety of kinds and, presumably, works of art will be created with new functions as yet unidentified.[7]

However, this assumption raises a problem in the very possibility of evaluating works of art with reference to their functions. If art as a kind is not essentially identified with any particular function or set of functions, how can one say that a given work's function is a relevant factor in deciding whether it is a good member (paradigm, model, successful example) of that kind?

Such kind-relative value has been taken by many philosophers to be a central form of normativity. Judith Jarvis Thomson, for example, defends the view that "there is such a property as being a good K if and only if K is a goodness-fixing kind."[8] So a given toaster has the property of being a good toaster only if there is a kind—toaster—associated with a specification of what it is to be a good member of the kind. A worry is that if, as I suggest, art is a kind that is not associated with any particular function or functions among its good-making characteristics, how is it possible for the function of any particular work of art to enter into the evaluation of it as good qua art? If there was no particular function associated with being a good toaster, one could not say that any given toaster is, by virtue of satisfying its function, good qua toaster. If works of art have functions but art as a kind is not associated with (the satisfaction of) any particular function, it seems that a work of art cannot be good qua art by virtue of its function.[9]

---

[7] It is consistent with there being no necessary function of art that there are constraints on what can be a function of art. There are, of course, some artistic ends that it would not be possible to satisfy—meaning that no intention that a work have that function could be successfully realized. The artist Piero Manzoni once installed a pedestal upside down on the earth and declared the planet-and-base his work of art. Although this succeeded in being a work of art, it was not as a sculpture which succeeded in making the actual earth a genuine constituent.

[8] Thomson (2008, 21).

[9] One potential way of avoiding that conclusion is to embrace a particularist form of evaluation that rejects the demand that the evaluation of a work of art qua art appeal to general reasons (such as the possession of a particular function) for why any instance of art is good. Purely procedural definitions of art, for example, do not require such particularism but allow that what makes something a work of art may be independent of what makes a work artistically valuable. See, e.g., Dickie (1997).

However, even if *art* is not a goodness-fixing kind, the function of a work of art can enter into an appraisal of it qua member of some more specific artistically relevant kind. That is, even if a work of art cannot be evaluated qua art, it can be judged with reference to its function qua a member of a style, movement, genre, or other category, subordinate to that of art as a kind.[10] In his *Poetics*, perhaps the first treatise based on such genre-relative criticism, Aristotle shows how the study of each type of poetry requires attending to its particular telos or aim, and he explains the comparative successes of different tragedies as due in part to how well their features contribute to their genre-specific ends.[11] Like Aristotle, we can identify a given work as belonging to a particular category of art, and evaluate it with reference to its satisfaction of whatever makes instances of such a category good qua instances of that category. The idea here is that works of have purposes indexed to the genres, styles, or other kinds they belong to (e.g., classical temple, picaresque novel, neo-impressionist painting), in addition to whatever particular, work-specific purposes they have. Or, rather, works of art often satisfy their category-specific ends in and through satisfying their particular ends. So we may evaluate any given work with a function, in part, in light of how well it satisfies the functions associated with its category. An evaluation of a particular detective story can thus be justified by noting whether it has the good-making features (e.g., a compelling, perhaps flawed, detective; clues that readers can follow) criterial of success in that genre.

Such reference to a work's category or categories in evaluating it is not ad hoc, for identifying a work as belonging to a category—such as cubist painting, still-life, sonata, political propaganda, romance novel, royal portrait, satire, body art, and so on—often depends upon an explanatory hypothesis about the kinds of problems and aims the work was designed to address.

Because any given work may belong to more than one category, it is possible for a work to be successful as one type of thing but unsuccessful as another. And it is possible for a work to fall short of satisfying all of its functions because they are mutually incompatible. *The Moonstone* by Wilkie Collins was described by T. S. Eliot as "the best of modern English detective novels," but that identity exists uneasily with its membership in a traditional category

---

[10] For a defense of the categorical approach in evaluation, see Walton (1970). For a defense of the approach in both evaluation and interpretation, see Carroll (2008).
[11] Aristotle (1987).

of mid-nineteenth-century Victorian melodrama or "sensation" fiction (a genre marked by social commentary, extended scenic descriptions, and digressions over several of a large cast of characters).

However, one caveat needs to be added to the theory that the evaluation of a work of art is a matter of appraising it qua a member of its genre, style, or other category: it is a feature of the practice of art in some traditions that, if a work of art is a member of one or more categories of art but does not conform to the good-making characteristics (including functions) associated with those categories, the work may nonetheless succeed in instantiating great artistic value.[12]

The thought here is that, while at any given time a work of art can be a good work of art through possessing the properties currently identified as the good-making characteristics of its kind, the possession of those particular good-making characteristics is not *necessary* for the work to be a good member of its kind. By contrast, an ordinary, non-idiosyncratic artifact typically belongs to a kind associated with certain characteristics, in the possession of which its members are good or defective. A can opener is a good can opener if and only if it possesses the good-making characteristics associated with that artifact kind. A can opener that was designed to radically depart from the norm of enabling the opening of cans could not be a good example of its type. However, a good work of art of some genre, style, or other category may be good qua art of that kind even as it rejects (modifies, elaborates, replaces, and so on) the heretofore good-making characteristics of that kind. The good-making characteristics (including functions) associated with categories of art are susceptible to revision through works that are instances of those very categories.[13] Works might be created, for example, that defy the conventional expectations of their kind, as in Merce Cunningham's choreographed dances that reproduce the behavior of people engaging in ordinary walking.

A work's constitutive function, as I will describe it, can typically be inferred from knowledge of the genre to which the work belongs. It is likely, e.g., that a given horror film has a constitutive function of causing audiences to feel

---

[12] This was Tom Stoppard's (1973) complaint: "There are two ways of becoming an artist. The first way is to do the things by which is meant art. The second way is to make art mean the things you do" (21).

[13] Sometimes the good-making characteristics before and after the revision can be characterized as different subordinate forms of a single higher-order value (such as the higher-order value of painterly realism achieved in the styles of impressionism and post-Impressionism) but often the values of art at different moments are incommensurable.

fear, and that a traditional novel aims to provide a rich representation of psychological interiority. However, works within a genre may reject its standard aims. Unlike standard detective stories, those by the Sicilian master Leonardo Sciascia leave little mystery about the identity of the guilty parties and eschew resolutions that would restore the moral order. And some works may be judged to "transcend" their genre. Leni Riefenstahl's *Triumph of the Will* and the collages of the Russian constructivists are indisputably instances of political propaganda, but many critics find that an appeal to any traditional understanding of that categorization obscures, rather than explains, what makes those works compelling.[14] John Ford's *The Searchers* would seem to fit squarely within the genre of the Western, but John Wayne's performance as the film's protagonist Ethan, a murderous and vengeful racist on an epic quest, makes the film much more significant than merely satisfying its genre's criteria would predict.

Thus, a work's membership in a category of art can offer only a defeasible reason for appraising it in light of the good-making properties associated with that category. For an artist may draw on the resources of a category of art without taking onboard its artistic standards for evaluation. Joseph Raz remarks that "The very idea of opera . . . is a normative idea in that we understand the concept of an opera . . . in part by understanding what a good opera is like."[15] The good-making characteristics (including the satisfaction of aims or functions) of a given kind of art, such as opera, are supplied by the good instances of that kind.

In the preceding discussion, I tried to show that there is no conceptual or practical reason why considerations of a particular work of art's function cannot enter into its evaluation. In §9.4 I show precisely how a work of art's satisfaction of its particular function always enters into its evaluation as art. But, for the moment, I want to better identify what sort of function is relevant in such evaluation. I call this function a *constitutive function*.

9.2. Constitutive Functions

A constitutive function of an artifact is a function that the artifact possesses in an essential manner. The function is a property of the artifact without

---

[14] For instance, Sontag (1966).
[15] Raz (2003, 31).

which the artifact would not be the particular artifact that it is. Having a constitutive function does not entail being able to serve or discharge that function. A very dull bread knife still has the function of slicing bread. Whether an artifact could lose *all* capacity to serve its essential function and still be said to have that function is unclear. Does a Polaroid camera have the function of taking pictures when the production of the self-developing film cartridges required for the camera has ceased? The important distinction I want to draw here holds between a constitutive function and a merely accidental or passing function, i.e., a use to which an artifact is put but which is not the artifact's function. A nonessential function that is given to an artifact may manifest a disposition of the artifact, but it does not reflect its identity.[16] Indeed, there is a strong temptation to redescribe any nonessential function of an artifact as merely the purpose for which the artifact is used on a particular occasion. In any case, if an artifact loses or does not have a capacity to serve such accidental functions, it does not have those accidental functions. An iron has the constitutive function of ironing clothes, but it may be given the only-accidental function of holding a door open. If it could not serve that accidental function, it would be odd to claim that it preserves that function nonetheless.

By contrast, if the iron broke or there was no electricity available and it thereby could not serve its constitutive function, it would still have that function. So a constitutive function is not "projected" onto or given to an artifact; rather, the artifact is such as to have that function. Of course, an artifact with one constitutive function can be employed in the constitution of another artifact with its own constitutive function, as a tire might be made into a playground swing or a urinal into a readymade work of art.[17] Here essential properties of one artifact (including functional properties) might not be essential to another artifact even though they are coexisting or realized in the same material.

A natural way of distinguishing constitutive and accidental functions that I've already appealed to identifies the constitutive functions with those that the creators of the works intended them to have.[18] Such attributions

---

[16] For the contrary view in which the function of a work of art is not a constituent of it but is accorded to it in the actions of an artist or an audience making use of the work, see Wolterstorff (1980).

[17] I assume here without argument that a work and the object that constitutes it are two numerically distinct coexisting objects, or that the work supersedes the object of which it is constituted. A way of making the distinction is to say that the work of art and the material object that constitutes it differ in essential properties. See Lamarque (2002a); Baker (2004).

[18] McLaughlin (2001) defends a general intentionalist theory of functions.

of an essential function to an artifact imply historical and explanatory commitments as to how the artifact came about. By contrast, attributions of accidental functions are not in principle constrained by facts about the origin of the object, although they may be constrained (like attributions of essential functions) by facts about the object's *capacity* to serve the proposed function. (These facts pertaining to capacities may be historical; for example, one cannot give a fossil the accidental function of revealing the diet of prehistoric animals unless the item really comes from that period.)

Some philosophers try to extend an etiological or "selected effects" account of biological function—in which the function of a trait is the effect of it favored by natural selection—to an analogous explanation of the function of artifacts.[19] That extension would identify the function of an artifact as a capacity, the desirable effect or performance of which explains why the artifact is reproduced. But this has the implausible consequence of making the attribution of an unprecedented or idiosyncratic function to an artifact wait on how history unfolds subsequent to the artifact's creation.[20] Attributing a naturalistic/non-teleological function to a biological trait may make sense only when assuming that the trait had been selected for. However, an artifact may have a novel function without its possession being explained as the result of its corresponding capacity having been present in earlier artifacts. A more plausible account of artifactual function would identify it with the intention with which an artifact is created, whatever the subsequent history of that artifact's kind turns out to be. Although perhaps at the cost of arriving at a concept of function that ranges invariantly across artifacts and biology, the intentional account allows novel functions to be discovered, not just derived from functions that already exist.

9.3. Intentions and Constitutive Functions

There is no direct entailment from an artifact having been intentionally created to its having a purpose or function. For one might intentionally create a wooden box just to refine one's skill in cutting dovetails or intentionally

---

[19] See, for example, Preston (1998); the theory of proper functions in Millikan (1984); Parsons and Carlson (2008, 73–89).

[20] Some etiological accounts propose a unitary notion of biological and artifactual function that allows for human intentions playing a role in the process of artifactual selection. But these also permit only a retrospective attribution of functions to original or once-idiosyncratic artifacts.

bake a cake to test the oven, without those products having any function or purpose in themselves. In such cases, performing the action has a purpose or function, but the object created thereby may not. And, of course, an artist might intend to create a work of art with a function but through, say, technical ineptitude or false beliefs fail to create such a work. The standard case, however, is that an artist intends to create a work of art that has a function and some capacity to discharge it, and it is in virtue of acting on that intention that the work she creates has that function and capacity.

However, it is unnecessary to maintain that when an artist's intentions play an explanatory role in our characterization of her work, those intentions must have been consciously represented. An artist may have unconscious goals, opaque to her in creating a work, but visible to us as we reflect on it against a background of knowledge about the context in which she worked.[21] An artist might also discover her intentions in the process of creating the work, where "discover" here means forming the intention in the work's very production.[22] Lionel Trilling thus remarked that "*Hamlet* is not merely the product of Shakespeare's thought, it is the very instrument of his thought."[23] Constraints of genre and medium may also cause a work to have certain properties qua work of art even if not intended by its author. Wayne Booth writes in this connection of how, despite Jane Austen's skepticism toward conventional patterns of desire, the formal structure of the novel as a genre led her to convey an endorsement of such patterns in *Emma*; and, how, despite Samuel Richardson's insistence that he intended in *Clarissa* for Lovelace to be seen as repugnant, rendering him in accord with conventions dictating the creation of plausible and engaging characters ended up inviting a sympathetic identification among some readers.[24]

Finally, an artist might also choose to incorporate some property in his work and thereby take on the functions of that property without explicitly thinking of himself as doing so. Through reverse engineering one can discover why a catenary arch was adopted in the construction of the earliest monumental Gothic cathedrals. Unlike less stable Roman arches and post-and-lintel systems, the Gothic shape redirects gravity's vertical forces into

---

[21] On unconsciously pursued goals, see Bargh et al. (2001); Gollwitzer and Bargh (2005). See also Walton (1990): "Even if we do understand a thing's function to be linked to the objectives of its creator, this may only be so because there happens to be a tradition or convention or understanding whereby this is so" (53).

[22] Forster, *Aspects of the Novel* (1927, 101).

[23] Trilling (2008, 52). See also Gilmore (2011b).

[24] See Booth (2010).

compressive forces that run through the arch's curves. Yet, even without such a discovery, creators of later cathedrals could unwittingly benefit from that design's function by merely copying the arch's shape and construction.

Can any kind of intended function be a constitutive function? Sometimes an artist intends to create a work of art with a particular function, and succeeds in creating a work of art, but the work cannot realize its intended function. If the reasons why the work cannot realize the function are external to it (such as would be the case if the work is no longer displayed or is written in a language of which there are no longer speakers) it seems plausible to say that it could possess its function without being able to discharge it. Analogously, we can attribute to a person's vote the function of helping elect a given candidate, even if, as is usually the case in large electorates, there is little probability of that vote being among those that make a difference. However, if a work is created with no capacity to fulfill a given function, it would fail to have that function altogether. Barnett Newman said that, understood properly, his abstract paintings of the 1940s "would mean the end of all state capitalism and totalitarianism."[25] Because there is no practical way in which those works could discharge that function, we should say, like the putative function of a perpetual-motion machine, the works don't possess it.

Note that in explaining how a creator's actions relate to the function of a work, we should adopt a liberal conception of creator. One can create a work of art through various means: by discovering—and reframing or giving a saliency to—an object without otherwise changing it; by appropriating an already created artifact; by employing others to fabricate one's work; by collaborative undertakings such that the creator is a corporate individual; and so on. What determines whether one is a work's creator is not typically the amount of labor one performs, but the degree of authority one has over such considerations as what constitutes the work, e.g., what properties belong to it and what properties belong only to the material by which it is constituted; when and whether it is finished; whether a copy or token is an adequate instance of it; and so on. Different contexts endow different individuals involved in the making of a work with different degrees of such authority: a sculptor's judgment typically trumps anyone else's as to whether a carving is completed; the director of a film may compete with its actors and screenwriters in realizing their respectively different ends; an architect is not the sole authority over a building's design; the contribution of an editor

---

[25] Newman (1962/1992, 251).

to a text in the early modern period was considered part of the work, not, as now, an external intervention to be ignored in uncovering the "original" composition.

Might a failure of fit between an intention and the artwork's possession of a corresponding function be due to the function not being an *artistic* one? If there are any such functions disqualified from being artistic, it seems that their identification must be made on a case-by-case basis. When, for example, musicians write pop songs with the aim of making money, that is typically not an artistic function of the resulting works. For we would tend to assume that the absence of such aims could have left the works unchanged. However, to stay with that example, such a function might not be disqualified from being artistic in a particular case, if making money was integral to a work's realization of an expressive function in, say, proclaiming art to be a commodity or artists to be only hucksters. Damien Hirst's 2007 *For the Love of God*, a platinum skull encrusted with diamonds, is only one extravagant example of work that exploits for expressive ends the price it commands at auction. One critic described Hirst as an artist who "uses the art market as his medium."[26] The obverse economic function, it should be said, has a more familiar pedigree in works made so as to offer little remuneration to their creators and owners, as in Russian constructivism's photographic collages disseminated in inexpensive popular magazines. Striking a symbolic blow against capitalism's hold on artistic production was a bona fide artistic function of these works, albeit unrealized as they became collected and curated, victims of their own success.

Finally, note that a work may possess a constitutive function for the sake of serving an external function. Velázquez's *Portrait of Juan de Pareja* renders its subject, the painter's assistant and an enslaved member of his household, with a beauty and realism that are internal to its aims. However, those artistic achievements served an external function as well. According to the painter's biographer Antonio Palomino, Velázquez had de Pareja carry the portrait to its first public exhibition, where the image could be compared to its original as an advertisement of the artist's skills. That commercial purpose essentially belonged to the action Velázquez performed in painting the canvas, without being a constitutive function of the work of art itself.

---

[26] Tomkins (2007). That expressive function is also illustrated in art such as J. S. G. Boggs's exchanges of his highly finished drawings of banknotes for goods and actual currency; and the productions of Takashi Murakami (e.g., a handbag designed for Louis Vuitton) that thematize, as well as straddle, the line between retail-commercial and high-art markets.

9.4. Normative Essentialism

Correlative to having an essential function is to be subject to a norm associated with that function. To say an artifact or work of art has a function entails that it is *supposed to* serve that function. It is a necessary condition of an object having a function that there be such a norm governing what capacities the object has.

Our evaluation of objects with reference to the kind of thing they are expresses this normative aspect of the assignment of functions. An object may have the capacity to serve as a weapon, paperweight, etc., but to identify it as an instance of a given functional kind, say as a hammer, is to identify it as subject to certain expectations grounding criticisms and evaluations associated with that kind of tool. Knowing that a given object is a hammer licenses certain forms of criticism, such as that it is too heavy, and silences others, e.g., that it isn't waterproof. Only through the application of some such norms is the *malfunctioning* of an artifact possible.[27] Identifying a pill as an antidote implies that it should counteract a poison; identifying a machine as a toaster implies that it ought to toast bread. Such a norm is internally related to the object's essential function. The artifact's normative essence is entailed by its functional essence.[28]

Such normativity of artifacts designed to serve a function is derived from the familiar, if not entirely understood, normativity of plans, intentions, desires, and rational behavior. If someone has a given end, he should adopt the means, other things being equal, that he believes will realize that end. Because such instrumental imperatives seem to lead to counterintuitive conclusions, such as that a person who happens to have murderous ends "ought" to use extremely lethal weapons, we should adopt a *wide-scope* interpretation of such imperatives. There we see the norm of rationality as applying to the conditional as a whole, i.e., that one ought to be means/end coherent, not that one ought to pursue whatever ends one happens to have.[29] That is, one can be means/end coherent by giving up some bad end, rather than by being forced to adopt whatever are the best means to reach it. Extending the instrumental norm to artifacts: if someone designs a tool

---

[27] The importance of a concept of function allowing (via a norm) the possibility of malfunctioning is a central feature of etiological accounts of biological function. See, e.g., Millikan (1989).

[28] See Fine (1995).

[29] See Broome (2004). Some philosophers argue that such instrumental imperatives are true only on the condition that the end is one the person ought to pursue. See, e.g., Korsgaard (1997).

to realize some function, the tool *should* be such (should be so designed) as to realize that function. I should note that it is compatible with it being the case that an artifact ought to satisfy its constitutive function that there ought not to be any such artifact. Someone who thought romantic comedies had a baneful influence on contemporary culture, or nuclear weapons should be eliminated, could still identify what features such artifacts ought to have.

When an artifact does not realize a constitutive function because of a feature essential to the artifact, that feature is a defect in the artifact qua a member of its functional kind. If it is a constitutive function of a plumber's wrench to loosen nuts around pipes but a particular wrench has a handle too short to allow the necessary torque, that short handle is a defect in the plumber's wrench qua plumber's wrench. That defect counts against it being a good instance (paradigm, model, exemplar, etc.) of its kind. I understand the "counting against" as diminishing the value of the thing in a pro tanto fashion. Insofar as the artifact has a defect—a defect that limits its satisfaction of its function—it is less good as an instance of the kind that it was designed to be.

When there is no general kind to which the artifact belongs, as with idiosyncratic artifacts, a defect counts against its being a good realization of the artifact it was intended to be.

The functional view of works of art that I propose is that just as ordinary artifacts should fulfill whatever constitutive functions they have, so works of art should fulfill their constitutive functions. Insofar as a feature of a work of art prevents it from satisfying its constitutive function, that feature is a defect in the work as a work of art. Specifically,

> If artwork A has constitutive function CF and an artistic property P in A counts against the satisfaction of CF, then P is a defect in A qua artwork A.

That last "qua" is intended to stress that I am speaking only of the relation between the properties of a work of art and the evaluation of it as a work of art. Those artistic properties may have a different relation to the value of the object under a description of some other kind. The visually dramatic story of a stained-glass window is internally related in a positive manner to its value as a work of art but perhaps detracts from its value as a window. And the reference to an *artistic* property in A (rather than just any property) is redundant, but meant to emphasize that the criticism of a work of art qua art should be based not just on any properties that it possesses (such as the weight of a painting), but only those it possesses as a work of art. One might suggest that we limit the features relevant to such artistic evaluation to those that are intrinsic, but that would inappropriately exclude the extrinsic or relational properties—for example, how the work affects its audience; its commentary on other works of art; its degree of originality—that may count for or against its artistic success.

The evaluative perspective on artistic functions that I describe here is similar to the idea in some eighteenth-century aesthetic theories of there being a degree of beauty in an object's "fitness for function." However, the value of such fitness in those contexts was explained typically as residing ultimately in the value of the realized function itself.[30] The view suggested here is that a work's fitness for (its constitutive) function can be an artistically relevant object of evaluation in addition to the function per se. In other words, we can evaluate a work of art as art from two interdependent perspectives pertaining to its functions: (1) whether it realizes its constitutive (essential and artistic) functions; and (2) whether its realization of those functions is worthy or valuable.

When applied to familiar kinds of artistic properties that frustrate the realization of the ends of a work, the functional view offers unsurprising results. If the constitutive function of a painting is to express some point of view on its subject, then it is an artistic defect in the work if that subject is so casually painted as to be unrecognizable. If an essential purpose of a particular mystery story is to elicit suspense but the identity of its villain is obvious, that feature is an artistic flaw—a flaw in light of the work's artistic ends.

However, the functional view has more interesting results when applied to the question of whether other—less obviously artistically germane—properties of a work may constitute artistic flaws. Can, for example, the property of being immoral count as a defect in art qua art? Or is the value of art as art untouched by its moral or immoral value? I address this question from the functional point of view in what follows.

---

[30] Hume (1739–40/1978), for example, observes that we can take pleasure in functional objects even though they are of no use to us: "This observation extends to tables, chairs, scritoires, chimneys, coaches, saddles, ploughs, and indeed to every work of art; it being an universal rule, that their beauty is chiefly deriv'd from their utility, and from their fitness for that purpose" (II.iii.5). However, his point is that such pleasure is possible because we can, via sympathy, see the objects from the perspective of those for whom they are useful.

9.5. The Functional View and Moral Value

As noted in earlier chapters, it may seem counterintuitive to judge morally defective responses elicited by a work of art as apt, rational, or fitting just because they conform to attitudes that the work is designed to elicit. Some theorists suggest that a moral defect in the attitude elicited by a work makes that response less fitting or appropriate.

Paisley Livingston and Alfred Mele, for example, distinguish between what they call "congruence," in our emotions for fictions, which is "determined by the story as told by the author," and "refinement," which is in part "a matter of responding to the story within one's own justified moral framework." For them, the congruence of a reader's emotional response with morally defective attitudes expressed or endorsed in a work renders the response inapt. Peter Goldie makes a comparable distinction between an apt emotion that follows the perspective of the fictional text and an "ethically" correct emotion that corresponds to how one should (morally) respond.[31]

Perhaps those arguments are sound when referring to aptness of our affective responses *all things considered*. My concern in this volume thus far has been with aptness in only the representational sense. One might feel offended by the bigoted attitudes and exploitative schemes of the narcissistic characters in the series *It's Always Sunny in Philadelphia*. But that would be to misrepresent the contents of the show (for one's responses to fail to fit it) because its fictional states of affairs are presented (usually with success) so as to elicit amusement and tolerance in relation to the characters' often morally deviant and always ill-advised plans. As in the cases of discrepant affect surveyed in the last chapter, we can distinguish between one's emotional response to the contents of a fiction being apt as a morally appropriate attitude to have toward those contents, and being apt in correctly presenting those contents.[32] As noted in §5.3, these two dimensions of a response can be independently evaluated.[33]

Still, it can seem counterintuitive to claim of some work of fiction that if it can successfully cause audiences to adopt morally defective attitudes as part of an appreciation of its contents, there is a relevant norm that says that one *ought to* respond as the work prescribes. How can a norm of

---

[31] Livingston and Mele (1997, 172); Goldie (2003, 59–61).

[32] See D'Arms and Jacobson (2000).

[33] Or, as Cohen (1999) notes, a joke's being morally objectionable, offensive, and so on, is compatible with it being funny.

representational accuracy call for one to respond as a fiction prescribes, when that prescription is to adopt attitudes that one ought not to have? I suggest that the worry here can be resolved if we identify an ambiguity over where the norms governing our engagements with fictions apply. I appeal here to the distinction discussed earlier between narrow- and wide-scope interpretations of norms. With a *narrow scope*, an application of the normative "ought" governing aptness in the representational sense would say:

> If one engages with a morally defective fiction, one ought to respond in conformity with how its contents are successfully represented.

This invites the concern already introduced. It just seems false to say that because a work of art succeeds in evoking its sought-after response from us through the use of morally offensive stereotypes, we ought to respond as it prescribes. It seems that even if we do go along with the work, we ought not to. Thus, I suggest that the norm governing the correctness of affective responses should be given a *wide-scope* interpretation, where the normative "ought" applies to the whole conditional:

> One ought, if one engages with a work of morally defective fiction, to respond in conformity with how its contents are successfully represented.

The latter interpretation allows the norm to be respected by negating the conditional's antecedent, rather than satisfying its consequent. If a given work is morally defective, one can decide not to engage with it and still abide by the preceding norm.

Of course, we often do seek to experience works of art in spite of finding them in one dimension or another morally problematic. What I want to do in this last section is ask: If a work exhibits a moral defect, does this entail the existence of an artistic defect too? I will suggest that the functional view I've outlined identifies at least one condition under which a work's moral defects and artistic defects are thus internally related.

There are a wide variety of ways in which works of art can invite moral criticism. Art may express racist, anti-Semitic, and homophobic points of view; objectify women; promote regressive politics; present violence in a seductive light; humiliate and degrade actual persons; violate privacy; destroy property; and so on.

Such morally troubling aspects are sometimes constitutive features of works of art; the flaws are not exclusively, say, properties of the motivations the artists had in creating them. Susan Sontag condemned Diane Arbus's celebrated and influential photographs of marginalized individuals (such as carnival performers, the indigent, spiritualists, and people with mental and physical disabilities) for showing people "who are pathetic, pitiable, as well as repulsive," from a vantage point "based on distance, on privilege, on a feeling that what the viewer is asked to look at is really other."[34] Whether Arbus knowingly adopted that attitude as she created those works is uncertain. However, the perspective is readily apparent as a feature of the works themselves. Her photographs, for example, are often composed as if to provide a taxonomy of oddities; and the images in many cases have an odd fisheye appearance—due to her use of a wide-angle lens in close quarters— that serves as a visual analogue of the putative "abnormality" of her subjects themselves.[35]

Even if we accept that works of art can exhibit or elicit such morally defective attitudes, we need a further argument to demonstrate that such moral defects can count as artistic defects. Perhaps partisans of artistic autonomy are right in holding moral and artistic value apart.[36]

9.6. Constitutive Moral Ends

I suggest that we can discover an internal relation between the artistic and moral value of a work in the relation between, broadly speaking, the moral vision of a work of art and the point, purpose, or function it was created to realize. We should consider, that is, that sometimes a work of art is designed to realize a given morally relevant aim, such as to express an ethical

---

[34] Sontag (1977, 34). Sontag's complaint echoes that of Walter Benjamin in "Author as Producer" (1934/1970), where he accuses the artists associated with the *Neue Sachlichkeit* (an emotionally cool style of apparently objective literary and photographic depiction) of "making misery itself an object of pleasure" (90).

[35] Related moral criticism of the artistic rendering of people in abject conditions has been raised in connection with works such as Dorothea Lange's surveys of Depression-era rural poverty, Nicholas Nixon's images of people dying from HIV/AIDS, James Nachtwey's depictions of victims of oppression and war, and Joel-Peter Witkin's baroque-like tableaux organized around dismembered corpses, social outcasts, and physically handicapped living models.

[36] The theory of *merited response* represents the most significant recent account of the internal connection between moral and artistic value. Two distinct formulations of the theory are developed, respectively, in Carroll (1996); and Gaut (2007). For criticism, and comparison to the functional view, see Gilmore (2011a, 2011c).

commitment, elicit a moral discovery, or create conditions under which audiences can empathize with people from whom they would otherwise be estranged. When a work has such a moral aim as a work of art, but fails, for morally relevant reasons, to achieve that aim, that is both a moral flaw in the work and an artistic flaw as well. Such a moral flaw instantiates a defect in the work in fully realizing the ends for which it was designed.

For example, in his photographs Sebastião Selgado no doubt intends to bear witness and call attention to the suffering of refugees, disenfranchised laborers, and other victims of famine and human depredation. That end is an essential and morally admirable artistic function of his works. However, the refined beauty and dramatic composition of his images sometimes present his subjects in a way that suggests that their degraded condition is the primary aspect or saliency under which they should be identified.[37] The artistic achievement of such works may thereby depend upon a kind of instrumental objectification that is in tension with full moral respect for those individuals as persons.[38] The images are designed to elicit from us moral emotions—empathetic pain, concern, indignation over rampant injustice—yet they do so while invoking morally defective responses—such as a distanced pleasure in their objectifying beauty. The works' admirable moral ends turn out to be compromised by their morally flawed artistic means.

By contrast, Arbus's works seem largely devoid of any such moral function. Her photographs are far less animated, that is, by any essential moral purpose or end. Sontag may have been right in identifying moral flaws in these works, but, if they were not made in light of any correlative moral standards, those flaws need not count as artistic ones. In other words, Arbus's work may be morally defective, but, if so, its defects seem not to tarnish the work's value as art.

When a work of art is designed to express some content, but fails in that respect, that failure is an artistic fault: it is a failure of the work to achieve at

---

[37] A standard indictment suggests that, despite the photographs having been composed to discharge a morally admirable expressive function, their beauty solicits the wrong (contemplative or pleasure-seeking) point of view on the abject subjects they represent. Selgado seems, one critic complained, "too busy with . . . finding the 'grace' and 'beauty' in the twisted forms of his anguished subjects. And this beautification of tragedy results in pictures that ultimately reinforce our passivity toward the experience they reveal" Sischy (1991, 92). See also Reinhardt, Edwards, and Duganne (2007).

[38] See Martha Nussbaum's (1995a) catalog of seven types of objectification, any one of which may come into play in these photographs: instrumentality, denial of autonomy, inertness (lacking in agency), fungibility (the particularity of the person being unimportant), violability (lacking in boundaries), ownership of another, and denial of subjectivity (not taking into account a person's own experience or feeling).

least one of its artistic aims. My claim, by extension, is that a moral flaw in a work with a constitutive moral function is a flaw in the work in light of its own standards for success. Thus, the violence enacted by the title character in the film *Dirty Harry* is supposed to express a notion of justice "higher" than what the law affords, but what the film actually appears to endorse is a false identification of justice with vengeance. Likewise, *A Clockwork Orange* putatively decries the violent anomie associated with its protagonists, yet its scenes of spectacular barbarity nonetheless invite us to be titillated by that which it allegedly condemns. Finally, films of Michael Haneke such as *Funny Games* disparage the cheap sentimental modes of popular movies and the too-sure effects they employ in manipulating our sensibilities, yet they exploit viewers' emotional vulnerabilities all the same.

In such cases, the realization of a constitutive function of expressing a moral point of view is compromised by a morally defective execution or means. Thus, criticizing those works for rendering their subjects in a morally offensive manner is not an *alternative* to criticizing them on artistic grounds, but rather a mode of such criticism on artistic grounds.

In the preceding examples, the moral defects count as artistic defects because they conflict with the aims of the works to express a moral attitude or stance concerning the subjects they depict. There are other ways in which moral defects might frustrate a work's realization of its defining ends, such as when they inadvertently curtail audiences' imaginative engagement with the work's content.[39] The functional view would count that as illustrating an alternative manner in which a moral defect may instantiate an artistic defect too.

However, contrary to such theories that tie moral defects to failures of uptake, the functional view allows that even when audiences are ignorant of the moral defects in a work—so insidious and camouflaged as they may be—the possession of such defects can still count against the work's artistic success. The judgment that a work employs immoral means to achieve some morally relevant end is independent of the determination that such immoral means have an effect on audiences' degree of imaginative engagement.

In the functional view, a moral flaw does not qualify as an artistic flaw under all conditions. A joke or farce may aim only at making an audience laugh; a satire may have the function only of ridiculing an individual or institution; a grotesquely brutal film of armed gangs stalking each other may

---

[39] See Carroll (1996).

aim only at entertainment, not at demonstrating how to peaceably settle differences. Such works may be criticized for the morally obnoxious attitudes they elicit and commitments they express, without those moral problems making an artistic difference if no moral ends are constitutive of the works.

I want to conclude by noting that the functional view offers a systematic account of how an internal relation may hold between a work's artistic value and many nonmoral kinds of value as well. Consider, for example, the question of whether a work's *cognitive* dimensions count in favor of or against its artistic worth. If, say, a work of art is designed to represent its subject in an enlightening way but the form in which that subject is depicted offers a distorting view, then the artwork has, to that extent, failed by its own lights. If the putative insight around which a work is organized is in fact flatly false or clichéd or if the putatively deep meditation that a work is designed to offer turns out to be ponderous, not profound, these cognitive failures are, by virtue of the artwork's ends or purposes, artistic failures as well.

This chapter's focus on the kinds of reasons that speak to the artistic value of a work is, of course, distinct from earlier chapters' examination of the reasons that speak to the aptness of our responses to a work. However, the two kinds of normative frameworks share a common structure: the criteria governing the evaluation of both works of art and the attitudes elicited in engaging with them are derived from the purposes of the works and engagements themselves. I acknowledge, of course, that one can always ask whether the functions of a given work of art or artistic engagement are worthy ones—aims that matter. Yet that is a question no longer about art's ends, but *our* ends—those that define our encounters with both the real world and the worlds conjured by the imagination.

Bibliography

Ackerman, Joshua M., Christopher C. Nocera, and John A. Bargh. 2010. "Incidental Haptic Sensations Influence Social Judgments and Decisions." *Science* 328(5986): 1712–15.

Adelmann, Pamela K., and Robert B. Zajonc. 1989. "Facial Efference and the Experience of Emotion." *Annual Review of Psychology* 40(1): 249–80.

Adolphs, Ralph, Daniel Tranel, Hanna Damasio, and Antonio Damasio. 1994. "Impaired Recognition of Emotion in Facial Expressions Following Bilateral Damage to the Human Amygdala." *Nature* 372(6507): 669.

Adorno, Theodor. 1983. *Prisms*. MIT Press.

Ainslie, George. 2013. "Grasping the Impalpable: The Role of Endogenous Reward in Choices, Including Process Addictions." *Inquiry: An Interdisciplinary Journal of Philosophy* 56(5): 446–69.

Ames, Daniel R. 2004. "Inside the Mind Reader's Tool Kit: Projection and Stereotyping in Mental State Inference." *Journal of Personality and Social Psychology* 87(3): 340.

Amodio, David M., Leah R. Zinner, and Eddie Harmon-Jones. 2007. "Social Psychological Methods of Emotion Elicitation." *Handbook of Emotion Elicitation and Assessment*, edited by James A. Coan and John Allen, 91–105. Oxford University Press.

Anderson, Craig A. 1983. "Imagination and Expectation: The Effect of Imagining Behavioral Scripts on Personal Influences." *Journal of Personality and Social Psychology* 45(2): 293–305.

Anderson, Craig A., and Brad J. Bushman. 2001. "Effects of Violent Video Games on Aggressive Behavior, Aggressive Cognition, Aggressive Affect, Physiological Arousal, and Prosocial Behavior: A Meta-analytic Review of the Scientific Literature." *Psychological Science* 12(5): 353–59.

Anderson, Craig A., and Brad J. Bushman. 2002. "The Effects of Media Violence on Society." *Science* 295(5564): 2377–79.

Anderson, Craig A., et al. 2010. "Violent Video Game Effects on Aggression, Empathy, and Prosocial Behavior in Eastern and Western Countries: A Meta-analytic Review." *Psychological Bulletin* 136(2): 151–73.

Anema, Helen A., Alyanne M. de Haan, Titia Gebuis, and H. Chris Dijkerman. 2012. "Thinking about Touch Facilitates Tactile but Not Auditory Processing." *Experimental Brain Research* 218(3): 373–80.

Anscombe, Elizabeth. 1957. *Intention*. Harvard University Press.

Antrobus, John S., Judith S. Antrobus, and Jerome L. Singer. 1964. "Eye Movements Accompanying Daydreaming, Visual Imagery, and Thought Suppression." *Journal of Abnormal and Social Psychology* 69(3): 244.

Appel, Markus. 2011. "A Story about a Stupid Person Can Make You Act Stupid (or Smart): Behavioral Assimilation (and Contrast) as Narrative Impact." *Media Psychology* 14(2): 144–67.

Appel, Markus, and Barbara Malečkar. 2012. "The Influence of Paratext on Narrative Persuasion: Fact, Fiction, or Fake?" *Human Communication Research* 38(4): 459–84.

Appel, Markus, and Martina Mara. 2013. "The Persuasive Influence of a Fictional Character's Trustworthiness." *Journal of Communication* 63(5): 912–32.

Appiah, Anthony. 2008. *Experiments in Ethics*. Harvard University Press.

Aristotle. 1987. *Poetics*. In *A New Aristotle Reader*, edited by J. L. Ackrill, 540–56. Princeton University Press.

Aristotle. 2016. *De Anima*. Trans. Christopher Shields. Oxford University Press.

Arnold, Magda B. 1960. *Emotion and Personality*. Columbia University Press.

Auden, Wystan Hugh. 2012. *The Dyer's Hand*. Faber & Faber.

Augustine. 2006. *Confessions*. Trans. F. J. Sheed. Hackett.

Badgaiyan, Rajendra D., Alan J. Fischman, and Nathaniel M. Alpert. 2009. "Dopamine Release during Human Emotional Processing." *Neuroimage* 47(4): 2041–45.

Baker, L. R. 2004. "The Ontology of Artifacts." *Philosophical Explorations* 7(2): 99–111.

Banerjee, Pronobesh, Promothesh Chatterjee, and Jayati Sinha. 2012. "Is It Light or Dark? Recalling Moral Behavior Changes Perception of Brightness." *Psychological Science* 23(4): 407–9.

Bargh, J. A., P. M. Gollwitzer, A. Lee-Chai, K. Barndollar, and R. Trötschel. 2001. "The Automated Will: Nonconscious Activation and Pursuit of Behavioral Goals." *Journal of Personality and Social Psychology* 81(6): 1014.

Bargh, John A., and Tanya L. Chartrand. 2000. "The Mind in the Middle." In *Handbook of Research Methods in Social and Personality Psychology*, edited by Harry T. Reis and Charles M. Judd, 253–85. Cambridge University Press.

Bargh, John A., and Lawrence E. Williams. 2007. "The Nonconscious Regulation of Emotion." In *Handbook of Emotion Regulation*, edited by James J. Gross, 429–45. Guilford Press.

Barkley, Russell A. 2001. "The Executive Functions and Self-Regulation: An Evolutionary Neuropsychological Perspective." *Neuropsychology Review* 11(1): 1–29.

Barlett, Christopher, Omar Branch, Christopher Rodeheffer, and Richard Harris. 2009. "How Long Do the Short-Term Violent Video Game Effects Last?" *Aggressive Behavior* 35(3): 225–36.

Barrett, Lisa Feldman. 2006. "Solving the Emotion Paradox: Categorization and the Experience of Emotion." *Personality and Social Psychology Review* 10(1): 20–46.

Barrett, Lisa Feldman. 2012. "Emotions Are Real." *Emotion* 12(3): 413–29.

Bastiaansen, Jojanneke A. C. J., Marc Thioux, and Christian Keysers. 2009. "Evidence for Mirror Systems in Emotions." *Philosophical Transactions of the Royal Society of London B: Biological Sciences* 364(1528): 2391–404.

Baumeister, J.-C., G. Papa, and F. Foroni. 2016. "Deeper Than Skin Deep: The Effect of Botulinum Toxin-A on Emotion Processing." *Toxicon* 118: 86–90.

Bavelas, Janet Beavin, Alex Black, Charles R. Lemery, and Jennifer Mullett. 1988. "Motor Mimicry as Primitive Empathy." In *Empathy and Its Development*, edited by Nancy Eisenberg and Janet Strayer, 317–38. Cambridge University Press.

Beardsley, Monroe C. 1981. *Aesthetics: Problems in the Philosophy of Criticism*. Hackett.

Beardsmore, R. W. 1971. *Art and Morality*. Macmillan.

Benjamin, Walter. 1934/1970. "The Author as Producer." *New Left Review* 62(1): 83–96.

Ben-Zeev, Aaron. 2010. "The Thing Called Emotion." In *Oxford Handbook of Philosophy of Emotion*, edited by Peter Goldie, 41–62. Oxford University Press.

Berger, Christopher C., and H. Henrik Ehrsson. 2018. "Mental Imagery Induces Cross-Modal Sensory Plasticity and Changes Future Auditory Perception." *Psychological Science* 29(6): 926–35.

Bernstein, Daniel M., and Elizabeth F. Loftus. 2009. "How to Tell If a Particular Memory Is True or False." *Perspectives on Psychological Science* 4(4): 370–74.

Berridge, Kent, and Piotr Winkielman. 2003. "What Is an Unconscious Emotion? (The Case for Unconscious 'Liking')." *Cognition & Emotion* 17(2): 181–211.

Birch, Susan A. J., and Paul Bloom. 2003. "Children Are Cursed: An Asymmetric Bias in Mental-State Attribution." *Psychological Science* 14: 283–86.

Bisiach, Edoardo, and Claudio Luzzatti. 1978. "Unilateral Neglect of Representational Space." *Cortex* 14(1): 129–33.

Black, John B., Terrence J. Turner, and Gordon H. Bower. 1979. "Point of View in Narrative Comprehension, Memory, and Production." *Journal of Verbal Learning and Verbal Behavior* 18(2): 187–98.

Blackburn, Simon. 1988. "Attitudes and Contents." *Ethics* 98(3): 501–17.

Blackburn, Simon. 1998. *Ruling Passions: A Theory of Practical Reasoning.* Clarendon Press.

Block, Ned. 1996. "What Is Functionalism?" In *The Encyclopedia of Philosophy Supplement*, edited by Donald Borchert. Macmillan.

Bloom, Paul. 2010. *How Pleasure Works: The New Science of Why We Like What We Like.* Random House.

Boden, Margaret A. 2004. *The Creative Mind: Myths and Mechanisms.* Psychology Press.

Bolivar, Valerie J., Annabel J. Cohen, and John C. Fentress. 1994. "Semantic and Formal Congruency in Music and Motion Pictures: Effects on the Interpretation of Visual Action." *Psychomusicology: A Journal of Research in Music Cognition* 13(1–2): 28–59.

Boltz, Marilyn G. 2001. "Musical Soundtracks as a Schematic Influence on the Cognitive Processing of Filmed Events." *Music Perception: An Interdisciplinary Journal* 18(4): 427–54.

Booth, Wayne C. 2010. *The Rhetoric of Fiction.* University of Chicago Press.

Botvinick, Matthew, Amishi P. Jha, Lauren M. Bylsma, Sara A. Fabian, Patricia E. Solomon, and Kenneth M. Prkachin. 2005. "Viewing Facial Expressions of Pain Engages Cortical Areas Involved in the Direct Experience of Pain." *Neuroimage* 25(1): 312–19.

Bourdieu, Pierre. 1984. *Distinction: A Social Critique of the Judgement of Taste.* Trans. Richard Nice. Harvard University Press.

Bourlon, Clémence, Bastien Oliviero, Nicolas Wattiez, Pierre Pouget, and Paolo Bartolomeo. 2011. "Visual Mental Imagery: What the Head's Eye Tells the Mind's Eye." *Brain Research* 1367: 287–97.

Bower, Gordon H., and Daniel G. Morrow. 1990. "Mental Models in Narrative Comprehension." *Science* 247(4938): 44–48.

Brady, Michael S. 2013. *Emotional Insight: The Epistemic Role of Emotional Experience.* Oxford University Press.

Brandom, Robert. 1982. "Points of View and Practical Reasoning." *Canadian Journal of Philosophy* 7(2): 321–33.

Brandt, Richard. 1979. *A Theory of the Good and the Right.* Oxford University Press.

Brandt, Stephan A., and Lawrence W. Stark. 1997. "Spontaneous Eye Movements during Visual Imagery Reflect the Content of the Visual Scene." *Journal of Cognitive Neuroscience* 9(1): 27–38.

Brecht, Bertolt. 1964. "A Short Organum for the Theatre." In *Brecht on Theatre*, trans. John Willet, 179–208. Hill and Wang.

Brickman, P., D. Coates, and R. Janoff-Bulman. 1978. "Lottery Winners and Accident Victims: Is Happiness Relative?" *Journal of Personality and Social Psychology* 36(8): 917–27.

Brock, Stuart, and Anthony Everett, eds. 2015. *Fictional Objects*. Oxford University Press.

Broome, J. 2004. "Reasons." In *Reason and Value: Themes from the Moral Philosophy of Joseph Raz*, edited by R. J. Wallace et al., 28–55. Oxford University Press.

Browne, Kevin D., and Catherine Hamilton-Giachritsis. 2005. "The Influence of Violent Media on Children and Adolescents: A Public-Health Approach." *The Lancet* 365(9460): 702–10.

Bryant, David, Barbara Tversky, and Nancy Franklin. 1992. "Internal and External Spatial Frameworks for Representing Described Scenes." *Journal of Memory and Language* 31: 74–98.

Buccino, Giovanni, Lucia Riggio, Giorgia Melli, Ferdinand Binkofski, Vittorio Gallese, and Giacomo Rizzolatti. 2005. "Listening to Action-Related Sentences Modulates the Activity of the Motor System: A Combined TMS and Behavioral Study." *Cognitive Brain Research* 24(3): 355–63.

Buccino, Giovanni, et al. 2001. "Action Observation Activates Premotor and Parietal Areas in a Somatotopic Manner: An FMRI Study." *European Journal of Neuroscience* 13(2): 400–404.

Budd, Malcolm. 1992. *Music and the Emotions: The Philosophical Theories*. Routledge.

Budd, Malcolm. 1995. *Values of Art: Pictures, Poetry, and Music*. Viking.

Bushman, Brad J., and Craig A. Anderson. 2009. "Comfortably Numb: Desensitizing Effects of Violent Media on Helping Others." *Psychological Science* 20(3): 273–77.

Byrne, Richard, and Andrew Whiten, eds. 1988. *Machiavellian Intelligence: Social Expertise and the Evolution of Intellect in Monkeys, Apes and Humans*. Clarendon Press.

Byrne, Ruth M. J. 2007. *The Rational Imagination: How People Create Alternatives to Reality*. MIT Press.

Cabeza, Roberto, and Lars Nyberg. 2000. "Imaging Cognition II: An Empirical Review of 275 PET and FMRI Studies." *Journal of Cognitive Neuroscience* 12(1): 1–47.

Cacioppo, John T., et al. 2000. "The Psychophysiology of Emotion." In *Handbook of Emotions*, 2nd ed., edited by Michael Lewis and Jeannette M. Haviland, 173–91. Guilford Press.

Camerer, Colin, George Loewenstein, and Martin Weber. 1989. "The Curse of Knowledge in Economic Settings: An Experimental Analysis." *Journal of Political Economy* 97(5): 1232–54.

Carlson, Stephanie M., Louis J. Moses, and Casey Breton. 2002. "How Specific Is the Relation between Executive Function and Theory of Mind? Contributions of Inhibitory Control and Working Memory." *Infant and Child Development* 11(2): 73–92.

Carr, Laurie, Marco Iacoboni, Marie-Charlotte Dubeau, John C. Mazziotta, and Gian Luigi Lenzi. 2003. "Neural Mechanisms of Empathy in Humans: A Relay from Neural Systems for Imitation to Limbic Areas." *Proceedings of the National Academy of Sciences* 100(9): 5497–502.

Carroll, James M., and James A. Russell. 1996. "Do Facial Expressions Signal Specific Emotions? Judging Emotion from the Face in Context." *Journal of Personality and Social Psychology* 70(2): 205.

Carroll, John S. 1978. "The Effect of Imagining an Event on Expectations for the Event: An Interpretation in Terms of the Availability Heuristic." *Journal of Experimental Social Psychology* 14(1): 88–96.

Carroll, Noël. 1992. "Art, Interpretation, and Conversation." In *Intention and Interpretation*, edited by Gary Iseminger, 97–131. Temple University Press.

Carroll, Noël. 1996. "Moderate Moralism." *British Journal of Aesthetics* 36(3): 223–39.

Carroll, Noël. 1997. "Art, Narrative, and Emotion." In *Emotion and the Arts*, edited by Mette Hjort and Sue Laver, 190–211. Oxford University Press.

Carroll, Noël. 1999. "Film, Emotion, and Genre." In *Passionate Views: Film, Cognition and Emotion*, edited by Carl Plantinga and Greg M. Smith, 21–47. Johns Hopkins University Press.

Carroll, Noël. 2003a. "Art and Mood: Preliminary Notes and Conjectures." *The Monist* 86(4): 521–56.

Carroll, Noël. 2003b. *The Philosophy of Horror: Or, Paradoxes of the Heart.* Routledge.

Carroll, Noël. 2004. "Sympathy for the Devil." In *The Sopranos and Philosophy: I Kill Therefore I Am*, edited by Richard Greene and Peter Vernezze, 121–36. Open Court.

Carroll, Noël. 2008. *On Criticism.* Routledge.

Carroll, Noël. 2014. "Creativity and the Insight That Literature Brings." In *The Philosophy of Creativity: New Essays*, ed. Elliott Samuel Paul and Scott Barry Kaufman. Oxford University Press.

Carruthers, Peter. 2006. "Why Pretend?" In *Architecture of the Imagination: New Essays on Pretence, Possibility, and Fiction*, edited by Shaun Nichols, 89–109. Oxford University Press.

Carruthers, Peter. 2007. "The Creative Action Theory of Creativity." *Innate Mind* 3: 154–71.

Carruthers, Peter. 2011. *The Opacity of Mind: An Integrative Theory of Self-Knowledge.* Oxford University Press.

Carruthers, Peter, and Peter K. Smith. 1996. *Theories of Theories of Mind.* Cambridge University Press.

Carver, C. S., et al. 1983. "Modeling: An Analysis in Terms of Category Accessibility." *Journal of Experimental Social Psychology* 19: 403–21.

Chalmers, David J. 2002. "Does Conceivability Entail Possibility?" In *Conceivability and Possibility*, edited by Tamar S. Gendler and John Hawthorne, 145–200. Oxford University Press.

Chan, Timothy, ed. 2014. *The Aim of Belief.* Oxford University Press.

Charland, Louis C. 1997. "Reconciling Cognitive and Perceptual Theories of Emotion: A Representational Proposal." *Philosophy of Science* 64(4): 555–79.

Chartrand, Tanya L., and John A. Bargh. 1999. "The Chameleon Effect: The Perception-Behavior Link and Social Interaction." *Journal of Personality and Social Psychology* 76(6): 893–910.

Choi, J. 2003. "All the Right Responses: Fiction Films and Warranted Emotions." *British Journal of Aesthetics* 43(3): 308–21.

Cichy, Radoslaw M., Jakob Heinzle, and John-Dylan Haynes. 2011. "Imagery and Perception Share Cortical Representations of Content and Location." *Cerebral Cortex* 22(2): 372–80.

Clore, Gerald L., and Stanley Colcombe. 2003. "The Parallel Worlds of Affective Concepts and Feelings." In *The Psychology of Evaluation: Affective Processes in Cognition and Emotion*, edited by Jochen Musch, Karl Christoph Klauer, 335–69. Lawrence Erlbaum Associates.

Clore, Gerald L., Karen Gasper, and Erika Garvin. 2001. "Affect as Information." In *Handbook of Affect and Social Cognition*, edited by Joseph P. Forgas, 121–44. Psychology Press.

Coan, James A., and John Allen, eds. 2007. *Handbook of Emotion Elicitation and Assessment.* Oxford University Press.

Cohen, Jonathan. 2004. "Parasocial Break-up from Favorite Television Characters: The Role of Attachment Styles and Relationship Intensity." *Journal of Social and Personal Relationships 21*(2): 187–202.

Cohen, Ted. 1999. *Jokes: Philosophical Thoughts on Joking Matters*. University of Chicago Press.

Coplan, Amy. 2004. "Empathic Engagement with Narrative Fictions." *Journal of Aesthetics and Art Criticism 62*(2): 141–52.

Coplan, Amy. 2006. "Catching Characters' Emotions: Emotional Contagion Responses to Narrative Fiction Film." *Film Studies 8*: 26–38.

Crane, Tim. 1992. *The Contents of Experience: Essays on Perception*. Cambridge University Press.

Craver-Lemley, Catherine, and Adam Reeves. 1992. "How Visual Imagery Interferes with Vision." *Psychological Review 99*(4): 633–49.

Currie, Gregory. 1990. *The Nature of Fiction*. Cambridge University Press.

Currie, Gregory. 1995a. *Image and Mind: Film, Philosophy and Cognitive Science*. Cambridge University Press.

Currie, Gregory. 1995b. "Imagination as Simulation: Aesthetics Meets Cognitive Science." In *Mental Simulation*, edited by Martin Davies and Tony Stone, 151–69. Blackwell.

Currie, Gregory. 1995c. "The Moral Psychology of Fiction." *Australasian Journal of Philosophy 73*(2): 250–59.

Currie, Gregory. 1997. "The Paradox of Caring: Fiction and the Philosophy of Mind." In *Emotion and the Arts*, edited by Mette Hjort and Sue Lever, 63–77. Oxford University Press.

Currie, Gregory. 2010a. *Narratives and Narrators: A Philosophy of Stories*. Oxford University Press.

Currie, Gregory. 2010b. "Tragedy." *Analysis 70*(4): 632–38.

Currie, Gregory. 2014. "Emotions Fit for Fiction." In *Emotion and Value*, edited by Sabine Roeser, 146–68. Oxford.

Currie, Gregory, and Ian Ravenscroft. 2002. *Recreative Minds: Imagination in Philosophy and Psychology*. Oxford University Press.

Cuthbert, Bruce N., Scott R. Vrana, and Margaret M. Bradley. 1991. "Imagery: Function and Physiology." In *Advances in Psychophysiology: A Research Annual*, edited by J. R. Jennings, P. K. Ackles, and M. G. H. Coles, Jessica Kingsley. Vol. 4: 1–42.

Dadlez, E. M. 1997. *What's Hecuba to Him?: Fictional Events and Actual Emotions*. Pennsylvania State University Press.

Damasio, Antonio R. 1994. *Descartes' Error: Emotion, Reason, and the Human Brain*. Putnam.

Damasio, Antonio R., Thomas J. Grabowski, Antoine Bechara, Hanna Damasio, Laura L. B. Ponto, Josef Parvizi, and Richard D. Hichwa. 2000. "Subcortical and Cortical Brain Activity during the Feeling of Self-Generated Emotions." *Nature Neuroscience 3*(10): 1049–56.

Dancy, Jonathan. 1985. "The Role of Imaginary Cases in Ethics." *Pacific Philosophical Quarterly 66*(1–2): 141–53.

Dancy, Jonathan. 2000. *Practical Reality*. Clarendon Press.

Dante Alighieri. 1980. *Inferno*. Trans. Allen Mandelbaum. University of California Press.

Danto, Arthur. 1981. *The Transfiguration of the Commonplace*. Harvard University Press.

D'Arms, Justin, and Daniel Jacobson. 2000. "The Moralistic Fallacy: On the 'Appropriateness' of Emotions." *Philosophical and Phenomenological Research* 61(1): 65–90.

Darnton, John. 1994. "Self-Made Monster: An Actor's Creation." *New York Times*, February 13.

Darwin, Charles. 1872. *The Expression of the Emotions in Man and Animals*. John Murray.

Davidson, Donald. 1982. "Paradoxes of Irrationality." In *Problems of Rationality*, edited by Donald Davidson, 169–88. Oxford University Press.

Davidson, Richard J. 2004. "Affective Style: Causes and Consequences." In *Essays in Social Neuroscience*, 77–91. MIT Press.

Davies, David. 2007. *Aesthetics and Literature*. Continuum.

Davies, David. 2011. "Infectious Music." In *Empathy: Philosophical and Psychological Perspectives*, edited by Amy Coplan and Peter Goldie, 134–48. Oxford University Press.

Davies, David. 2015. "Fictive Utterance and the Fictionality of Narratives and Works." *British Journal of Aesthetics* 55(1): 39–55.

Davies, Stephen. 2006. "Aesthetic Judgements, Artworks and Functional Beauty." *Philosophical Quarterly* 56(223): 224–41.

Davies, Stephen. 1991. *Definitions of Art*, Cornell University Press.

Davis, M. H., et al. 1996. "Effect of Perspective-Taking on the Cognitive Representation of Persons: A Merging of Self and Other." *Journal of Personality and Social Psychology* 70: 713–26.

De Sousa, Ronald. 1987. *The Rationality of Emotion*. MIT Press.

De Vega, Manuel, José M. Diaz, and Inmaculada León. 1997. "To Know or Not to Know: Comprehending Protagonists' Beliefs and Their Emotional Consequences." *Discourse Processes* 23(2): 169–92.

Decety, Jean, and Thierry Chaminade. 2003. "Neural Correlates of Feeling Sympathy." *Neuropsychologia* 41(2): 127–38.

Decety, Jean, and Thierry Chaminade. 2005. "The Neurophysiology of Imitation and Intersubjectivity." *Perspectives on Imitation: From Neuroscience to Social Science*, edited by Susan L. Hurley and Nick Chater. 1: 119–40.

Decety, Jean, and Julie Grèzes. 2006. "The Power of Simulation: Imagining One's Own and Other's Behavior." *Brain Research* 1079(1): 4–14.

Decety, Jean, and Philip L. Jackson. 2006. "A Social-Neuroscience Perspective on Empathy." *Current Directions in Psychological Science* 15(2): 54–58.

Decety, Jean, Marc Jeannerod, and Claude Prablanc. 1989. "The Timing of Mentally Represented Actions." *Behavioural Brain Research* 34(1): 35–42.

Deigh, J. 1994. "Cognitivism in the Theory of Emotions." *Ethics* 104(4): 824–54.

Demarais, Ann M., and Barry H. Cohen. 1998. "Evidence for Image-Scanning Eye Movements during Transitive Inference." *Biological Psychology* 49(3): 229–47.

Denis, Michel, and Stephen M. Kosslyn. 1999. "Scanning Visual Mental Images: A Window on the Mind." *Cahiers de Psychologie Cognitive / Current Psychology of Cognition* 18(4): 409–65.

Deonna, Julien, and Fabrice Teroni. 2012. *The Emotions: A Philosophical Introduction*. Routledge.

Derryberry, Douglas, and Don M. Tucker. 1994. "Motivating the Focus of Attention." In *The Heart's Eye: Emotional Influences in Perception and Attention*, edited by P. M. Niedenthal and S. Kitayama, 167–96. Academic Press.

Descartes, René. 1988. *Descartes: Selected Philosophical Writings*. Translated by John Cottingham et al. Cambridge University Press.

DeSteno, David, Richard E. Petty, Duane T. Wegener, and Derek D. Rucker. 2000. "Beyond Valence in the Perception of Likelihood: The Role of Emotion Specificity." *Journal of Personality and Social Psychology* 78(3): 397–416.

Dickie, G. 1997. "Art: Function or Procedure: Nature or Culture?" *Journal of Aesthetics and Art Criticism* 55(1): 19–28.

Diderot, Denis. 1761. "Eloge de Richardson." In *Oeuvres Complètes*, vol. 5, 127–46. Le Club Français du Livre.

Dietrich, Arne. 2008. "Imaging the Imagination: The Trouble with Motor Imagery." *Methods* 45(4): 319–24.

Dijksterhuis, Ap. 2005. "Why We Are Social Animals: The High Road to Imitation as Social Glue." *Perspectives on Imitation: From Neuroscience to Social Science* 2: 207–20.

Dimberg, Ulf, and Maria Petterson. 2000. "Facial Reactions to Happy and Angry Facial Expressions: Evidence for Right Hemisphere Dominance." *Psychophysiology* 37(5): 693–96.

Dimberg, Ulf, et al. 2000. "Unconscious Facial Reactions to Emotional Facial Expressions." *Psychological Science* 11(1): 86–89.

Dion, Karen, Ellen Berscheid, and Elaine Walster. 1972. "What Is Beautiful Is Good." *Journal of Personality and Social Psychology* 24(3): 285–90.

Doggett, Tyler, and Andy Egan. 2012. "How We Feel About Terrible, Non-existent Mafiosi." *Philosophy and Phenomenological Research* 84(2): 277–306.

Döring, Sabine A. 2003. "Explaining Action by Emotion." *Philosophical Quarterly* 53(211): 214–30.

Döring, Sabine A. 2007. "Seeing What to Do: Affective Perception and Rational Motivation." *Dialectica* 61(3): 363–94.

Doris, J. M. 2002. *Lack of Character: Personality and Moral Behavior*. Cambridge University Press.

Dostoevsky, Fyodor. 1866/1993. *Crime and Punishment*. Translated by Richard Pevear and Larissa Volokhonsky. Vintage.

Dretske, Fred I. 1997. *Naturalizing the Mind*. MIT Press.

Edwards, George. 2008. *Collected Essays on Modern and Classical Music*. Scarecrow Press.

Ehrsson, H. Henrik, Stefan Geyer, and Eiichi Naito. 2003. "Imagery of Voluntary Movement of Fingers, Toes, and Tongue Activates Corresponding Body-Part-Specific Motor Representations." *Journal of Neurophysiology* 90(5): 3304–16.

Ekman, Paul. 1992. "An Argument for Basic Emotions." *Cognition & Emotion* 6(3–4): 169–200.

Ekman, Paul. 1994. "Moods, Emotions, and Traits." In *The Nature of Emotion: Fundamental Questions*, edited by Paul Ekman and Richard J. Davidson, 56–58. Oxford University Press.

Eldridge, Richard. 1989. *On Moral Personhood: Philosophy, Literature, Criticism, and Self-Understanding*. University of Chicago Press.

Eliot, George. 1998. *Middlemarch*. Oxford.

Elster, Jon. 1999. *Alchemies of the Mind*. Cambridge University Press.

Eslick, Andrea N., Lisa K. Fazio, and Elizabeth J. Marsh. 2011. "Ironic Effects of Drawing Attention to Story Errors." *Memory* 19(2): 184–91.

Farah, Martha J. 1984. "The Neurological Basis of Mental Imagery: A Componential Analysis." *Cognition* 18(1): 245–72.

Feagin, Susan. 1983. "The Pleasures of Tragedy." *American Philosophical Quarterly* 20(1): 95–104.

Feagin, Susan. 1984. "Some Pleasures of Imagination." *Journal of Aesthetics and Art Criticism* 43(1): 41–55.

Feagin, Susan. 1996. *Reading with Feeling: The Aesthetics of Appreciation.* Cornell University Press.

Feagin, Susan. 2011. "Empathizing as Simulating." In *Empathy: Philosophical and Psychological Perspectives*, edited by Amy Coplan and Peter Goldie, 149–61. Oxford University Press.

Fehige, Christoph. 2001. "Instrumentalism." In *Varieties of Practical Reasoning*, edited by Elijah Millgram, 49–76. MIT Press.

Ferguson, Christopher J., Cheryl K. Olson, Lawrence A. Kutner, and Dorothy E. Warner. 2014. "Violent Video Games, Catharsis Seeking, Bullying, and Delinquency: A Multivariate Analysis of Effects." *Crime & Delinquency* 60(5): 764–84.

Fernández-Dols, José-Miguel, Flor Sanchez, Pilar Carrera, and Maria-Angeles Ruiz-Belda. 1997. "Are Spontaneous Expressions and Emotions Linked? An Experimental Test of Coherence." *Journal of Nonverbal Behavior* 21(3): 163–77.

Ferstl, Evelyn C., Mike Rinck, and D. Yves Von Cramon. 2005. "Emotional and Temporal Aspects of Situation Model Processing during Text Comprehension: An Event-Related FMRI Study." *Journal of Cognitive Neuroscience* 17(5): 724–39.

Fielding, Henry. 1750/1999. *Tom Jones.* Wordsworth Classics.

Fine, Kit. 1995. "Ontological Dependence." *Proceedings of the Aristotelian Society* 95(1): 269–90.

Finzi, Eric, and Norman E. Rosenthal. 2014. "Treatment of Depression with OnabotulinumtoxinA: A Randomized, Double-Blind, Placebo Controlled Trial." *Journal of Psychiatric Research* 52: 1–6.

Firestone, Chaz, and Brian J. Scholl. 2016. "Cognition Does Not Affect Perception: Evaluating the Evidence for 'Top-Down' Effects." *Behavioral and Brain Sciences* 39: E229. doi:10.1017/S0140525X15000965.

Fischer, M. H., and R. A. Zwaan. 2008. "Embodied Language: A Review of the Role of the Motor System in Language Comprehension." *Quarterly Journal of Experimental Psychology* 61(6): 825–50.

Fischhoff, Baruch. 1975. "Hindsight Is Not Equal to Foresight: The Effect of Outcome Knowledge on Judgment under Certainty." *Journal of Experimental Psychology: Human Perception and Performance* 1(3): 288–99.

Fish, Stanley. 1998. *Surprised by Sin: The Reader in "Paradise Lost".* Harvard University Press.

Flaubert, Gustave. 1992. *Madame Bovary.* Translated by Francis Steegmuller. Random House.

Fodor, Jerry A. 1975. *The Language of Thought.* Vol. 5. Harvard University Press.

Forgas, Joseph P., and Patrick T. Vargas. 2000. "The Effects of Mood on Social Judgment and Reasoning." In *Handbook of Emotions*, 2nd ed., edited by Michael Lewis and Jeannette M. Haviland, 350–68. Guilford Press.

Foroni, Francesco, and Gün R. Semin. 2009. "Language That Puts You in Touch with Your Bodily Feelings: The Multimodal Responsiveness of Affective Expressions." *Psychological Science* 20(8): 974–80.

Forster, E. M. 1927. *Aspects of the Novel*. Harcourt.

Frankfurt, Harry G. 1971. "Freedom of the Will and the Concept of a Person." *Journal of Philosophy* 68(1): 5–20.

Fredrickson, Barbara L., and Christine Branigan. 2005. "Positive Emotions Broaden the Scope of Attention and Thought-Action Repertoires." *Cognition & Emotion* 19(3): 313–32.

Friend, Stacie. 2003. "How I Really Feel about JFK." In *Imagination, Philosophy and the Arts*, edited by Matthew Kieran and Dominic Lopes, 35–53. Routledge.

Friend, Stacie. 2007. "Fictional Characters." *Philosophy Compass* 2(2): 141–56.

Friend, Stacie. 2008. "Imagining Fact and Fiction." In *New Waves in Aesthetics*, edited by Kathleen Stock and Katherine Thomson-Jones, 150–69. Palgrave Macmillan.

Frijda, Nico H. 2007. *The Laws of Emotion*. Erlbaum.

Gallese, V. 2001. "The Shared Manifold Hypothesis: From Mirror Neurons to Empathy." *Journal of Consciousness Studies* 85(7): 33–50.

Ganis, Giorgio, William L. Thompson, and Stephen M. Kosslyn. 2004. "Brain Areas Underlying Visual Mental Imagery and Visual Perception: An FMRI Study." *Cognitive Brain Research* 20(2): 226–41.

Gaut, Berys. 1998. "The Ethical Criticism of Art." In *Aesthetics and Ethics: Essays at the Intersection*, edited by Jerrold Levinson, 182–203. Cambridge.

Gaut, Berys. 2003. "Reasons, Emotions, and Fictions." In *Imagination, Philosophy, and the Arts*, edited by Matthew Kieran and Dominic Lopes, 15–34. Routledge.

Gaut, Berys. 2006. "Imaginative Contagion." *Metaphilosophy* 37(2): 183–203.

Gaut, Berys. 2007. *Art, Emotion and Ethics*. Oxford University Press.

Gaut, Berys. 2010. "Empathy and Identification in Cinema." *Midwest Studies in Philosophy* 34(1): 136–57.

Gaut, Berys. 2010. *Intuition, Imagination, and Philosophical Methodology*. Oxford University Press.

Gaut, Berys. 2003. "Creativity and Imagination." In *The Creation of Art: New Essays in Philosophical Aesthetics*, edited by Berys Gaut and Paisley Livingston, 148–73. Cambridge University Press.

Gell, Alfred. 1998. *Art and Agency: An Anthropological Theory*. Clarendon Press.

Gendler, Tamar. 2000. "The Puzzle of Imaginative Resistance." *Journal of Philosophy* 97(2): 55–81.

Gendler, Tamar, and John Hawthorne. 2002. *Conceivability and Possibility*. Clarendon Press.

Gendler, Tamar, and Karson Kovakovich. 2006. "Genuine Rational Fictional Emotions." In *Contemporary Debates in Aesthetics and the Philosophy of Art*, edited by Matthew Kieran, 241–53. Blackwell.

Gernsbacher, M. A., H. H. Goldsmith, and R. R. W. Robertson. 1992. "Do Readers Mentally Represent Characters' Emotional States?" *Cognition & Emotion* 6(2): 89–111.

Gibbard, Allan. 1992. *Wise Choices, Apt Feelings: A Theory of Normative Judgment*. Oxford University Press.

Gilbert, Daniel, and Timothy Wilson. 2007. "Prospection: Experiencing the Future." *Science* 317: 1351–54.

Gilbert, Daniel, et al. 1998. "Immune Neglect: A Source of Durability Bias in Affective Forecasting." *Journal of Personality and Social Psychology* 75: 617–38.

Gilmore, Jonathan. 2000. *The Life of a Style: Beginnings and Endings in the Narrative History of Art*. Cornell University Press.

Gilmore, Jonathan. 2005. "Internal Beauty." *Inquiry 48*(2): 145–54.

Gilmore, Jonathan. 2011a. "Ethics, Aesthetics, and Artistic Ends." *Journal of Value Inquiry 45*(2): 203–14.

Gilmore, Jonathan. 2011b. "Expression as Realization: Speakers' Interests in Freedom of Speech." *Law and Philosophy 30*(5): 517–39.

Gilmore, Jonathan. 2011c. "A Functional View of Artistic Evaluation." *Philosophical Studies 155*(2): 289–305.

Gilmore, Jonathan. 2013. "Criticism." In *The Routledge Companion to Aesthetics*, 3rd ed., edited by Berys Gaut and Dominic Lopes, 375–83. Routledge.

Gilovich, Thomas, Kenneth Savitsky, and Victoria Medvec. 1998. "The Illusion of Transparency: Biased Assessments of Others' Ability to Read One's Emotional States." *Journal of Personality and Social Psychology 75*: 332–46.

Glanz, James. 2009. "Historians Reassess Battle of Agincourt." *New York Times*. Oct. 25.

Gleason, Tracy R. 2013. "Imaginary Relationships." In *The Oxford Handbook of the Development of Imagination*, edited by Marjorie Taylor, 251–71. Oxford University Press.

Glenberg, Arthur M., Marion Meyer, and Karen Lindem. 1987. "Mental Models Contribute to Foregrounding during Text Comprehension." *Journal of Memory and Language 26*(1): 69–83.

Gold, Herbert. 1967. "Interview with Vladimir Nabokov: The Art of Fiction, No. 40." *Paris Review 41* (Summer–Fall).

Goldie, Peter. 2000. *The Emotions: A Philosophical Exploration*. Clarendon.

Goldie, Peter. 2003. "Narrative, Emotion, and Perspective." In *Imagination, Philosophy, and the Arts*, edited by Matthew Kieran and Dominic Lopes, 54–68. Routledge.

Goldie, Peter. 2004. "Emotion, Feeling, and Knowledge of the World." In *Thinking about Feeling: Contemporary Philosophers on Emotions*, edited by Robert C. Solomon, 91–106. Oxford University Press.

Goldie, Peter. 2009. "Getting Feelings into Emotional Experience in the Right Way." *Emotion Review 1*(3): 232–39.

Goldie, Peter. 2011. "Anti-empathy." In *Empathy: Philosophical and Psychological Perspectives*, edited by Amy Coplan and Peter Goldie, 302–317. Oxford University Press.

Goldman, Alvin. 1992. *Liaisons: Philosophy Meets the Cognitive and Social Sciences*. MIT Press.

Goldman, Alvin. 1995. "Empathy, Mind, and Morals." In *Mental Simulation: Evaluations and Applications*, edited by Martin Davies and Tony Stone, 185–208. Blackwell.

Goldman, Alvin. 2006a. "Imagination and Simulation in Audience Responses to Fiction." In *The Architecture of Imagination: New Essays on Pretence, Possibility, and Fiction*, edited by Shaun Nichols, 41–56. Oxford University Press.

Goldman, Alvin. 2006b. *Simulating Minds: The Philosophy, Psychology, and Neuroscience of Mindreading*. Oxford University Press.

Goldman, Alvin. 2011. "Two Routes to Empathy." In *Empathy: Philosophical and Psychological Perspectives*, edited by Amy Coplan and Peter Goldie, 31–44. Oxford University Press.

Goldstein, Noah J., and Robert B. Cialdini. 2007. "The Spyglass Self: A Model of Vicarious Self-Perception." *Journal of Personality and Social Psychology 92*(3): 402–17.

Gollwitzer, Peter M., and John A. Bargh. 2005. "Automaticity in Goal Pursuit." In *Handbook of Competence and Motivation*, edited by A. Elliot and C. Dweck, 624–46. Guilford Press.

Gordon, Robert M. 1986. "Folk Psychology as Simulation." *Mind & Language* 1(2): 158–71.

Gordon, Robert M. 1990. *The Structure of Emotions: Investigations in Cognitive Philosophy.* Cambridge University Press.

Gordon, Robert M. 1995. "Sympathy, Simulation, and the Impartial Spectator." *Ethics* 105(4): 727–42.

Gould, Stephen Jay, and Richard C. Lewontin. 1979. "The Spandrels of San Marco and the Panglossian Paradigm: A Critique of the Adaptationist Programme." *Proceedings of the Royal Society of London B: Biological Sciences* 205(1161): 581–98.

Gray, Elizabeth K., David Watson, Roy L. Payne, and Cary R. Cooper. 2001. "Emotion, Mood, and Temperament: Similarities, Differences, and a Synthesis." In *Emotions at Work: Theory, Research and Applications for Management*, edited by Roy L. Payne, and Cary R. Cooper, 21–43. John Wiley & Sons.

Green, Melanie C., and John K. Donahue. 2009. "Simulated Worlds: Transportation into Narratives." In *Handbook of Imagination and Mental Simulation*, edited by Keith D. Markman, William Klein, and Julie A. Suhr, 241–56. Psychology Press.

Green, Melanie C., Jennifer Garst, Timothy C. Brock, and Sungeun Chung. 2006. "Fact versus Fiction Labeling: Persuasion Parity Despite Heightened Scrutiny of Fact." *Media Psychology* 8(3): 267–85.

Green, Otis Howard. 1992. *The Emotions: A Philosophical Theory.* Springer Science & Business Media.

Greenberg, Clement. 1971. "Avant-Garde and Kitsch." In *Art and Culture: Critical Essays*, 3–21. Beacon Press.

Greene, Joshua D., Leigh E. Nystrom, Andrew D. Engell, John M. Darley, and Jonathan D. Cohen. 2004. "The Neural Bases of Cognitive Conflict and Control in Moral Judgment." *Neuron* 44(2): 389–400.

Greenspan, Patricia S. 1980. "A Case of Mixed Feelings: Ambivalence and the Logic of Emotion." In *Explaining Emotions*, edited by Amélie O. Rorty, 223–50. University of California Press.

Greenspan, Patricia. S. 1988. *Emotions and Reasons: An Inquiry into Emotional Justification.* Routledge.

Gregory, W. Larry, Robert B. Cialdini, and Kathleen M. Carpenter. 1982. "Self-Relevant Scenarios as Mediators of Likelihood Estimates and Compliance: Does Imagining Make It So?" *Journal of Personality and Social Psychology* 43(1): 89–99.

Griffiths, P. E. 1997. *What Emotions Really Are: The Problem of Psychological Categories.* University of Chicago Press.

Gross, Cornelius T., and Newton Sabino Canteras. 2012. "The Many Paths to Fear." *Nature Reviews Neuroscience* 13(9): 651–58.

Gross, James J., and Robert W. Levenson. 1995. "Emotion Elicitation Using Films." *Cognition & Emotion* 9(1): 87–108.

Gupta, Anil. 2012. "An Account of Conscious Experience." *Analytic Philosophy* 53(1): 1–29.

Gurlyand. 1904. "Reminiscences of A. P. Chekhov." *Teatr i iskusstvo* 28(11).

Gygax, Pascal, Jane Oakhill, and Alan Garnham. 2003. "The Representation of Characters' Emotional Responses: Do Readers Infer Specific Emotions?" *Cognition & Emotion* 17(3): 413–28.

Haidt, Jonathan. 2001. "The Emotional Dog and Its Rational Tail: A Social Intuitionist Approach to Moral Judgment." *Psychological Review* 108(4): 814–34.

Halliwell, Stephen. 2002. *The Aesthetics of Mimesis: Ancient Texts and Modern Problems.* Princeton University Press.

Halpern, Andrea R. 2001. "Cerebral Substrates of Musical Imagery." *Annals of the New York Academy of Sciences 930*(1): 179–92.

Hampson, Peter John, and Christine Duffy. 1984. "Verbal and Spatial Interference Effects in Congenitally Blind and Sighted Subjects." *Canadian Journal of Experimental Psychology 38*: 411.

Hanakawa, Takashi, Ilka Immisch, Keiichiro Toma, Michael A. Dimyan, Peter Van Gelderen, and Mark Hallett. 2003. "Functional Properties of Brain Areas Associated with Motor Execution and Imagery." *Journal of Neurophysiology 89*(2): 989–1002.

Harold, James. 2000. "Empathy with Fictions." *British Journal of Aesthetics 40*(3): 340–55.

Harold, James. 2005. "Infected by Evil." *Philosophical Explorations 8*(2): 173–87.

Harold, James. 2007. "Imagining Evil (Or, How I Learned to Stop Worrying and Love the Sopranos)." In *The Proceedings of the Twenty-First World Congress of Philosophy 12*: 7–14.

Harris, Paul. 2000. *The Work of the Imagination.* Blackwell.

Harris, Paul, Robert D. Kavanaugh, Henry M. Wellman, and Anne K. Hickling. 1993. "Young Children's Understanding of Pretense." *Monographs of the Society for Research in Child Development 58*(1): 1–107.

Hatfield, Elaine, John T. Cacioppo, and Richard L. Rapson. 1992. "Primitive Emotional Contagion." *Review of Personality and Social Psychology 14*: 151–77.

Hatfield, Elaine, John T. Cacioppo, and Richard L. Rapson. 1994. *Emotional Contagion, 1.* Cambridge University Press.

Hauk, Olaf, Ingrid Johnsrude, and Friedemann Pulvermüller. 2004. "Somatotopic Representation of Action Words in Human Motor and Premotor Cortex." *Neuron 41*(2): 301–7.

Hazlett, Allan. 2009. "How to Defend Response Moralism." *British Journal of Aesthetics 49*(3): 241–55.

Helm, Bennett W. 2002. "Felt Evaluations: A Theory of Pleasure and Pain." *American Philosophical Quarterly 39*(1): 13–30.

Helm, Bennett W. 2007. *Emotional Reason: Deliberation, Motivation, and the Nature of Value.* Cambridge University Press.

Hennenlotter, Andreas, et al. 2005. "A Common Neural Basis for Receptive and Expressive Communication of Pleasant Facial Affect." *Neuroimage 26*(2): 581–91.

Hennenlotter, Andreas, et al. 2008. "The Link between Facial Feedback and Neural Activity within Central Circuitries of Emotion: New Insights from Botulinum Toxin-Induced Denervation of Frown Muscles." *Cerebral Cortex 19*(3): 537–42.

Heyes, Cecilia. 2010. "Where Do Mirror Neurons Come From?" *Neuroscience & Biobehavioral Reviews 34*(4): 575–83.

Heyworth, Peter. 1996. *Otto Klemperer. Vol. 1, 1885–1933: His Life and Times.* Cambridge University Press.

Hickok, Gregory. 2009. "Eight Problems for the Mirror Neuron Theory of Action Understanding in Monkeys and Humans." *Journal of Cognitive Neuroscience 21*(7): 1229–43.

Higgins, E. T., W. S. Rholes, and C. R. Jones. 1977. "Category Accessibility and Impression Formation." *Journal of Experimental Social Psychology 13*: 141–54.

Holland, Peter C., and Michela Gallagher. 1999. "Amygdala Circuitry in Attentional and Representational Processes." *Trends in Cognitive Sciences 3*(2): 65–73.

Holmes, Emily A., and Andrew Mathews. 2005. "Mental Imagery and Emotion: A Special Relationship?" *Emotion* 5(4): 489.

Hopkins, Robert. 2010. "Inflected Pictorial Experience: Its Treatment and Significance." In *Philosophical Perspectives on Depiction*, edited by Catharine Abell, and Katerina Bantinaki, 151–80. Oxford.

Horgan, Terence, and John Tienson. 2002. "The Intentionality of Phenomenology and the Phenomenology of Intentionality." In *Philosophy of Mind: Classical and Contemporary Readings*, edited by David Chalmers, 520–33. Oxford.

Horowitz, Tamara. 1998. "Philosophical Intuitions and Psychological Theory." *Ethics* 108(2): 367–85.

Hume, David. 1739–40/1978. *Treatise of Human Nature*, edited by L. A. Selby-Bigge. Oxford University Press.

Hume, David. 1777/1975. *Enquiries Concerning the Human Understanding and Concerning the Principles of Morals*, edited by L. A. Selby-Bigge. Oxford University Press.

Hume, David. 1987. "Of Tragedy." In *Essays: Moral, Political, and Literary*, edited by E. F. Miller. Liberty.

Humphrey, Katherine, and Geoffrey Underwood. 2008. "Fixation Sequences in Imagery and in Recognition during the Processing of Pictures of Real-World Scenes." *Journal of Eye Movement Research* 2(2): 1–15.

Hurley, Susan. 2008. "The Shared Circuits Model (SCM): How Control, Mirroring, and Simulation Can Enable Imitation, Deliberation, and Mindreading." *Behavioral and Brain Sciences* 31(1): 1–22.

Ichikawa, Jonathan, and Benjamin Jarvis. 2009. "Thought-Experiment Intuitions and Truth in Fiction." *Philosophical Studies* 142(2): 221–46.

Intraub, Helene, and James E. Hoffman. 1992. "Reading and Visual Memory: Remembering Scenes That Were Never Seen." *American Journal of Psychology* 105(1): 101–14.

Isenberg, Nancy, David Silbersweig, Almut Engelien, Sylvia Emmerich, Kishor Malavade, Bradley Beattie, Andrew C. Leon, and Emily Stern. 1999. "Linguistic Threat Activates the Human Amygdala." *Proceedings of the National Academy of Sciences* 96(18): 10456–59.

Ishai, Alumit, and Dov Sagi. 1995. "Common Mechanisms of Visual Imagery and Perception." *Science* 268(5218): 1772–74.

Izard, Carroll E. 1991. *The Psychology of Emotions*. Springer Science & Business Media.

Jabbi, Mbemba, Jojanneke Bastiaansen, and Christian Keysers. 2008. "A Common Anterior Insula Representation of Disgust Observation, Experience and Imagination Shows Divergent Functional Connectivity Pathways." *PloS One* 3(8): e2939.

Jabbi, Mbemba, Marte Swart, and Christian Keysers. 2007. "Empathy for Positive and Negative Emotions in the Gustatory Cortex." *Neuroimage* 34(4): 1744–53.

Jackson, Philip L., Eric Brunet, Andrew N. Meltzoff, and Jean Decety. 2006. "Empathy Examined through the Neural Mechanisms Involved in Imagining How I Feel versus How You Feel Pain." *Neuropsychologia* 44(5): 752–61.

Jeannerod, Marc. 1994. "The Representing Brain: Neural Correlates of Motor Intention and Imagery." *Behavioral and Brain Sciences* 17(2): 187–202.

Jeannerod, Marc. 2001. "Neural Simulation of Action: A Unifying Mechanism for Motor Cognition." *Neuroimage* 14(1): S103–9.

Johansson, Petter, Lars Hall, Sverker Sikström, and Andreas Olsson. 2005. "Failure to Detect Mismatches between Intention and Outcome in a Simple Decision Task." *Science* 310(5745): 116–19.

Johnson, Marcia K. , Shahin Hashtroudi, and D. Stephen Lindsay. 1993. "Source Monitoring." *Psychological Bulletin 114*(1): 3–28.

Johnson, Samuel. 1751. *The Rambler 1*, no. 125.

Johnson, Samuel. "Preface to Shakespeare." 1765/1978. In *Johnson on Shakespeare*, edited by Arthur Sherbo. Yale University Press.

Johnson-Laird, Philip N. 1983. *Mental Models: Towards a Cognitive Science of Language, Inference, and Consciousness*. Harvard University Press.

Johnston, M. 2001. "Is Affect Always Mere Effect?" *Philosophy and Phenomenological Research 63*(1): 225–28.

Jordens, Karen, and Frank Van Overwalle. 2005. "Cognitive Dissonance and Affect: An Initial Test of a Connectionist Account." *Psychologica Belgica 45*(3): 157–84.

Joyce, James. 1914/*2006*. *Dubliners*. Norton.

Joyce, Richard. 2000. "Rational Fear of Monsters." *British Journal of Aesthetics 40*(2): 209–24.

Kael, Pauline. 1965/2011. "McCall's." In *5001 Nights at the Movies*. Holt Paperbacks.

Kahneman, Daniel. 2003. "A Perspective on Judgment and Choice: Mapping Bounded Rationality." *American Psychologist 58*(9): 697–720.

Kahneman, Daniel, and Amos Tversky. 2000. *Choices, Values, and Frames*. Cambridge University Press.

Kaufman, Geoff F., and Lisa K. Libby. 2012. "Changing Beliefs and Behavior through Experience-Taking." *Journal of Personality and Social Psychology 103*(1): 1–19.

Kawin, Bruce F. 1992. *How Movies Work*. University of California Press.

Kehner, Dacher, Kenneth D. Locke, and Paul C. Aurain. 1993. "The Influence of Attributions on the Relevance of Negative Feelings to Personal Satisfaction." *Personality and Social Psychology Bulletin 19*(1): 21–29.

Keillor, Jocelyn M., Anna M. Barrett, Gregory P. Crucian, Sarah Kortenkamp, and Kenneth M. Heilman. 2002. "Emotional Experience and Perception in the Absence of Facial Feedback." *Journal of the International Neuropsychological Society 8*(1): 130–35.

Kelly, T. 2003. "Epistemic Rationality as Instrumental Rationality: A Critique." *Philosophy and Phenomenological Research 66*(3): 612–40.

Kenny, Anthony. 1963. *Action, Emotion, and Will*. Routledge and Kegan Paul.

Keysers, Christian, Bruno Wicker, Valeria Gazzola, Jean-Luc Anton, Leonardo Fogassi, and Vittorio Gallese. 2004. "A Touching Sight: SII/PV Activation during the Observation and Experience of Touch." *Neuron 42*(2): 335–46.

Kidd, David Comer, and Emanuele Castano. 2013. "Reading Literary Fiction Improves Theory of Mind." *Science 342*(6156): 377–80. https://doi.org/10.1126/science.1239918.

Kind, Amy. 2011. "The Puzzle of Imaginative Desire." *Australasian Journal of Philosophy 89*(3): 421–39.

Kind, Amy. 2013. "The Heterogeneity of the Imagination." *Erkenntnis 78*(1): 141–59.

Kinsbourne, Marcel. 2005. "Imitation as Entrainment: Brain Mechanisms and Social Consequences." *Perspectives on Imitation: From Neuroscience to Social Science 2*: 163–72.

Koehler, Derek J. 1991. "Explanation, Imagination, and Confidence in Judgment." *Psychological Bulletin 110*(3): 499–519.

Korsgaard, Christine. 1997. "The Normativity of Instrumental Reason." In *Ethics and Practical Reason*, edited by Garrett Cullity and Berys Gaut, 215–54. Clarendon Press, Oxford University Press.

Korsgaard, Christine. 2009. "The Activity of Reason." In *Proceedings and Addresses of the American Philosophical Association 83*(2): 23–43.

Kosslyn, Stephen. 1973. "Scanning Visual Images: Some Structural Implications." *Attention, Perception, & Psychophysics 14*(1): 90–94.

Kosslyn, Stephen, Giorgio Ganis, and William L. Thompson. 2001. "Neural Foundations of Imagery." *Nature Reviews Neuroscience 2*(9): 635–42.

Kosslyn, Stephen, William L. Thompson, Irene J. Klm, and Nathaniel M. Alpert. 1995. "Topographical Representations of Mental Images in Primary Visual Cortex." *Nature 378*(6556): 496–98.

Kovács, Ágnes Melinda, Ernő Téglás, and Ansgar Denis Endress. 2010. "The Social Sense: Susceptibility to Others' Beliefs in Human Infants and Adults." *Science 330*(6012): 1830–34.

Krahé, Barbara. 2010. *Situation Cognition and Coherence in Personality: An Individual-Centred Approach.* Cambridge University Press.

Kreiman, Gabriel, Christof Koch, and Itzhak Fried. 2000. "Imagery Neurons in the Human Brain." *Nature 408*(6810): 357–61.

Laeng, Bruno, and Dinu-Stefan Teodorescu. 2002. "Eye Scanpaths during Visual Imagery Reenact Those of Perception of the Same Visual Scene." *Cognitive Science 26*(2): 207–31.

Lamarque, Peter. 1981. "How Can We Fear and Pity Fictions?" *British Journal of Aesthetics 21*(4): 291–304.

Lamarque, Peter. 1996. *Fictional Points of View.* Cornell University Press.

Lamarque, Peter. 2002a. "Work and Object." *Proceedings of the Aristotelian Society 102*: 141–62.

Lamarque, Peter. 2002b. "Appreciation and Literary Interpretation." In *Is There a Single Right Interpretation?*, edited by M. Krausz, 285–306. Penn State University Press.

Lamarque, Peter. 2007. "On the Distance between Literary Narratives and Real-Life Narratives." *Royal Institute of Philosophy Supplements 60*: 117–32.

Lamarque, Peter. 2010. "The Uselessness of Art." *Journal of Aesthetics and Art Criticism 68*(3): 205–14.

Lamarque, Peter. 2014. *The Opacity of Narrative.* Rowman & Littlefield.

Lamarque, Peter, and Stein Haugom Olsen. 1996. *Truth, Fiction, and Literature: A Philosophical Perspective.* Oxford University Press.

Lamm, Claus, C. Daniel Batson, and Jean Decety. 2007. "The Neural Substrate of Human Empathy: Effects of Perspective-Taking and Cognitive Appraisal." *Journal of Cognitive Neuroscience 19*(1): 42–58.

Lamm, Claus, Eric C. Porges, John T. Cacioppo, and Jean Decety. 2008. "Perspective Taking Is Associated with Specific Facial Responses during Empathy for Pain." *Brain Research 1227*: 153–61.

Lang, Peter J. 1984. "Cognition in Emotion: Concept and Action." In *Emotions, Cognition, and Behavior*, edited by Carroll E. Izard, Jerome Kagan, and Robert Zajonc, 192–226. Cambridge.

Langland-Hassan, Peter. 2012. "Pretense, Imagination, and Belief: The Single Attitude Theory." *Philosophical Studies 159*(2): 155–79.

Lawrence, Andrew D., Andrew J. Calder, Stephen W. McGowan, and Paul M. Grasby. 2002. "Selective Disruption of the Recognition of Facial Expressions of Anger." *Neuroreport 13*(6): 881–84.

Lazarus, Richard. 1984. "On the Primacy of Cognition." *American Psychologist 39*: 124–29.

Lazarus, Richard. 1991. *Emotion and Adaptation.* Oxford University Press.

LeDoux, Joseph. 1996. *The Emotional Brain*. Simon and Schuster.

LeDoux, Joseph. 2000. "Cognitive-Emotional Interactions: Listen to the Brain." In *Cognitive Neuroscience of Emotion*, edited by R. D. Lane and L. Nadel, 129–55. Oxford University Press.

Lee, Daniel H., Reza Mirza, John G. Flanagan, and Adam K. Anderson. 2014. "Optical Origins of Opposing Facial Expression Actions." *Psychological Science 25*(3): 745–52.

Leslie, A. M. 1987. "Pretense and Representation: The Origins of 'Theory of Mind.'" *Psychological Review 94*(4): 412–26.

Leslie, A. M. 1994. "Pretending and Believing: Issues in the Theory of ToMM 1." *Cognition 50*(1–3): 211–38.

Levin, Irwin P., Sandra L. Schneider, and Gary J. Gaeth. 1998. "All Frames Are Not Created Equal: A Typology and Critical Analysis of Framing Effects." *Organizational Behavior and Human Decision Processes 76*(2): 149–88.

Levenson, Robert W., Paul Ekman, and Wallace V. Friesen. 1990. "Voluntary Facial Action Generates Emotion-Specific Autonomic Nervous System Activity." *Psychophysiology 27*(4): 363–84.

Levinson, Jerrold. 2006. "Hypothetical Intentionalism: Statement, Objections, and Replies." In *Contemplating Art*, 302–15. Oxford University Press.

Lewis, David. 1972. "Psychophysical and Theoretical Identifications." *Australasian Journal of Philosophy 50*(3): 249–58.

Lewis, David. 1978. "Truth in Fiction." *American Philosophical Quarterly 15*(1): 37–46.

Lewis, David. 1986. *On the Plurality of Worlds*. Oxford University Press.

Lhermitte, François, Bernard Pillon, and Michel Serdaru. 1986. "Human Autonomy and the Frontal Lobes. Part I: Imitation and Utilization Behavior: A Neuropsychological Study of 75 Patients." *Annals of Neurology 19*(4): 326–34.

Lillard, Angeline S. 2013. "Fictional Worlds, the Neuroscience of the Imagination, and Childhood." In *The Oxford Handbook of the Development of Imagination*, edited by Marjorie Taylor, 137–60. Oxford University Press.

Lindquist, Kristen A., Tor D. Wager, Hedy Kober, Eliza Bliss-Moreau, and Lisa Feldman Barrett. 2012. "The Brain Basis of Emotion: A Meta-analytic Review." *Behavioral and Brain Sciences 35*(3): 121–43.

Livingston, Paisley, and Alfred R. Mele. 1997. "Evaluating Emotional Responses to Fiction." *Emotion and the Arts*, edited by Mette Hjort and Sue Laver, 157–76. Oxford University Press.

Loewenstein, George, and Jennifer S. Lerner. 2003. "The Role of Affect in Decision Making." In *Handbook of Affective Science*, edited by Richard Davidson, Klaus Sherer, and H. Hill Goldsmith, 619–42. Oxford.

Loftus, Elizabeth F. 2003. "Make-Believe Memories." *American Psychologist 58*(11): 867–73.

Lopes, Dominic McIver. 2005. *Sight and Sensibility*. Clarendon Press.

Lotze, Martin, Pedro Montoya, Michael Erb, Ernst Hülsmann, Herta Flor, Uwe Klose, Niels Birbaumer, and Wolfgang Grodd. 1999. "Activation of Cortical and Cerebellar Motor Areas during Executed and Imagined Hand Movements: An FMRI Study." *Journal of Cognitive Neuroscience 11*(5): 491–501.

Lucretius. 2001. *De Rerum Natura*. Translated by M. F. Smith. Hackett.

Lutz, Catherine, and Geoffrey M. White. 1986. "The Anthropology of Emotions." *Annual Review of Anthropology 15*(1): 405–36.

Lyons, William. 1980. *Emotion*. Cambridge University Press.

Maio, Gregory R., and Victoria M. Esses. 2001. "The Need for Affect: Individual Differences in the Motivation to Approach or Avoid Emotions." *Journal of Personality* 69(4): 583–614.

Mantel, Hillary. 2005. *Beyond Black*. Harper Collins.

Mar, Raymond A. 2011. "The Neural Bases of Social Cognition and Story Comprehension." *Annual Review of Psychology 62*: 103–34.

Mar, Raymond A., and Keith Oatley. 2008. "The Function of Fiction Is the Abstraction and Simulation of Social Experience." *Perspectives on Psychological Science 3*(3): 173–92.

Mar, Raymond A., Keith Oatley, Jacob Hirsh, Jennifer dela Paz, and Jordan B. Peterson. 2006. "Bookworms versus Nerds: Exposure to Fiction versus Non-fiction, Divergent Associations with Social Ability, and the Simulation of Fictional Social Worlds." *Journal of Research in Personality 40*(5): 694–712.

Marsh, Elizabeth J., and Lisa K. Fazio. 2006. "Learning Errors from Fiction: Difficulties in Reducing Reliance on Fictional Stories." *Memory & Cognition 34*(5): 1140–49.

Martin, Michael G. F. 2002. "The Transparency of Experience." *Mind & Language* 17(4): 376–425.

Matravers, Derek. 2001. *Art and Emotion*. Oxford University Press.

Matravers, Derek. 2014. *Fiction and Narrative*. Oxford University Press.

Mazzoni, Giuliana, and Amina Memon. 2003. "Imagination Can Create False Autobiographical Memories." *Psychological Science 14*(2): 186–88.

McDowell, John Henry. 1998. *Mind, Value, and Reality*. Harvard University Press.

McGinn, Colin. 1997. *Ethics, Evil, and Fiction*. Oxford University Press.

McGinn, Colin. 2004. *Mindsight: Image, Dream, Meaning*. Harvard University Press.

McGlone, Matthew S., and Jessica Tofighbakhsh. 1999. "The Keats Heuristic: Rhyme as Reason in Aphorism Interpretation." *Poetics 26*(4): 235–44.

McGlone, Matthew S., and Jessica Tofighbakhsh. 2000. "Birds of a Feather Flock Conjointly(?): Rhyme as Reason in Aphorisms." *Psychological Science 11*(5): 424–28.

McLaughlin, Peter. 2001. *What Functions Explain*. Cambridge University Press.

Meier, Brian P., Michael D. Robinson, L. Elizabeth Crawford, and Whitney J. Ahlvers. 2007. "When 'Light' and 'Dark' Thoughts Become Light and Dark Responses: Affect Biases Brightness Judgments." *Emotion 7*(2): 366–76.

Meskin, Aaron, and Jonathan M. Weinberg. 2003. "Emotions, Fiction, and Cognitive Architecture." *British Journal of Aesthetics 43*(1): 18–34.

Meyer, D. E., and W. Schvaneveldt. 1971. "Facilitation in Recognizing Pairs of Words: Evidence of a Dependence between Retrieval Operations." *Journal of Experimental Psychology 90*: 227–34.

Miall, David S. 2000. "On the Necessity of Empirical Studies of Literary Reading." *Frame: Utrecht Journal of Literary Theory 14*(2–3): 43–59.

Millikan, Ruth Garrett. 1984. *Language, Thought, and Other Biological Categories: New Foundations for Realism*. MIT Press.

Millikan, Ruth Garrett. 1989. "In Defense of Proper Functions." *Philosophy of Science* 56(2): 288–302.

Montaigne, Michel de. 2004. "Apology for Raymond Sebond." In *The Complete Works*, translated by Donald M. Frame. Alfred A. Knopf.

Moran, Richard. 1994. "The Expression of Feeling in Imagination." *Philosophical Review* 103(1): 75–106.

Morris, John S., Arne Öhman, and Raymond J. Dolan. 1998. "Conscious and Unconscious Emotional Learning in the Human Amygdala." *Nature 393*(6684): 467–70.

Moses, Louis J. 2001. "Executive Accounts of Theory-of-Mind Development." *Child Development* 72(3): 688–90.

Mulligan, Kevin. 1998. "From Appropriate Emotions to Values." *Monist* 81(1): 161–88.

Munzert, Jörn, Britta Lorey, and Karen Zentgraf. 2009. "Cognitive Motor Processes: The Role of Motor Imagery in the Study of Motor Representations." *Brain Research Reviews* 60(2): 306–26.

Murdoch, Iris. 2013. *The Sovereignty of Good*. Routledge.

Naccache, Lionel, et al. 2005. "A Direct Intracranial Record of Emotions Evoked by Subliminal Words." *Proceedings of the National Academy of Sciences of the United States of America* 102(21): 7713–17.

Nehamas, Alexander. 2007. *Only a Promise of Happiness: The Place of Beauty in a World of Art*. Princeton University Press.

Nehamas, Alexander. 2015. "Pity and Fear in the Rhetoric and the Poetics." In *Aristotle's "Rhetoric": Philosophical Essays*, edited by Alexander Nehamas and David J. Furley, 257–82. Princeton University Press.

Nehamas, Alexander. 2016. *On Friendship*. Basic Books.

Neill, Alexander. 1993. "Fiction and the Emotions." *American Philosophical Quarterly* 30(1): 1–13.

Neill, Alexander. 1996. "Empathy and (Film) Fiction." In *Post-theory: Reconstructing Film Studies*, edited by David Bordwell and Noël Carroll, 175–94. University of Wisconsin Press.

Neill, Alexander, and Aaron Ridley. 2010. "Religious Music for Godless Ears." *Mind* 119(476): 999–1023.

Newman, Barnett. 1962/1992. Interview with Dorothy Seckler. In *Selected Writings and Interviews*. University of California Press.

Nichols, Shaun. 2004. "Imagining and Believing: The Promise of a Single Code." *Journal of Aesthetics and Art Criticism* 62(2): 129–39.

Nichols, Shaun, ed. 2006a. *The Architecture of the Imagination: New Essays on Pretence, Possibility, and Fiction*. Oxford University Press.

Nichols, Shaun. 2006b. "Just the Imagination: Why Imagining Doesn't Behave like Believing." *Mind & Language* 21(4): 459–74.

Nichols, Shaun, and Stephen Stich. 2000. "A Cognitive Theory of Pretense." *Cognition* 74(2): 115–47.

Nichols, Shaun, and Stephen Stich. 2003. *Mindreading: An Integrated Account of Pretence, Self-Awareness, and Understanding Other Minds*. Oxford University Press.

Nichols, Shaun, et al. 1996. "Varieties of Off-line Simulation." In *Theories of Theories of Mind*, Peter Carruthers and Peter K. Smith, eds. Cambridge University Press. 39–74.

Niedenthal, Paula M., et al. 2001. "When Did Her Smile Drop? Facial Mimicry and the Influences of Emotional State on the Detection of Change in Emotional Expression." *Cognition & Emotion* 15(6): 853–64.

Niedenthal, Paula M., et al. 2005. "Embodiment in Attitudes, Social Perception, and Emotion." *Personality and Social Psychology Review* 9(3): 184–211.

Nietzsche, Friedrich. 2001. *The Gay Science*, Bernard Williams, edited by Cambridge University Press.

Nietzsche, Friedrich. 2006. "On the Genealogy of Morality." In *On the Genealogy of Morality and Other Writings*, edited by Keith Ansell-Pearson and Carol Diethe. Cambridge University Press.

Nisbett, Richard E., and Timothy D. Wilson. 1977. "The Halo Effect: Evidence for Unconscious Alteration of Judgments." *Journal of Personality and Social Psychology* 35(4): 250.

Noordman, Leo G. M., and Wietske Vonk. 1992. "Readers' Knowledge and the Control of Inferences in Reading." *Language and Cognitive Processes* 7(3–4): 373–91.

Norton, Michael I., Benoit Monin, Joel Cooper, and Michael A. Hogg. 2003. "Vicarious Dissonance: Attitude Change from the Inconsistency of Others." *Journal of Personality and Social Psychology* 85(1): 47–62.

Norton, Robert E. 1997. *The Beautiful Soul: Aesthetic Morality in the Eighteenth Century.* Cornell.

Nussbaum, Martha. 1992. *Love's Knowledge: Essays on Philosophy and Literature.* Oxford University Press.

Nussbaum, Martha. 1995a. "Objectification." *Philosophy & Public Affairs* 24(4): 249–91.

Nussbaum, Martha. 1995b. *Poetic Justice: The Literary Imagination and Public Life.* Beacon Press.

Nussbaum, Martha. 2001. *Upheavals of Thought: The Intelligence of Emotions.* Cambridge University Press.

Nussbaum, Martha. 2004. "Emotions as Judgments of Value and Importance." In *Thinking about Feeling: Contemporary Philosophers on Emotions,* edited by Robert C. Solomon, 183–99. Oxford University Press.

Oatley, Keith. 1999. "Meetings of Minds: Dialogue, Sympathy, and Identification in Reading Fiction." *Poetics* 26(5–6): 439–54.

Oatley, Keith, Raymond A. Mar, and Maja Djikic. 2012. "The Psychology of Fiction: Present and Future." In *Cognitive Literary Studies: Current Themes and New Directions,* edited by Isabel Jaén and Julien J. Simon, 235–49. University of Texas Press.

Obhi, Sukhvinder S., and Jeremy Hogeveen. 2010. "Incidental Action Observation Modulates Muscle Activity." *Experimental Brain Research* 203(2): 427–35.

O'Craven, Kathleen M., and Nancy Kanwisher. 2000. "Mental Imagery of Faces and Places Activates Corresponding Stimulus-Specific Brain Regions." *Journal of Cognitive Neuroscience* 12(6): 1013–23.

Öhman, Arne. 2002. "Automaticity and the Amygdala: Nonconscious Responses to Emotional Faces." *Current Directions in Psychological Science* 11(2): 62–66.

Otten, Sabine, and Gordon B. Moskowitz. 2000. "Evidence for Implicit Evaluative In-Group Bias: Affect-Biased Spontaneous Trait Inference in a Minimal Group Paradigm." *Journal of Experimental Social Psychology* 36(1): 77–89.

Owens, David. 2012. *Shaping the Normative Landscape.* Oxford University Press.

Paik, Haejung, and George Comstock. 1994. "The Effects of Television Violence on Antisocial Behavior: A Meta-analysis 1." *Communication Research* 21(4): 516–46.

Paluck, E. L., and D. P. Green. 2009. "Prejudice Reduction: What Works? A Review and Assessment of Research and Practice." *Annual Review of Psychology* 60: 339–67.

Parfit, Derek. 2001. "Rationality and Reasons." In *Exploring Practical Philosophy: From Action to Values,* edited by D. Egonsson et al., 17–39. Ashgate.

Parsons, Glenn, and Allen Carlson. 2008. *Functional Beauty.* Oxford University Press.

Pascual-Leone, Alvaro. 2001. "The Brain That Plays Music and Is Changed by It." *Annals of the New York Academy of Sciences* 930(1): 315–29.

Peacocke, Christopher. 1985. "Imagination, Experience, and Possibility." In *Essays on Berkeley: A Tercentennial Celebration,* edited by John Foster and Howard Robinson, 19–35. Oxford University Press.

Peacocke, Christopher. 1992. *A Study of Concepts*. MIT Press.

Pitt, David. 2004. "The Phenomenology of Cognition, or What Is It Like to Think That P?" *Philosophy and Phenomenological Research 69*(1): 1–36.

Plantinga, Carl. 1999. "The Scene of Empathy and the Human Face on Film." In *Passionate Views: Film, Cognition, and Emotion*, edited by Carl Plantinga and Greg M. Smith, 239–55. Johns Hopkins University Press.

Plato. 1975. *Republic*. Translated by G. M. A. Grube and C.D. C. Reeve. Hackett.

Preston, Beth. 1998. "Why Is a Wing Like a Spoon? A Pluralist Theory of Function." *Journal of Philosophy 95*(5): 215–54.

Preston, Stephanie D., and Frans B. M. De Waal. 2002. "Empathy: Its Ultimate and Proximate Bases." *Behavioral and Brain Sciences 25*(1): 1–20.

Prinz, Jesse. 2004. *Gut Reactions: A Perceptual Theory of Emotion*. Oxford University Press.

Prinz, Jesse. 2006. "Is Emotion a Form of Perception?" *Canadian Journal of Philosophy 36*: 137–60.

Prinz, Jesse. 2007. *The Emotional Construction of Morals*. Oxford University Press.

Prinz, Wolfgang. 2005. "An Ideomotor Approach to Imitation." *Perspectives on Imitation: From Neuroscience to Social Science 1*: 141–56.

Pulvermüller, Friedemann. 2005. "Brain Mechanisms Linking Language and Action." *Nature Reviews Neuroscience 6*(7): 576–82.

Pushkin, Alexander. 2003. *Eugene Onegin*. Translated by Charles Johnston. Penguin.

Putnam, Hilary. 2013. *Meaning and the Moral Sciences*. Routledge.

Rabinowicz, W., and T. Ronnow-Rasmussen. 2004. "The Strike of the Demon: On Fitting Pro-attitudes and Value." *Ethics 114*(3): 391–423.

Radford, Colin. 1975. "How Can We Be Moved by the Fate of Anna Karenina?" *Proceedings of the Aristotelian Society, Supplementary Volumes 49*: 67–93.

Raz, Joseph. 2003. *The Practice of Value*. Clarendon Press.

Reddy, Leila, Naotsugu Tsuchiya, and Thomas Serre. 2010. "Reading the Mind's Eye: Decoding Category Information during Mental Imagery." *NeuroImage 50*(2): 818–25.

Reinhardt, Mark, Holly Edwards, and Erina Duganne. 2007. *Beautiful Suffering: Photography and the Traffic in Pain*. University of Chicago Press.

Ridley, Aaron. 2005. "Tragedy." In *The Oxford Handbook of Aesthetics*, edited by Jerrold Levinson, 408–20. Oxford University Press.

Rizzolatti, Giacomo, and Laila Craighero. 2004. "The Mirror-Neuron System." *Annual. Review of Neuroscience. 27*: 169–92.

Roberts, Robert C. 1988. "What an Emotion Is: A Sketch." *Philosophical Review 97*(2): 183–209.

Roberts, Robert C. 2003. *Emotions: An Essay in Aid of Moral Psychology*. Cambridge University Press.

Robinson, Jenefer. 2005. *Deeper Than Reason: Emotion and Its Role in Literature, Music, and Art*. Oxford University Press.

Rolls, Edmund T. 2000. "Neurophysiology and Functions of the Primate Amygdala, and the Neural Basis of Emotion." In *The Amygdala: A Functional Analysis*, edited by J. Aggleton, 447–78. Oxford University Press.

Rosen, Gideon. 1990. "Modal Fictionalism." *Mind 99*(395): 327–54.

Ross, Lee, David Greene, and Pamela House. 1977. "The 'False Consensus Effect': An Egocentric Bias in Social Perception and Attribution Processes." *Journal of Experimental Social Psychology 13*(3): 279–301.

Roth, Muriel, et al. 1996. "Possible Involvement of Primary Motor Cortex in Mentally Simulated Movement: A Functional Magnetic Resonance Imaging Study." *Neuroreport* 7(7): 1280–84.

Rousseau, Jean-Jacques. 1761/1997. *Julie, or the New Heloise*. 1761/1997. *The Collected Writings of Rousseau*. Trans. Philip Stewart and Jean Vaché. Ed. Roger D. Masters and Christopher Kelly.

Rousseau, Jean-Jacques. 1758/1968. *Politics and the Arts: Letter to M. D'Alembert on the Theatre*. Cornell University Press.

Ruskin, John. 1860. "Of the Pathetic Fallacy." In *Modern Painters*, edited by Edward Tyas Cook, vol. 3, pt. 4. Cambridge.

Ryan, Marie-Laure. 1991. *Possible Worlds, Artificial Intelligence and Narrative Theory*. University of Indiana Press.

Sabatinelli, Dean, et al. 2006. "The Neural Basis of Narrative Imagery: Emotion and Action." *Progress in Brain Research 156*: 93–103.

Saenger, Paul. 1997. *Space between Words: The Origins of Silent Reading*. Stanford University Press.

Sapone, A., et al. 2009. "Hidden Paradoxes in Generic Drug Substitution Affecting Pharmacotherapy." *Journal of Biomedicine and Biotechnology 2009*: 1–2.

Sartre, Jean-Paul. 1948. "Outline of a Theory of the Emotions." Translated by Bernard Frechtman. *Philosophical Library*.

Scanlon, Thomas. 1998. *What We Owe to Each Other*. Harvard University Press.

Schacter, Daniel L., et al. 2012. "The Future of Memory: Remembering, Imagining, and the Brain." *Neuron 76*(4): 677–94.

Schacter, Stanley, and Jerome Singer. 1962. "Cognitive, Social, and Physiological Determinants of Emotional State." *Psychological Review 69*(5): 379–99.

Scheffler, Samuel. 2010. "Valuing." In *Equality and Tradition: Questions of Value in Moral and Political Theory*. Oxford University Press.

Scherer, Klaus R., Angela Schorr, and Tom Johnstone. 2001. *Appraisal Processes in Emotion: Theory, Methods, Research*. Oxford University Press.

Schier, Flint. 1983. "Tragedy and the Community of Sentiment." In *Philosophy and Fiction: Essays in Literary Aesthetics*, edited by Peter Lamarque, 73–92. Aberdeen University Press.

Schlegel, Friedrich. 1849/1956. *The Aesthetic and Miscellaneous Works of Frederick von Schlegel*. Trans. E. J. Millington. London: HG Bohn.

Schnall, Simone, Jonathan Haidt, Gerald L. Clore, and Alexander H. Jordan. 2008. "Disgust as Embodied Moral Judgment." *Personality and Social Psychology Bulletin* 34(8): 1096–109.

Schroeder, Timothy, and Carl Matheson. 2006. "Imagination and Emotion." In *The Architecture of the Imagination: New Essays on Pretence, Possibility, and Fiction*, edited by Shaun Nichols, 19–40. Oxford University Press.

Schueler, G. 1991. "Pro-attitudes and Direction of Fit." *Mind 100*: 277–81.

Schwartz, Gary E., Daniel A. Weinberger, and Jefferson A. Singer. 1981. "Cardiovascular Differentiation of Happiness, Sadness, Anger, and Fear Following Imagery and Exercise." *Psychosomatic Medicine 43*(4): 343–64.

Segal, Sydney J., and Vincent Fusella. 1970. "Influence of Imaged Pictures and Sounds on Detection of Visual and Auditory Signals." *Journal of Experimental Psychology* 83(3.1): 458–64.

Seidel, Angelika, and Jesse Prinz. 2013. "Sound Morality: Irritating and Icky Noises Amplify Judgments in Divergent Moral Domains." *Cognition 127*(1): 1–5.

Shaftsbury. 1714. *Characteristicks of Men, Manners, Opinions, Times.* 2nd ed. Oxford.

Shanks, David R. , et al. 2013. "Priming Intelligent Behavior: An Elusive Phenomenon." *PloS One 8*(4).

Shelley, Percy Bysshe. 1821/1909. "A Defence of Poetry." In *English Essays: From Sir Philip Sidney to Macaulay. With Introductions and Notes*, edited by Charles W. Eliot. P.F. Collier and Son.

Sherman, Steven J., Robert B. Cialdini, Donna F. Schwartzman, and Kim D. Reynolds. 1985. "Imagining Can Heighten or Lower the Perceived Likelihood of Contracting a Disease: The Mediating Effect of Ease of Imagery." *Personality and Social Psychology Bulletin 11*(1): 118–27.

Shidlovski, Daniella, Yaacov Schul, and Ruth Mayo. 2014. "If I Imagine It, Then It Happened: The Implicit Truth Value of Imaginary Representations." *Cognition 133*(3): 517–29.

Shoemaker, Sidney. 1984. "Some Varieties of Functionalism." In *Identity, Cause, and Mind*, 261–86. Cambridge University Press.

Siemer, Matthias, and Rainer Reisenzein. 1998. "Effects of Mood on Evaluative Judgements: Influence of Reduced Processing Capacity and Mood Salience." *Cognition & Emotion 12*(6): 783–805.

Singer, Tania, Ben Seymour, John O'Doherty, Holger Kaube, Raymond J. Dolan, and Chris D. Frith. 2004. "Empathy for Pain Involves the Affective but Not Sensory Components of Pain." *Science 303*(5661): 1157–62.

Sinnott-Armstrong, Walter. 2008. "Framing Moral Intuitions." In *Moral Psychology, vol 2: The Cognitive Science of Morality: Intuition and Diversity*, 47–76. MIT Press.

Sischy, Ingrid. 1991. "Photography: Good Intentions." *New Yorker*, September 9, 89–95.

Skolnick, Deena, and Paul Bloom. 2006. "The Intuitive Cosmology of Fictional Worlds." In *The Architecture of the Imagination: New Essays on Pretence, Possibility, and Fiction*, edited by Shaun Nichols, 73–88. Oxford University Press.

Slotnick, Scott D., William L. Thompson, and Stephen M. Kosslyn. 2005. "Visual Mental Imagery Induces Retinotopically Organized Activation of Early Visual Areas." *Cerebral Cortex 15*(10): 1570–83.

Slovic, Paul, Melissa Finucane, Ellen Peters, and Donald G. MacGregor. 2002. "The Affect Heuristic." In *Heuristics and Biases: The Psychology of Intuitive Judgment*, edited by T. Gilovich, D. Griffin, and D. Kahneman, 397–420. Cambridge University Press.

Smith, Adam. 1759/2010. *The Theory of Moral Sentiments*. Penguin.

Smith, Craig A., and Phoebe C. Ellsworth. 1985. "Patterns of Cognitive Appraisal in Emotion." *Journal of Personality and Social Psychology 48*(4): 813.

Smith, Craig A., and Richard S. Lazarus. 1990. "Emotion and Adaptation." In *Handbook of Personality: Theory and Research*, edited by Oliver John, Richard Robins, and Lawrence Pervin, 609–37. Guilford Press.

Smith, Craig A., and Richard S. Lazarus. 1993. "Appraisal Components, Core Relational Themes, and the Emotions." *Cognition & Emotion 7*(3–4): 233–69.

Smith, Greg M. 2003. *Film Structure and the Emotion System*. Cambridge University Press.

Smith, Murray. 1995. *Engaging Characters: Fiction, Emotion, and the Cinema*. Oxford University Press.

Smith, Murray. 1999. "Gangsters, Cannibals, Aesthetes, or Apparently Perverse Allegiances." In *Passionate Views: Film, Cognition, and Emotion*, edited by Carl Plantinga and Greg M. Smith, 217–38. Johns Hopkins University Press.

Solomon, Robert C. 1976. *The Passions: Emotions and the Meaning of Life*. Anchor Press / Doubleday.

Solomon, Robert C. 1993. *The Passions: Emotions and the Meaning of Life*. Hackett.

Song, Hyunjin, and Norbert Schwarz. 2008. "If It's Hard to Read, It's Hard to Do: Processing Fluency Affects Effort Prediction and Motivation." *Psychological Science 19*(10): 986–88.

Sontag, Susan. 1966. *Against Interpretation: And Other Essays*. Farrar, Straus and Giroux.

Sontag, Susan. 1977. *On Photography*. Macmillan.

Sorensen, Roy A. 1992. *Thought Experiments*. Oxford University Press.

Spark, Muriel. 2014. "The Desegregation of Art." In *The Informed Air*, edited by Penelope Jardine, 77–82. New Directions.

Spaulding, Shannon. 2015. "Imagination, Desire, and Rationality." *Journal of Philosophy 112*(9): 457–76.

Speer, Nicole K., Jeremy R. Reynolds, Khena M. Swallow, and Jeffrey M. Zacks. 2009. "Reading Stories Activates Neural Representations of Visual and Motor Experiences." *Psychological Science 20*(8): 989–99.

Sperduti, M., et al. 2016. "The Paradox of Fiction: Emotional Response toward Fiction and the Modulatory Role of Self-Relevance." *Acta Psychologica 165*: 53–59.

Spivey, Michael, Melinda Tyler, Daniel Richardson, and Ezekiel Young. 2000. "Eye Movements during Comprehension of Spoken Scene Descriptions." In *Proceedings of the 22nd Annual Conference of the Cognitive Science Society 2000*: 487–92.

Stampe, Dennis W. 1987. "The Authority of Desire." *Philosophical Review 96*(3): 335–81.

Starek, Joanna E., and Caroline F. Keating. 1991. "Self-Deception and Its Relationship to Success in Competition." *Basic and Applied Social Psychology 12*(2): 145–55.

Stecker, Robert. 2006. "Moderate Actual Intentionalism Defended." *Journal of Aesthetics and Art Criticism 64*(4): 429–38.

Stel, M., and A. van Knippenberg. 2008. "The Role of Facial Mimicry in the Recognition of Affect." *Psychological Science 19*: 984–85.

Sterelny, Kim. 2003. *Thought in a Hostile World: The Evolution of Human Cognition*. Blackwell.

Stich, Stephen. 1978. "Beliefs and Subdoxastic States." *Philosophy of Science 45*(4): 499–518.

Stich, Stephen. 1979. "Do Animals Have Beliefs?" *Australasian Journal of Philosophy 57*(1): 15–28.

Stich, Stephen, and Shaun Nichols. 1992. "Folk Psychology: Simulation or Tacit Theory?" *Mind & Language 7*(1–2): 35–71.

Stock, Kathleen. 2014. "Physiological Evidence and the Paradox of Fiction." In *Aesthetics and the Sciences of Mind*, edited by Gregory Currie et al, 205–26. Oxford University Press.

Stock, Kathleen. 2017. *Only Imagine: Fiction, Interpretation, and Imagination*. Oxford University Press.

Stocker, Michael. 1979. "Desiring the Bad: An Essay in Moral Psychology." *Journal of Philosophy 76*(12): 738–53.

Stokes, Mark, Russell Thompson, Rhodri Cusack, and John Duncan. 2009. "Top-Down Activation of Shape-Specific Population Codes in Visual Cortex during Mental Imagery." *Journal of Neuroscience 29*(5): 1565–72.

Stone, Alex. 2012. *Fooling Houdini: Magicians, Mentalists, Math Geeks, and the Hidden Powers of the Mind*. Bond Street Books.

Stoppard, Tom. 1973. *Artist Descending a Staircase & Where Are They Now? Two Plays for Radio*. Faber & Faber.

Strawson, Galen. 2009. *Mental Reality*. MIT Press.

Szpunar, Karl K., and Daniel L. Schacter. 2013. "Get Real: Effects of Repeated Simulation and Emotion on the Perceived Plausibility of Future Experiences." *Journal of Experimental Psychology: General* 142(2): 323–27.

Tal-Or, N., and Y. Papirman. 2007. "The Fundamental Attribution Error in Attributing Fictional Figures' Characteristics to the Actors." *Media Psychology* 9: 331–45.

Tamietto, Marco, and Beatrice De Gelder. 2010. "Neural Bases of the Non-conscious Perception of Emotional Signals." *Nature Reviews Neuroscience* 11(10): 697–709.

Tan, Siu-Lan, Matthew P. Spackman, and Matthew A. Bezdek. 2007. "Viewers' Interpretations of Film Characters' Emotions: Effects of Presenting Film Music before or after a Character Is Shown." *Music Perception: An Interdisciplinary Journal* 25(2): 135–52.

Tappolet, Christine. 2016. *Emotions, Value, and Agency*. Oxford University Press.

Taylor, Marjorie. 2001. *Imaginary Companions and the Children Who Create Them*. Oxford University Press on Demand.

Taylor, Marjorie, Sara D. Hodges, and Adèle Kohányi. 2003. "The Illusion of Independent Agency: Do Adult Fiction Writers Experience Their Characters as Having Minds of Their Own?" *Imagination, Cognition and Personality* 22(4): 361–80.

Teasdale, John D., Robert J. Howard, Sally G. Cox, Yvonne Ha, Michael J. Brammer, Steven C. R. Williams, and Stuart A. Checkley. 1999. "Functional MRI Study of the Cognitive Generation of Affect." *American Journal of Psychiatry* 156(2): 209–15.

Thagard, Paul. 2014. "Thought Experiments Considered Harmful." *Perspectives on Science* 22(2): 288–305.

Thirion, Bertrand, Edouard Duchesnay, Edward Hubbard, Jessica Dubois, Jean-Baptiste Poline, Denis Lebihan, and Stanislas Dehaene. 2006. "Inverse Retinotopy: Inferring the Visual Content of Images from Brain Activation Patterns." *Neuroimage* 33(4): 1104–16.

Thomas, Ayanna K., John B. Bulevich, and Elizabeth F. Loftus. 2003. "Exploring the Role of Repetition and Sensory Elaboration in the Imagination Inflation Effect." *Memory & Cognition* 31(4): 630–40.

Thomas, Dylan. 2010. "A Refusal to Mourn the Death . . ." In *The Collected Poems of Dylan Thomas: The Original Edition*. New Directions Publishing.

Thomasson, Amie L. 1999. *Fiction and Metaphysics*. Cambridge University Press.

Thomson, Judith J. 2008. *Normativity*. Open Court.

Todd, Andrew, and Adam Galinsky. 2014. "Perspective Taking as a Strategy for Improving Intergroup Relations." *Social and Personality Psychology Compass* 8/7: 374–87.

Todorov, A., and A. Bargh. 2002. "Automatic Sources of Aggression." *Aggression and Violent Behavior* 7: 53–68.

Tolstoy, Leo. 1978. *Tolstoy's Letters*. 2 vols. Scribner's.

Tomkins, Calvin. 2007. "A Fool for Art." *New Yorker*, November 12, 64–75.

Toon, Adam. 2012. *Models as Make-Believe: Imagination, Fiction and Scientific Representation*. Springer.

Trilling, Lionel. 2008. *The Liberal Imagination: Essays on Literature and Society*. New York Review of Books.

Tversky, Amos, and Daniel Kahneman. 1971. "Belief in the Law of Small Numbers." *Psychological Bulletin* 76(2): 105–10.

Tversky, Amos, and Daniel Kahneman. 1981. "The Framing of Decisions and the Psychology of Choice." *Science* 211(4481): 453–58.

Tye, Michael. 1995. *Ten Problems of Consciousness: A Representational Theory of the Phenomenal Mind*. MIT Press.

Upton, Candace L. 2009. *Situational Traits of Character: Dispositional Foundations and Implications for Moral Psychology and Friendship*. Lexington Books.

Van Boven, Leaf, David Dunning, and George Loewenstein. 2000. "Egocentric Empathy Gaps between Owners and Buyers: Misperceptions of the Endowment Effect." *Journal of Personality and Social Psychology* 79(1): 66–76.

Van Den Broek, P., R. F. Lorch, T. Linderholm, and M. Gustafson. 2001. "The Effects of Readers' Goals on Inference Generation and Memory for Texts." *Memory & Cognition* 29(8): 1081–87.

Van Inwagen, Peter. 1977. "Creatures of Fiction." *American Philosophical Quarterly* 14(4): 299–308.

Velleman, David. 1992. "The Guise of the Good." *Nous* 26(1): 3–26.

Velleman, David. 2000. "On the Aim of Belief." In *The Possibility of Practical Reason*, 244–81. Clarendon.

Vrana, Scott R., Bruce N. Cuthbert, and Peter J. Lang. 1989. "Processing Fearful and Neutral Sentences: Memory and Heart Rate Change." *Cognition & Emotion* 3(3): 179–95.

Wallbott, Harald G. 1988. "In and out of Context: Influences of Facial Expression and Context Information on Emotion Attributions." *British Journal of Social Psychology* 27(4): 357–69.

Wallentin, Mikkel, Andreas Højlund Nielsen, Peter Vuust, Anders Dohn, Andreas Roepstorff, and Torben Ellegaard Lund. 2011. "Amygdala and Heart Rate Variability Responses from Listening to Emotionally Intense Parts of a Story." *Neuroimage* 58(3): 963–73.

Walton, Kendall. 1970. "Categories of Art." *Philosophical Review* 79(3): 334–67.

Walton, Kendall. 1978a. "Fearing Fictions." *Journal of Philosophy* 75(1): 5–27.

Walton, Kendall. 1978b. "How Remote Are Fictional Worlds from the Real World?" *Journal of Aesthetics and Art Criticism* 37(1): 11–23.

Walton, Kendall. 1990. *Mimesis as Make-Believe: On the Foundations of the Representational Arts*. Harvard University Press.

Walton, Kendall. 1994. "Morals in Fiction and Fictional Morality" *Proceedings of the Aristotelian Society* 68: 27–50.

Walton, Kendall. 1997/2015. "Spelunking, Simulation, and Slime: On Being Moved by Fiction." In *In Other Shoes: Music, Metaphor, Empathy, Existence*, 273–286. Oxford University Press.

Walton, Kendall. 1999. "Projectivism, Empathy, and Musical Tension." *Philosophical Topics* 26(1–2): 407–40.

Walton, Kendall. 2006. "On the (So-Called) Puzzle of Imaginative Resistance." In *The Architecture of the Imagination: New Essays on Pretence, Possibility, and Fiction*, edited by Shaun Nichols, 137–48. Oxford University Press.

Walton, Kendall. 2015a. *In Other Shoes: Music, Metaphor, Empathy, Existence*. Oxford University Press.

Warnock, Mary. 1957. "The Justification of Emotions I." *Proceedings of the Aristotelian Society* 31: 43–58.

Wedgwood, R. 2001. "Sensing Values?" *Philosophy and Phenomenological Research* 63(1): 215–23.

Wicker, B., C. Keysers, J. Plailly, J. P. Royet, V. Gallese, and G. Rizzolatti. 2003. "Both of Us Disgusted in My Insula: The Common Neural Basis of Seeing and Feeling Disgust." *Neuron* 40(3): 655–64.

Wiggins, David. 1998. *Needs, Values, Truth: Essays in the Philosophy of Value*. Oxford University Press.

Williams, Bernard. 1976. *Problems of the Self: Philosophical Papers, 1956–1972.* Cambridge University Press.

Williams, Bernard. 1981. *Moral Luck: Philosophical Papers, 1973–1980*. Cambridge University Press.

Williams, Leanne M., et al. 2006. "Amygdala-Prefrontal Dissociation of Subliminal and Supraliminal Fear." *Human Brain Mapping 27*(8): 652–61.

Williamson, Timothy. 2007. "Philosophical Knowledge and Knowledge of Counterfactuals." *Grazer Philosophische Studien 74*(1): 89–123.

Wilson, Catherine. 2013. "Grief and the Poet." *British Journal of Aesthetics 53*(1): 77–91.

Wilson, George M. 1986. *Narration in Light: Studies in Cinematic Point of View*. Johns Hopkins University Press.

Wilson, Timothy. 2004. *Strangers to Ourselves*. Harvard University Press.

Wilson, Timothy, and Nancy Brekke. 1994. "Mental Contamination and Mental Correction: Unwanted Influences on Judgments and Evaluations." *Psychological Bulletin 116*: 117–42.

Winkielman, Piotr, and Kent C. Berridge. 2004. "Unconscious Emotion." *Current Directions in Psychological Science 13*(3): 120–23.

Winkielman, Piotr, Paula M. Niedenthal, and Lindsay M. Oberman. 2008. "Embodied Perspective on Emotion-Cognition Interactions." In *Mirror Neuron Systems*, edited by Jaime A. Pineda, 235–57. Springer.

Wittgenstein, Ludwig. 1934/1958. *The Blue and Brown Books*. Harper & Row.

Wolterstorff, N. 1980. *Works and Worlds of Art*. Oxford University Press.

Zadra, Jonathan R., and Gerald L. Clore. 2011. "Emotion and Perception: The Role of Affective Information." *Wiley Interdisciplinary Reviews: Cognitive Science 2*(6): 676–85.

Zajonc, Robert B. 1980. "Feeling and Thinking: Preferences Need No Inferences." *American Psychologist 35*(2): 151.

Zajonc, Robert B. , et al. 1989. "Feeling and Facial Efference: Implications of the Vascular Theory of Emotion." *Psychological Review 96*(3): 395–416.

Zalta, Edward N. 1988. *Intensional Logic and the Metaphysics of Intentionality*. MIT Press.

Zatorre, Robert J., Andrea R. Halpern, David W. Perry, Ernst Meyer, and Alan C. Evans. 1996. "Hearing in the Mind's Ear: A PET Investigation of Musical Imagery and Perception." *Journal of Cognitive Neuroscience 8*(1): 29–46.

Zunshine, Lisa. 2006. *Why We Read Fiction: Theory of Mind and the Novel*. Ohio State University Press.

Zwaan, Rolf A., Joseph P. Magliano, and Arthur C. Graesser. 1995. "Narrative Comprehension." *Learning, Memory 21*(2): 386–83.

Zwaan, Rolf A., and Lawrence J. Taylor. 2006. "Seeing, Acting, Understanding: Motor Resonance in Language Comprehension." *Journal of Experimental Psychology: General 135*(1): 1–11.

Index

For the benefit of digital users, indexed terms that span two pages (e.g., 52–53) may, on occasion, appear on only one of those pages.

affect heuristic, 119–20
affective contagion, 68–70, 121–23
affective forecasting, 100–1
affective mindreading. *See* simulation
Apocalypse Now, 115–16
aptness, 86–94
    as correctness, 92–93
    as justification, 92–93
    formal characterization of, 93
Arbus, Diane, 222, 223
Aristotle, 129n.69, 158n.7, 209
artistic medium, 117–19, 145–46
asymmetries between fictional and real-world emotions, 71–84
attribution effects. *See* projection
Augustine, 159n.17
autonomy, 1–8

beauty of soul, 116–17
behavioral motivation and fiction-directed emotions, 74–77, 166–67
beliefs from fictions, 24–26
biases and heuristics, 148–51, 152–53
Booth, Wayne, 193–94
brain regions involved in motor imagining, 29–30
brain regions involved in perception and imagination, 29

Caravaggio, 162
Carroll, Noël, 70–71n.95, 119–20n.30, 177n.2, 209n.10, 222n.36, 224
Chalmers, David, 3–4n.5
Clore, Gerald, Gasper, Karen and Garvin, Erika, 123n.49
cognitive theory of the imagination, 17–30

continuity
    affective, 85
    conative, 155–71
    doxastic, 139–43
    empirical, 17–30, 57–71
    evaluative, 176
    history of debate over, 5–7
    in discovery of fictional content, 136, 139–43
    in visual perception and imagining, 27–29
    normative, 95–101
Crime and Punishment, 117
Currie, Gregory, 9, 13–14, 35, 100n.32, 108n.12, 125n.57, 138, 161n.22, 162n.24, 186n.22
Currie, Gregory and Ravenscroft, Ian, 23, 62n.60, 139n.7

Damasio, Antonio, 54–55n.28, 90n.7
Dante, 159
Darwin, Charles, 68n.81
Davidson, Donald, 174n.42
Descartes, René, 3–4
Desires
    and discrepant affects, 181–82
    direction of fit, 155–56
    imaginative counterparts of, 166–68
    presenting their objects as good, 156
    pro tanto reasons for, 165
    puzzle of conflicts among, 163, 168–71
    rationality of, 169–75
    second-order desires, 172–73
Dickens, Charles, 145
discontinuity, normative argument for, 102

discontinuity, normative (*cont.*)
  framing effects in service of, 110–13
  in discovery of fictional content,
    136, 143–52
  three theories threatened by, 102–7
  two kinds of opponents of, 8–14
discrepant affects, 176
disgust elicitors, 124–25
Doggett, Tyler and Egan, Andy, 166n.32,
  168n.34
Don Quixote, 140
Dr. Strangelove, 177

emotions
  and desires, 160–61n.21, 181–82
  and functions, 131–33
  as evaluative appraisals, 44–57
  as revealing a person's character, 103
  automatic processes of, 51–52
  cognitive bases of, 45–46
  concepts of, 71–84
  criterial qualities of, 46–47
  dual process theories of, 55–56
  elicited by fictions, (*see* fiction-directed
    emotions)
  justification of, 94
  lower and higher processes in
    production of, 56–57
  perceptual theories of, 50–53
  phenomenology of, 49–50
  strict cognitivist theories of, 47–48
  using fictional narratives to study, 107
empathy, 69–70. *See* simulation

Feagin, Susan, 64, 67n.76, 99–100
fiction-directed emotions, 57–71
  and concepts of real-world
    emotions, 79–81
  dangers of, 58–60, 190–91
  edifying effects of, 106
  experimental problems in
    measuring, 77–78
  explanatory stakes in debate over
    realism of, 79–81
  paradox of, 90, 100
  psychology and neurophysiology
    of, 60–61
  realism and irrealism about, 71–77

fictional characters
  concern for, 165
  evaluation of, 177–78
  identification with, 65, 146–47, 186–95
  names of, 119, 146, 151
  simulation of, 64–68, 140–41
fictional content, 85–98, 126–27. *See* truth
  in fiction
fictional import, 40
fictional representation, 12–14
fictional worlds, 13–14, 31, 138
Fielding, Henry, 1–2
Fiennes, Ralph, 193–94
fit. *See* aptness
framing effects, 110–13, 182–83
functions
  aesthetic, 207–8
  and evaluation of art, 218–19
  and kind-relative value, 208
  and moral evaluation of art, 220–22
  artifactual, 210
  artistic, 202, 204–11
  constitutive, 203–4, 211–13
  etiological accounts of, 213
  fitness for, 219
  intentions and, 213–16
  of fictional engagements,
    10–11, 153–54
fundamental attribution error, 148

Gaut, Berys, 65n.71, 104–5, 184n.17,
  222n.36
Gendler, Tamar, 60n.53, 178n.4
Goldie, Peter, 49, 76n.75, 102
guilty pleasures, 183, 199

Hamlet, 2, 39–40
Harold, James, 186, 199–200n.70
Harris, Paul, 61n.59
Hirst, Damien, 216
Horace, 17
Humbert Humbert, 183–84
Hume, David, 3–4, 68, 127–28, 157,
  219n.30

imagination and belief interactions, 22–23
imaginative resistance, 178
imagining

correctly, 96–98
deviant, 176
experiential, 23–24, 40–41
functions of, 131–33
individuated from other mental
    states, 19–20
prescriptions for, 13n.24, 96–97
propositional, 17–30
reduced to belief, 20–22
vs. truth-apt thinking, 11–12
See also quarantine; simulation
inflection, 118–19
internal and external perspectives on a
    fiction, 35–43
and explanation of emotions, 66, 70–71
and explanation of story
    content, 141–43
invariance. See continuity

Johnson, Samuel, 3–4, 58–59, 158,
    174n.43
Joyce, James, 40–41

Kaufman, Geoff and Libby, Lisa, 192,
    195n.63
Kind, Amy, 3–4n.5
King Lear, 161n.23, 162n.25
kitsch, 129
Kuleshov Effect, 66

Lamarque, Peter, 41–42, 160
Lamarque, Peter, and Olsen, Stein,
    35n.56, 179–80
Leslie, Alfred, 21–22
Lewis, David, 31–34, 38
literary fiction vs. counterfactual
    representations, 30–35
Livingston, Paisley and Mele, Alfred, 220
Locke, John, 3–4
Loftus, Elizabeth, 26
Lucretius, 158n.13

Mar, Raymond, 67–68
mental states and functional roles, 17–18
merited response, 222n.36
    See also moral defects and artistic
        evaluation
Middlemarch, 140–41

Mirroring
    and behavior, 123–24, 192–93
    and facial expression, 68–69, 122
    and simulation, 191–92
    See also affective contagion
Montaigne, Michel de, 51n.19
moods, 119–21
moral defects and artistic evaluation, 221–25
Moran, Richard, 128–29
Mutual Belief Principle, 33, 34, 37–38. See
    also Lewis, David

Nehamas, Alexander, 126n.59, 185n.19
Nichols, Shaun, 39n.64, 60n.53, 176, 181–82
normative discontinuity
    arguments for, 102
    framing effects in support of, 110–13
    in discovery of fictional content,
        136, 143–52
    three theories threatened by, 102–7
    two kinds of opponents, 8–14
normative essentialism, 217–19
Nussbaum, Martha, 59, 98–99n.27,
    223n.38

opacity of literary representation,
    41–42, 179–80

Paradise Lost, 126, 184, 199–200
Peacocke, Christopher, 3–4n.5
Plato, 3–4, 58, 68n.83, 159
Positive Opera Company, 157n.5
priming, 193
Prinz, Jesse, 50, 51–52
projection, 123, 126–28, 149
Proust, Marcel, 147

quarantine, 24–27, 186–95
"quasi-emotions." See realism about
    fiction-directed emotions

Radford, Colin, 3n.4
Raz, Joseph, 211
Reality Principle, 31–32, 34. See also
    Lewis, David
response moralism, 104–5
    See also merited response
Robinson, Jenefer, 50, 52, 99

Rousseau, Jean-Jacques, 58–59
Ruskin, John, 127–28

Selgado, Sebastião, 223
sentimentalism, 86n.1
Serrano, Andres, 131
simulation, 61–64, 186–95
    and diminution of self, 192
    and neuropsychology, 67–68 (*see also* empathy)
    socially negative effects of, 190
    socially positive effects of, 191
Smith, Murray, 182n.14, 199n.70
Sontag, Susan, 222
source-monitoring errors, 24–27
Spark, Muriel, 129, 142–43
Star Trek, 39
Stock, Kathleen, 78
sui generis experiences, 8, 9n.15
"surprised by sin," 184

Tappolet, Christine, 52–53
theoretical rationality, 137–38
Thomas, Dylan, 129–30
Thomson, Judith Jarvis, 208
Tom Jones, 1–2
tragedy, 155

artistic success of, 175
paradox of, 157–60
three desires constitutive of, 171–75
Trilling, Lionel, 214
truth in fiction, 31–35
    discovery of, 134–39, 151–52, 166–67
    See also fictional content
The Elephant Man, 126
The Moonstone, 209–10
The Searchers, 210–11
The Wire, 184–85
typography, 118, 119

valuing, 178–79
Velázquez, 216
video games, 190
visual imagery in brain and mind, 27–29

Wagner, 194–95
Wallentin, Mikkel, 60
Walton, Kendall, 8–9, 34, 35, 73, 128–29, 180, 209n.10
Warhol, Andy, 157
wide-scope interpretations of practical norms, 217–18, 220–21
Wittgenstein, Ludwig, 97n.22
Wodehouse, 142